CYPHER CULTURE

CYPHER CULTURE

Conspiracy, Fandom, and the Messages That Were Not There

JOSEPH PACKER
AND
ETHAN STONEMAN

Louisiana State University Press | Baton Rouge

Published by Louisiana State University Press
lsupress.org

LSU Press Paperback Original

DESIGNER: Emily Ann Olson
TYPEFACES: Minion Pro, text; Tomarik, Felt Tip Woman, display

Cover illustration: Adobe Stock (adapted).

The manufacturer's authorized representative in the EU for product safety is Mare Nostrum Group B.V., Doelen 72, 4831 GR Breda, The Netherlands. Email: gpsr@mare-nostrum.co.uk.

Portions of this book first appeared in Joseph Packer and Ethan Stoneman, "Where We Produce One, We Produce All: The Platform Conspiracism of QAnon," *Cultural Politics* 17, no. 3 (2021): 255–78; and Packer and Stoneman, "The White Knight: Batman as Esoteric Hero for the Dissident Right," *Transformative Works and Cultures* 40 (2023).

CATALOGING-IN-PUBLICATION DATA ARE AVAILABLE FROM THE LIBRARY OF CONGRESS.

ISBN 978-0-8071-8734-0 (pbk.: alk. paper) — ISBN 978-0-8071-8776-0 (pdf) —
ISBN 978-0-8071-8775-3 (epub)

The Blank Page, the blank notebooks. I can tell you what I like and keep back what I like. You may read between the lines, there is nothing to stop you.

—Muriel Spark, notes for *A Far Cry from Kensington*

CONTENTS

ACKNOWLEDGMENTS

I would like to start by thanking my coauthor. Academic writing has become a pleasure in my life even though so many parts of it are rather miserable. This owes itself entirely to my brilliant writing partner and good buddy. The author order in no way reflects unequal contribution. The order was originally reversed until a powerful case of presentiment moved us to action.

I also would like to thank Tim O'Donnell for changing the direction of my life by encouraging me to go to grad school over law school.

I would like to thank the anonymous reviewers at *Cultural Politics* and *Transformative Works and Cultures* for their thoughtful comments. John Armitage for believing in our work and publishing the first piece of what would become *Cypher Culture.* Mel Stanfield for providing insight related to fan studies and guiding us through the editorial process at *Transformative Works and Cultures.*

I would like to thank everyone at Louisiana State University Press, but specifically James W. Long for taking a chance on the book and shepherding us through this project.

I would like to thank Todd Manza for his careful edits of the manuscript. His suggestion to change *poseur* to *poser* helped us not look like posers.

I would like to thank my friends who help me engage in my passions: paleontology (STEGOSAURUS), video games (*Civ V* and *Huns*), walkathons, NO work days, ASTROGRAPHY.

I would like to thank the anonymous reviewers who offered enormously valuable suggestions, which worked to drastically shape the manuscript for the better.

I would like to thank S. J. Cardswall, a friend with whom I share half my spiritual DNA. I find our projects intertwined like Spanish moss and the southern live oak.

Finally, I would like to thank my family: my parents for always supporting and encouraging me, my sister for just being awesome, Drea for being a loving partner on a dying planet.

—JP

What is best in life? To read books, to write books, to feel the soft glow of the moon upon one's naked flesh while muttering sentences that may or may not make sense in the daylight. This book, if it can be called that, is the result of many long nights spent chasing the ghost of meaning through the labyrinth of desire.

First, to Dr. Butler, whose miraculous tinctures kept the black bile at bay and replaced my blood with a fine and jittery electricity.

To Polyhymnia, solemn muse of sacred song and sacred silence. Your whisper guided my trembling hand when all I could see were the ghosts of worlds forgotten.

To my writing partner, my comrade in delirium, Joe Packer. Your soul burns bright across the ages, a beacon to all who stagger in the dark pursuit of sentences that will not die.

To my parents and my sister, who raised me among relics and candlesmoke, where saints and specters keep equal company. I carry the blessings you gave me like a quiet litany in the marrow.

To my wife, whose sacred bond nourishes my soul and anchors my otherwise vaporous existence.

To my spawn, I see the hunger in their eyes, and I know one day they shall dismantle me like Ymir, fashioning from my bones and words a world more terrible and beautiful than this one. May they build well.

To the moon, for watching me without judgment.

If there is any wisdom here, it belongs to others. So mote it be!

—ES

CYPHER CULTURE

INTRODUCTION

Conspiracy Theory, Rhetorical Esotericism, and Pronoiac Fandom

I learned to read the secret meaning of things.

—Richard Condon, *The Manchurian Candidate*

You are Kanye West. You are transported to a dystopian future and forced to battle with clones of famous twentieth- and twenty-first-century rappers. This is the catchy plot of the 2013 indie role-playing video game *Kanye Quest 3030*, which made a brief splash after being released to generally positive reviews. "Kanye," however, along with other in-game features such as time portals, rap battles, and many other rap artist clones—of the likes of 2Pac, Lil B (The Based-God), MF Doom, and RZA—was all a ruse. When players successfully solved some of the puzzles, they were greeted with the following message:

> Congratulations! You have proven yourself to be an open-minded and curious thinker. We must apologize for deceiving you, but we can reveal that the game you were playing until this point was a "front" constructed to protect what you are currently accessing. . . . The following is a thought exercise designed to teach you something beneficial. By undertaking this exercise, you will hopefully be affected in a positive way. Due to the nature of the exercise, this "something" cannot be revealed immediately.[1]

Kanye Quest 3030, in other words, is different from what it seems. Playing through secret parts of the game introduces players to the ideas of ascen-

Figure 1. A turn-based, role-playing game battle against a clone of the rapper The BasedGod from the game *Kanye Quest 3030*. Clara Hope (2013).

sionism, a religious group often referred to as a cult. What better way to attract and test potential new recruits than through the anthropological constant of competitive play? And by "better," we mean not only effective but also safe. Regardless of whether ascensionism could be better described as a religion or a cult, it is a minority belief system and therefore runs the risk of being perceived as outré.

Religious minorities, however, are not the only groups who may have cause to be circumspect in their ways and means of communicating. Philosophers, queer people, fascists, and others situated outside what passes for the mainstream have also found themselves occupying a hostile world bent on their containment or destruction. The cultural manifestations of such a world include a sea of malevolent movies, books, plays, and video games—all media, really—that call into question their values, beliefs, truths, and oftentimes their very right to exist.

Within this hostile cultural space, however, exist texts that these and other vilified groups have identified as only superficially antagonistic toward their way of life. From that perspective, some media artifacts are encoded so that while they outwardly reflect and reinforce a culture's symbolic boundaries of inclusion and exclusion, interstitially they whisper forbidden and welcome knowledge to those who experience the pangs of social ostracism. Whether as a marketing stunt or a sincere vehicle for transferring occult wisdom, the game harks back to a media era in which the flow of information was considerably more restricted than after the successive revolutions of print, electric communication, and digitality. In that era, characterized by orality and chirography, the world was seemingly (but not too seemingly) full of hidden knowledge intended only for the elect—whether of ancient mystery cults, kabbalah, or gnosticism.

Knowledge is sometimes hidden by necessity. The great psychic wound of the Western philosophical tradition arguably originates with the trial and execution of Socrates at the behest of Athens's public censors. This event arguably fostered the self-preserving tendency of philosophers and public intellectuals to keep their more controversial views close to the chest. Persecution—or the belief in its likelihood—can cause potentially targeted knowledge to retreat from the public to the private realm, where it knows only a conscientious or interpersonal existence. However, controversial facts and information can occasionally remain obstinately lodged in the public sphere, gaining "operational security" from superposable layers of textual obfuscation. On the surface, such texts often speak in the language of common belief or public opinion—what the ancient Greeks called *doxa*. To most, such texts appear anodyne and unremarkable, but for the initiated or those with the desire and skill to decode, they suggest layers of hidden signification.

In the 1952 collection *Persecution and the Art of Writing*, twentieth-century German American political philosopher Leo Strauss famously asserted that before the nineteenth century, most philosophers felt compelled, out of fear of persecution, to write and teach esoterically, that is, to disguise multiple levels of meaning within an exoteric structure of philosophical communication.[2] Using a variety of rhetorical stratagems and compositional techniques to encrypt the true meaning of texts—including obscure references, irony or paradox, hyperbole, or even deliberate self-contradictions—premodern philosophers like al-Farabi, Marsilius of Padua, and Xenophon deployed esoteric writing to safely reach a select readership consisting of what Strauss describes as "thoughtful . . . careful readers."[3] On that view, the ordinary, exoteric meaning of a work like Plato's *Republic* functions principally as a discursive means of bypassing the censors of a punitive society and safely distributing a truth that is potentially inimical to common belief and opinion.

Although Strauss and his followers regard esoteric hermeneutics as a lost art—at least in the Western philosophical tradition—instances of dual-audience messaging can also be clearly observed in the contemporary era. Twentieth-century Soviet dissidents, for example, often communicated with one another via allegory to avoid imprisonment by the General Directorate for the Protection of State Secrets in the Press. Something of that practice persists today behind China's Great Firewall, where cultural "subversives" use coded language to evade Chinese internet censorship.

Apart from the historical parameters that Strauss and some contemporary Straussians may impose on the practice of esoteric writing, they would probably qualify the above examples as "prosaic" rather than philosophical esotericism. Yet as today's foremost chronicler of esoteric hermeneutics, Arthur Melzer, argues, esotericism is best conceived of as "a form of rhetoric."[4] The case is not difficult to make, given Strauss's emphasis on the use of rhetorical devices to conceal while selectively revealing an author's true meaning. Metaphor, allegory, hyperbole, and irony are all classic rhetorical tropes that allow writers (as well as speakers) to make a point without stating it explicitly—a helpful strategy that becomes a practical necessity when one's purpose is not only to achieve eloquence but also to ensure that one's true message slips past the cultural censors. As Jorge Luis Borges was purported to have said, "Censorship is the mother of metaphor."[5] That rhetorical fecundity goes beyond the tropological and according to Melzer includes such maneuvers as the odd use of italics and even putting one's true message in the mouth of a villain. Straussians, by and large, believe that when faced with an esoteric text, careful readers will key in to the writer's hidden purpose and "read between the lines," identifying and interpreting esoteric clues for what they are: invitations to investigate a text more deeply and discern what other, more casual readers are likely to miss.

Behind these invitations, Melzer identifies four motives. Two relate to the rhetor's perceived need to hide their thoughts. The first, "defensive esotericism," emanates from the specter of Socrates's untimely death while hinging on a desire to protect oneself from persecution; the second, "protective esotericism," consists in the impulse to protect society from dangerous truths. In contrast to defensive esotericism, which is perhaps self-explanatory, the motive to protect society through esotericism may strike some as puzzling. Yet history abounds with instances of the paternalistic concealment of information—from the obfuscation of state secrets and reports on the health of political leaders to the suppression of information likely to cause panic. Protective esotericism shares these paternalistic concerns but is internally constrained to communicate the potential cause of disturbance to a select audience. For example, we can imagine that atheists who recognize religion's social value may esoterically restrict communication about their religious views to help maintain order. Whereas the first two esoteric motives are precautionary, the remaining two concern the rhetor's need to communicate at all.

The third motive, "political esotericism," is opposed to protective esotericism; rather than limiting one's audience to preserve the social order, it disguises its message from authorities to overturn that order and replace it with something better. (Any instance of dissidents using hidden, "propagandistic" messages to foment regime change would fit the bill.) Melzer refers to the fourth reason for esoteric communication as "pedagogical esotericism." Like the motive for protection, it is also solicitous. Still, while protective esotericism strives to protect at the societal level, pedagogical esotericism is more concerned with protecting individuals from "dangerous" ideas—ideas for which they may be intellectually or emotionally unprepared. At the same time, like the political motive, the pedagogical is animated by a positive aim of providing for "the philosophical education of the rare and gifted individual" through hints and insinuation.[6] For Straussians—specifically, those followers of Strauss predisposed to read texts esoterically—the pedagogical form of esotericism traverses time and place. In their view, messages hidden by ancient philosophers like Plato or early modern playwrights like William Shakespeare were intended to be decoded by thoughtful, careful readers throughout the ages, not just ancient Athenians or Elizabethans.[7]

This hermeneutic enjoys a certain magic: brilliant people writing to each other covertly across eras and cultures while evading myriad censors through clever codes and double entendres. Unfortunately, the very nature of the esoteric enterprise makes it somewhat difficult to map with any kind of definitiveness. As the noted Straussian Paul Cantor writes, "a demonstrably esoteric text is a contradiction in terms."[8] Occasionally, an author or authors will publicly admit to having produced an esoteric work, though this typically occurs only after a change in given circumstances of censorship. A recent example is the admission that from 1995 to 1997 a public art project created by the GALA Committee (from Georgia/Los Angeles, where the project originated) covertly inserted more than two hundred art objects into episodes of the prime time television soap opera *Melrose Place* (1992–1999), mainly in the form of props and set dressing.[9] Such instances, however, tend to be exceptions that prove the rule. They also almost exclusively fall into the category of political esotericism, since any explicit disclosure of an esoteric motive would work against the purpose of seeking to maintain a pedagogical or protective esotericism for careful readers of any time or place.

But whatever the species, the intrinsically secret nature of esotericism means that while individuals can provide esoteric readings of texts, there is typically no way to confirm the veracity of any esoteric interpretation. If there were, then the esotericism of a work would become a relic. That feature alone, however, has not resulted in a contemporary aversion to such a hermeneutic; in fact, the opposite may be closer to the truth. Today, the piecing together of inscribed clues to uncover hidden authorial intent enjoys a certain cachet—at least when the bricolage appears in places such as academic journal articles about secret messages in Shakespeare or entertainment news sites cataloging social media posts that Britney Spears fans thought were a cry for help.[10]

There is, however, an obverse to this appreciative cultural reception. As the conspiracy theory researcher Timothy Melley argues, esoteric hermeneutics—specifically that brand of esotericism advocated by Strauss—is "structurally indistinguishable" from cult leader Charles Manson's claims that The Beatles' music contained coded messages encouraging an apocalyptic race war—encrypted codes that only Charlie, conveniently, could crack.[11] Melley's remark about the structural homology between conspiracy discourse and Strauss's esoteric hermeneutics is a throwaway comment in a groundbreaking work about turn-of-the-century conspiracy culture. But now, more than two decades into the twenty-first century, Melley's observation strikes us as deserving more critical attention. (It was arguably more deserving of focused analysis at the turn of the century, too.) Given esotericism's central conceit of uncovering hidden truths, the hermeneutic certainly appears to constellate with the detection of plots and conspiracies. For that reason, scholarly approaches to the phenomenon of conspiracy theories suggest a useful starting point for resituating esotericism as a hermeneutic practice.

THE THEORY OF CONSPIRACY THEORY

Conspiracy theories are nothing new. Indeed, they are probably as old as the first human societies, dating back to whenever rumors began circulating in primary oral cultures—to a time preceding the very invention or practice of affixing dates. Evolutionary psychologists have even recently proposed an "adaptive-conspiracism hypothesis," which stipulates that "conspiracy thinking is an adaptive feature of the human coalitional" present in all human societies.[12] While the term *conspiracy theory* is a comparatively recent coinage that only entered popular usage to any significant degree in the 1970s, the phenomenon it describes is evident in the historical record as far back as classical antiquity. According to Joseph Roisman and Victoria Pagán, the Greco-Roman world was suffused with a conspiratorial mindset, its pages filled with stories about suspected plots.[13] In ancient Athens, the rhetoric of conspiracy functioned as a dynamic and fluid strategy in a variety of forensic and deliberative settings; in Rome, it operated as a driving force of political culture, from rumors that Emperor Nero had engineered the Great Fire of 64 CE in order to rebuild Rome according to his personal desires to talk of secret assassinations and other suspicious circumstances surrounding the accession of Emperor Hadrian in 117.[14]

Evidence of a conspiracy-theorizing culture is also imprinted on certain episodes of medieval history. Accusations of anti-Christian collusion among Jews, Muslims, and lepers spread rampantly in southern France between 1320 and 1321.[15] It was also during that century that King Philip IV of France (called Philip the Fair) destroyed the Knights Templar, a French military order of the Roman Catholic faith. At the time, rumors about the Templars' secret initiation ceremony had created distrust among the populace. Philip, to free himself from debts to the Templars incurred during his war against England, exploited this mistrust to pressure Pope Clement V to have many of the order's members in France arrested and tortured. Members' false confessions, obtained under duress, often claimed that during Templar admission ceremonies, recruits were forced to spit on the cross, deny Christ, worship idols, and engage in "indecent kissing."[16] Many of the arrested were burned at the stake, while others were sentenced to life imprisonment or exiled. By 1312, Pope Clement had disbanded the order.

Conspiracy theories, however, did not die off with the dissolution of the Knights Templar, or even the close of the Middle Ages, but continued apace with the modern period, from the Renaissance to the present, developing in unexpected ways in the contemporary era. One such development, arguably the most important in the history of American conspiracy theories, is what Katharina Thalmann characterizes as the stigmatization of conspiracy theories in the 1950s and 1960s.[17] This problematization, she argues, consisted in a shift in the status of conspiracy theory from orthodox to heterodox knowledge. Whereas discussions in previous centuries and decades had focused on whether a particular conspiracy theory was true, beginning in the 1950s, political elites, along with the news and entertainment industries, began interrogating the foundations of the conspiracist mode of thinking and expressing concerns about its possible psychosocial effects. In postwar America, fear of conspiracy theory—or what Jack Bratich calls conspiracy panic—quickly supplanted fear of actual or alleged conspiracies.[18]

Thalmann and Michael Butter both provide thorough and nuanced accounts of the reasons for this shift, which they argue occurred in three waves.[19] Essentially, conspiracy theories lost their status as orthodox knowledge and moved to the margins of society because they became a subject of academic discourse among American historians and political scientists. Following the Second World War, social scientists began to challenge the claims of conspiracist knowledge. On the one hand, European émigrés from the Frankfurt School (such as Theodor Adorno, Norbert Guterman, and Leo Lowenthal) emphasized the potential sociopolitical dangers posed by conspiracist thinking; on the other hand, scholars like Karl Popper, in *The Open Society and Its Enemies*, criticized conspiracy theories on epistemological grounds as overestimating intentional action while underestimating systemic conditions and unintended or structural effects.

Initially confined to the ivory towers of academia, these critical perspectives were soon popularized by a younger generation of American scholars concerned with the effects of the Red Scare in the United States. This popularization was accelerated by the GI Bill and its "unprecedented growth in audiences who were receptive to and interested in scientific ideas."[20] According to Mark Fenster's now classic *Conspiracy Theories*, these trends coincided with the efforts of pluralist democratic theorists and consensus historians to elaborate an account of ordered political disagreement capable of avoiding the collective irrationalities they identified in political extremism, mass movements, consumerism, and other dangers to the prevailing "consensus" and "pluralism" of American democracy.[21] Although conspiracism was only one issue associated with the study of pluralism and consensus, these historians' and political scientists' discussions of "the fear of conspiracy" took place in the wake of McCarthyism and the throes of the Cold War and thus their work was widely disseminated among concerned intellectuals and the general reading public.

The marginalization of conspiracy theory culminated in 1964 with the seminal essay "The Paranoid Style in American Politics." Written by the consensus historian Richard Hofstadter and originally published in the widely read *Harper's Magazine,* the essay builds on the then-recent shift in the status of conspiracy theory by pathologizing conspiracism as a form of paranoia, symptoms of which were objectively discernible in its political rhetoric. In the introduction to his 1966 collection of essays on the style and practices of paranoid politics, Hofstadter explains that by "style" he means "above all, a way of seeing the world and of expressing oneself," one that is principally concerned with "the way in which ideas are believed and advocated rather than with the truth or falsity of their content." A distinctly paranoid style, he argues, sees the world through an "apocalyptic and absolutist framework" of "absolute good and absolute evil" that emphasizes evil's machinations against good. Through this paranoia-infused lens, enemies are satanically elevated into "a perfect model of malice, a kind of amoral superman—sinister, ubiquitous, powerful, cruel, luxury-loving." This absolutism is complemented by an overwhelming coherence that "leaves no room for mistakes, failures, or ambiguities": "it believes that it is up against an enemy who is as infallibly rational as he is totally evil, and it seeks to match his imputed total competence with its own, leaving nothing unexplained and comprehending all of reality in one overreaching consistent theory."[22]

For Hofstadter, such epistemological extremism was not tied to a particular ideology but could be located at both ends of the political spectrum. Although he devoted far more attention to far-right paranoiacs like Barry Goldwater, Joseph McCarthy, and their followers, as Fenster argues, "this is undoubtedly less because he saw, in the early to mid-1960s, any essential distinction between the far left and the far right, and more because of the prominence of the far right at the time in which wrote."[23] According to Hofstadter's interpretation, extremes on both the left and right were prone to offering totalizing systems mapping the hidden plots or schemes of malefic Others. In a list of movements that fit within the paranoid style, Hofstadter cites the "popular left-wing press," along with abolitionists who suspected a slaveholders' conspiracy, anti-Masonic and anti-Catholic groups, nineteenth-century Populist Party fears of international bankers, and right-wing anxieties about communist infiltration.[24] From Hofstadter's perspective of consensual Cold War liberalism, the paranoid style provided a big tent or cudgel for diagnosing and dismissing illegitimate political opposition.

Hofstadter was not the first historian to turn a critical eye to conspiracy theory. Decades prior to Hofstadter's essay, historians challenged the conspiracist historiography of the French Revolution, the New England Illuminati scare of the 1790s, and conspiracist explanations of the origins of the First World War.[25] Nevertheless, Hofstadter's stigmatizing conceptualization of conspiracy theory as paranoid phenomenon set the template, for decades, for research in the history of conspiracy theories. The publication of "Paranoid Style" in *Harper's* shows what "broad impact . . . [Hofstadter's], and others,' dismissal of conspiracy theory as paranoia could develop at the time."[26] By all accounts, the essay remains "the most prominent and influential account of conspiracy theory and populist 'extremism.'"[27]

By the 1970s, in large part because of the influence of Hofstadter's essay, conspiracy theorizing had become so thoroughly stigmatized as pathological that the very term "conspiracy theory" had become an insult. As Peter Knight writes, "Calling something a conspiracy theory is not infrequently enough to end discussion."[28] Despite recent indications that conspiracy theories are enjoying a current "renaissance" (for instance, in the rise of populist movements and the high visibility and accessibility of conspiracies made possible by Web 2.0), they are still stigmatized in some domains, particularly those we continue to regard, rightly or wrongly, as mainstream.[29]

In the field of cultural studies, too, Hofstadter's interpretation of the paranoid style of American politics served as a model for many subsequent studies of conspiracy theories, directing scholarly attention to elements perceived as unscientific, irrational, and extremist. Key works in this vein include those by Robert Robins and Jerrold Post, and Michael Barkun.[30] Robins and Post explore the psychological underpinnings of political paranoia and its manifestations in political movements and leaders, highlighting how paranoid thinking can undermine rational debate and lead to polarization. In *A Culture of Conspiracy* (now in its second edition), Barkun corrects Hofstadter's claim that conspiracy theories have always been "the preferred style only of *minority* movements," arguing that they have moved from the fringes of society into the mainstream.[31] Barkun then identifies several key features of conspiracy theories: their tendency to draw on ideas that are rejected by mainstream institutions, their frequent attempts to connect disparate events and phenomena into a single overarching narrative, and their incorporation of apocalyptic or millenarian themes predicting catastrophe or transformative events.[32]

Hofstadter's notion of the paranoid style continues to exert influence in the realm of cultural studies.[33] Calum Matheson recently explored the rhetoric and media discourse that fueled widespread fear and suspicion that the military exercise known as Jade Helm 15 was a prelude to martial law or an invasion of Texas.[34] Although Matheson does not explicitly draw on Hofstadter's framework, he links the Jade Helm 15 conspiracy theories to paranoia's close relative, anxiety. Even more recently, and nearly sixty years after the publication of Hofstadter's essay, Frida Beckman's *The Paranoid Chronotope* delved into the interplay between paranoia, time, and narrative structures, examining how these elements shape and are shaped by power dynamics, concepts of truth, and identity formation. She argues that paranoia is not just an individual psychological condition but a pervasive cultural phenomenon—a "looming specter"—that influences how people perceive and interact with the world, shaping narratives of history, politics, and personal identity. Her concept of the paranoid chronotope refers to the specific ways in which time and space are constructed in paranoid narratives, which often feature a sense of urgency, a collapsing of past and future, and a heightened perception of threats that distort reality.[35]

However, despite the staying power of Hofstadter's paranoia thesis, around the turn of the twenty-first century a number of cultural studies scholars began articulating alternative approaches to the study of conspiracy theories.[36] According to Butter and Knight, these revisionist scholars "started from the assumption that the task is not to condemn popular manifestations of conspiracy theory, but to understand their appeal and assess their cultural significance . . . [and] to make sense of why conspiracist narratives have become so attractive, both for individual believers and cultural forms such as postmodern novels and Hollywood thrillers."[37] In a review essay announcing the cultural studies turn, Jodi Dean noted that these studies—specifically those by Fenster, Marcus, and Melley—opposed the focus on conspiracy theory's alleged pathological motivations, as well as its style and preoccupation with plot, adopting instead a critical-theoretical approach to the all-too-real problems of power, secrecy, and political agency that make conspiracy narratives plausible in the first place.[38]

For these and similarly minded scholars, the focus of analysis is less on disordered reasoning and psychopathology than on the particular ways of making sense of reality that communities use to link facticity, causality, motive, coherence, and rationality. As George Marcus remarks in the introduction to *Paranoia Within Reason,* conspiracy theories are not necessarily irrational disturbances to an otherwise rational, discursive, procedural public sphere but, in certain contexts, can make up "a 'reasonable' component of rational and commonsensical thought and experience."[39] Melley likewise argues that conspiracy theories constitute "logical responses to technological and social change," offering "an odd sort of comfort in an uncertain age: it makes sense of the inexplicable, accounting for complex events in a clear, if frightening way."[40] As Knight puts it, conspiracism as a worldview "provides an everyday epistemological quick-fix to often intractably complex problems."[41] From this critical standpoint, seeing the world in terms of the behind-the-scenes workings of powerful and obscure entities is an understandable response to a techno-social reality marked by increasing globalization, corporatization, and datafication.[42]

Many of these and later studies draw on and continue the analysis of Marxist literary critic Fredric Jameson. In a well-known essay, Jameson describes conspiracy theories as "the poor person's cognitive mapping in the postmodern age," noting that "it is a degraded figure of the total logic of late capital, a desperate attempt to represent the latter's system, whose failure is marked by its slippage into sheer theme and content."[43] According to this account, the fascination with conspiracy theories in popular media reflects our current struggle to comprehend the interconnectedness of social, political, and economic factors. Conspiracism, according to this perspective, can be a creative response and a means of questioning existing power structures despite its inaccuracies.

Dean encapsulates both sides of this critical-creative potentiality. On the one hand, she argues, conspiracy theory provides an endless series of possible connections, stoking desire with the discovery of each connective piece in a puzzle that is never quite finalized.[44] On the other hand, it may also serve as "an appropriate vehicle for political contestation," a method for thinking critically when caught within the governing assumptions of "consensus reality."[45] In *Conspiracy Panics,* Jack Bratich makes a different but complementary intervention, arguing that the term *conspiracy theory* is never neutral but is a discursive maneuver used by those in power to discredit certain beliefs and exclude them from the boundaries of rational political discourse. This allows for the delegitimizing of alternative political dissent by labeling it as extreme or irrational. Similarly, in *Knowledge Goes Pop,* Clare Birchall delves into the ways in which conspiracy theories challenge the boundaries between reason and irrationality, as well as between official and marginalized knowledge. She argues that any attempt to establish certain forms of knowledge as legitimate is ultimately a construct, as there is no definitive basis for determining what is inherently true or valid. By shifting the focus from the content of conspiracy theories to the social and cultural dynamics surrounding them, these scholars call for a more nuanced understanding of conspiracy theories and the situated contexts from which they emerge and persist.

Other scholars working in the critical-cultural mode tend to focus less on how definitions of conspiracy theory come about—the interests and techniques that shape any given definition—and more on how conspiracy theories come to function persuasively in their appeal to subjective adherence. Writing from the perspective of rhetorical and argumentation studies, Jenny Rice and Calum Matheson both explore conspiracy theories as case studies that reveal the limitations of traditional argumentative structures—or, as Rice puts it, "to raise a question that many people (both inside and outside academic circles) are asking: *Why do traditional modes of argument often fail in the face of claims that rely on bad evidence?*"[46] Rice argues that conspiracy theories are constructed and disseminated through what she terms "awful archives"—collections of information whose curation and presentation rely on the nonlogical dimensions of persuasion. These archives are often characterized by selective use of evidence as well as evidentiary excess, misinterpretation of data, the blending of fact and fiction, and rhetorical techniques such as the strategic use of language, emotional appeals, and the manipulation of narrative structures—all in a bid to create compelling and seemingly credible conspiracy theories. Similarly, Matheson, drawing on Lacanian psychoanalysis, suggests that conspiracy theories function as a form of cathexis, in which individuals emotionally invest in signifiers—such as "Make America Great Again" or "Drain the Swamp"—that provide coherence to an otherwise chaotic world. In this view, conspiracy theories are not simply about argumentation but about the affective structures that shape political and social identities.[47]

Building on Melley's notion of agency panic, Casey Ryan Kelly and Matheson both argue that conspiracy theories emerge from anxieties over individual autonomy in a world increasingly governed by impersonal systems of power.[48] Whereas Matheson explores the rhetoric and media discourse that fueled widespread fear and suspicion that Jade Helm 15 was a prelude to martial law (or an invasion of Texas, take your pick), Kelly examines COVID-19 conspiracy theories, showing how fears surrounding vaccines, digital passports, and lockdowns reflect deeper concerns about the erosion of a self-possessed, property-owning (white) liberal subject. In a parallel move, Matheson explores how conspiracy discourse offers a sense of agency in an uncertain world by investing in emotionally charged narratives. Both scholars suggest that conspiracy theories provide psychological compensation for the diminishing sense of personal control in an era of globalization, digital surveillance, and bureaucratic governance.

The rhetorical dimensions of conspiracy discourse also hinge on the interplay between secrecy and revelation, a theme explored by Atilla Hallsby and Joshua Gunn. Like Rice, Hallsby approaches conspiracy theory through a lens like Rice's awful archive but places greater emphasis on tropes than on argumentation, specifically tropes pertaining to the duality of secrecy and transparency—"the sense of expectation and desire that accompanies every encounter with the secret." He argues that conspiracy theories operate through an affective economy of anticipation, where the pleasure of secrecy lies not in the discovery of hidden truths but in the process of uncovering them—what he describes as the perpetual deferral of complete revelation that "keeps the promise of release in indefinite suspense."[49] Gunn extends this analysis by linking conspiracy theories to occult rhetoric, showing how both function as structuring forces that shape how people interpret the world. He argues that secrecy generates desire, fascination, and paranoia, particularly in media-saturated societies, where the unknown often feels more compelling than the known. Like esoteric ("occult") traditions that claim hidden knowledge available only to the initiated, conspiracy theories thrive on the belief that nothing is as it seems and that uncovering secret truths grants power or enlightenment.[50]

These scholars illustrate that conspiracy theories are not merely epistemological errors or cognitive biases but complex rhetorical formations that mobilize affect, narrative structure, and secrecy. Whether understood through the lens of argumentation, psychoanalysis, or rhetorical tropes, conspiracy discourse functions by drawing adherents into a recursive process of meaning-making that resists closure. These theories do not simply persuade through rational appeals; rather, they offer adherents a framework for understanding the world—one that is emotionally, politically, and existentially charged.

ESOTERICISM AS PRONOIAC CONSPIRACY THEORY

Treating conspiracy theory as a potentially dangerous cultural symptom is related to another salient feature of much research on the topic, the presumption that malevolence is the sine qua non of conspiracism. Many scholars adopt the presumption made explicit by social psychologists Karen Douglas and Robbie Sutton that the conspiracies alleged by the conspiracy-minded "are almost always malevolent—that is, against the public interest."[51] In this view, secrecy prominently features in conspiracy theory because it is necessary for the execution of the alleged malefic plot and to sustain the deception that may have motivated it. After all, an uncovered plot taken seriously by the authorities stands a chance of being interrupted.

As we have seen, however, philosophical esotericism suggests a contrasting alternative motive for concealment: benevolence. There are indeed those among the conspiracy-minded who attribute to supposed plots a benevolent purposiveness—a motive to subserve rather than subvert public interest, or for that matter the interests of private groups and individuals. Yet, while critical discourse about conspiracism allows for the possibility of imputing altruistic motives, it still tends, as a matter of practice, to diminish the benignity of any given conspiracy theory—theoretically as well as attentively—while amplifying the prohibitory quality.[52] This is true even among scholars who put a premium on the interrelations among texts, contexts, and audiences; they tend to recontextualize audiences' attribution of kind and positive intentions against an interpretive background highlighting hostility. When it comes to discussing conspiracy theories, hidden benevolent forces generally do not occupy a central position in the academic or even popular imagination.

Despite this tendency, any decent survey of contemporary American conspiracy theories would be remiss if it did not at least mention QAnon, arguably the most popular conspiracy theory in recent history to spotlight the role of benevolence. From its inception as a sprawling constellation of conspiracy narratives, QAnon has depicted President Donald Trump and the anonymous poster "Q" (said to be a senior official with Q clearance, or access to top-secret government materials) as coconspirators tasked with neutralizing an alleged satanic cabal of pedophilic global elites.[53] This narrative includes belief in adrenochrome markets, elite pedophile rings, and political traitors—all classic tropes of hostile conspiracy theories.

But these features only make up half of the story. To counter these nefarious forces, proponents argue, Trump, Q, and an internet-savvy network of private individuals are actively engaged in a counterconspiracy to uncover and disrupt the elite's satanic, pedophilic designs. Much of the benevolent subversion allegedly consists of the circulation and interpretation of secretly coded messages among right-thinking Americans. Some messages are believed to be revelations concerning the cabal's hidden agenda and activities, while others are said to be messages indicating Trump's considered countermeasures, occasionally including specific dates and times.

For critics strictly adhering to a malevolent paradigm, Trump and Q's counterconspiracy probably would still be characterized primarily by its deviation from legal norms and its opposition to the interests of the so-called deep state, which would suppress the counterconspiracy if given a chance.[54] This interpretation is not wrong per se, but it does overlook a distinctive and interesting aspect of the QAnon conspiracy theory—if, indeed, the term *conspiracy* still applies. Most conspiracy theories of the malevolent variety virtually presuppose an antagonistic method of decoding, whereby secrecy is peeled back, layer after investigative layer, in opposition to the conspirators' hidden plans and desires. Conspiracy theories with benevolent conspirators, in contrast, frequently position conspirators and decoders as working in tandem. Here, conspirators (like Trump and Q) do not make encryption errors that their enemies will seek to exploit so much as they leave deliberate breadcrumbs to be deciphered by what Strauss called "thoughtful . . . careful readers."[55]

Thus, if one is inclined to pathologize conspiracism, one should attend not only to paranoia but also to pronoia, its far less discussed counterpart. Whereas the origin of the term *paranoia* was the Greek word *par-a-noy'a* (meaning "derangement" or "departure from the normal" in thinking), and the word itself appeared in Greek tragic drama and Platonic dialogues, *pronoia* was probably not coined until the 1980s.[56] One of its earliest appearances, if not the earliest, occurred in an article published in *Social Problems*.[57] According to its author, Fred Goldner, pronoia is a person's belief or perception that the world around them is conspiring to do them good, in contrast to paranoia, where one believes that the world is out to harm them. It is a state of mind in which individuals feel that others have positive intentions and that life events will lead to favorable outcomes. Pronoia fosters optimism, trust, and a sense of connection with others, often leading to a more positive and proactive approach to life's challenges.

The call for a pronoiac lens does not seek to replace other vectors of analysis; many conspiracies with benevolent conspirators assume (almost as a condition of possibility) a paranoia-inducing world of mysterious, harmful forces. To view QAnon only through the lens of pronoia thus obstructs the picture. That said, some of our case studies are so defined by benevolence that they may not even register as conspiracy theories for those who use paranoia as a litmus test. For what is pronoiac conspiracy theory if not a species of esoteric hermeneutics? Some conspiracies we discuss, like that of the so-called Gaylors, are primarily driven by benevolent conspiring (so much so that they may not even register as conspiracy theories). Others, like QAnon, have a mix of paranoid and pronoiac elements.

The case could even be made that philosophical esotericism may be the urtext of benevolent conspiracy theorization in the Western intellectual tradition. While one imagines the Straussian stables rejecting this association, for the general public, the critical determination of whether something is to be branded a "conspiracy theory" is an assessment of that something's truth claim. Birchall and Bratich maintain that such assessments are not made in a mediological, cultural, or political vacuum, yet despite the myriad factors that condition people's judgment—as well as differences in judgments themselves—whatever counts as truth typically serves as an epistemological bifurcation separating conspiracy theories from the discovery of actual conspiracies. At this point, it is worth reiterating that the esoteric nature of any given esoteric text is nondemonstrable and that structurally speaking esotericism and conspiracism appear to be cut from the same cloth. The present book aims to elaborate on this homology by critiquing select, contemporary examples of pop cultural esotericism/pronoiac speculation, from Disney, Taylor Swift, and Batman to QAnon and Shakespeare.

RHETORICAL ESOTERICISM AND PRONOIAC FANDOM

Like most of the scholars mentioned above, our approach is primarily informed by a media and cultural studies paradigm focusing on what Vilém Flusser describes as the interrelations among scene, surface, and receiver (or context, text/image, and audience).[58] This means that we do not presume Strauss's nonfalsifiable principle of logographic necessity, according to which all features of a text are intentional and authors exercise complete control over their texts. Instead, we maintain that, irrespective of authorial intent, some texts possess features that invite or are seen to invite politically charged esoteric readings. In other words, we approach texts subjected to esoteric readings as *rhetorically* esoteric, as esoteric by design, not necessarily by intent.

That framework enables us to identify certain communicative features that encourage audiences to engage esoterically with pop cultural phenomena. Expressed as a series of alternatives, the most important esoterically invitational tropes are whether an object is popular and intertextual, whether it rewards close attention to details, whether it offers a lens for interpretation or a method of reading, and whether there exists (for the sender or receiver) a threat of persecution. None of these features are strictly subjective/epistemological or objective/ontological but are distributed among the interrelations among scene, surface, and receiver, inviting, almost alchemically, an esoteric response.

In developing our framework, our methodological approach embraces surface reading as an alternative to the hermeneutics of suspicion that has dominated interpretive paradigms in critical theory. Building upon the insights of Stephen Best and Sharon Marcus in "Surface Reading" and of Eve Kosofsky Sedgwick in "Paranoid Reading and Reparative Reading," we argue for a rhetorical esotericism that privileges surface-level textual engagements over depth-based hermeneutics. Traditionally, critical methods rooted in depth hermeneutics—such as those advanced by thinkers like Hans-Georg Gadamer, Paul Ricoeur, and Fredric Jameson—operate on the assumption that meaning is hidden, repressed, or obfuscated within a text and must be excavated by the reader. The hermeneutics of suspicion, characterized by Ricoeur as the shared stance of Karl Marx, Friedrich Nietzsche, and Sigmund Freud, fosters an interpretive ethos wherein texts are treated as sites of ideological mystification, demanding exegesis to reveal their latent truths.[59] This approach, as Sedgwick critiques, has become almost synonymous with critical inquiry itself, positioning paranoia as a mandatory methodological imperative.[60] Surface reading, by contrast, seeks to move beyond the reflexive suspicion that treats textual surfaces as mere veils for deeper meaning. Best and Marcus propose that symptomatic reading—rooted in the assumption that texts require unmasking—can occlude what is manifestly present. Surface reading, in contrast, emphasizes description, materiality, and the structures operating in plain sight, thereby offering a methodological shift away from the compulsive disclosure of hidden depths.[61]

Rhetorical esotericism does not align directly with either of these methodologies. It examines surface-level textual elements not to ascertain a text's probable meaning but to identify rhetorical features that actively invite a specific mode of paranoid interpretation—namely, forms of Straussian esotericism. Unlike classical Straussian esotericism, a type of Sedgwickian paranoid (pronoiac) reading which presumes an intentional concealment of meaning by an author, rhetorical esotericism acknowledges that some texts have features that solicit esoteric readings due to their structural and aesthetic properties. Sidestepping the question of whether a paranoid reading is appropriate, esoteric rhetorical analysis asks what brings about such a reading. Thus, instead of treating esotericism as an authorial strategy, we examine how audiences engage with pop cultural texts—Disney films, Taylor Swift's lyrics, Batman narratives, and QAnon messaging—by treating them as encrypted surfaces inviting interpretive labor.

Sedgwick's distinction between paranoid and reparative reading is also central to our approach. Paranoid reading, which begins by assuming deception and on that basis seeks to expose hidden meanings, has long shaped critical engagement with conspiracy theories. In contrast, reparative reading offers a mode of interpretation that embraces openness, curiosity, and the creative possibilities of textual engagement. When examining esoteric fandom, we see how certain interpretive communities adopt a reparative stance, engaging with texts in ways that generate new meanings and foster affirmative readings rather than focusing solely on ideological critique or subtextual exposure. By adopting surface reading as a guiding methodology, we depart from both paranoid suspicion and depth hermeneutics, instead emphasizing the rhetorical, aesthetic, and affective dimensions of cultural texts. This approach allows us to map the ways in which esoteric readings emerge not from the necessity of unveiling hidden truths but from the structured, intertextual play of signs and surfaces that invite audiences into the interpretive act.

Our perspective thus departs from the author-centered humanism of classical rhetoric as much as from its counterpart in philosophical hermeneutics. On that model, rhetoric is conceived as a rational art—a technique—for maximizing one's persuasive impact, just as esoteric hermeneutics is regarded as a rational process for maximizing a reader's ability to decode a rhetor's intentionally hidden messages. Our pronoiac case studies proceed differently—one could say less agentially. On the one hand, we bracket off questions of author intentionality and reader truth claims, assuming instead an agnostic position concerning both; on the other hand, we support, up to a point, the esoteric guideline that some texts, under certain conditions, invite esoteric readings. The following chapters shed light on this process, analyzing esotericism's distributed, tropological nature while examining how pop cultural forms of esoteric decoding occasionally take hold of the persecuted but simultaneously pronoiac imagination. Our project thus contributes to the rhetorical criticism of conspiracy theory undertaken by scholars such as Jenny Rice, Calum Matheson, and Atilla Hallsby, with a pop cultural twist.

In addition to hermeneutic and media and cultural studies approaches to conspiracy theory, the present work also draws upon fan studies. As with the study of conspiracy theory, fan studies is an interdisciplinary field of academic research situated at the intersection of the humanities and the social sciences. In contrast to cultural studies research examining the reception of popular media by fans (audience studies), fan studies examines the activities, cultures, and communities of fans, fandoms, and fan works.[62] It explores how fans engage with media, texts, celebrities, and popular culture through various forms of participation, such as fan fiction, fan art, conventions, online communities, and cosplay, while also investigating the social, cultural, and economic impacts of fan practices and how fans create and negotiate meanings within their fandoms. Key topics include how fans form identities and communities around shared interests, the creation of new content (such as fan fiction and fan art) based on existing media, how fans mobilize around causes related to their interests, the power relationships between fans and producers (including issues of control and influence over media content), and how digital platforms and social media have transformed fan practices.[63]

Like esotericism and conspiracism, fandom constitutes a multiform system of expression that individuals and groups use to make sense of daily life, apprehend reality, communicate with others, articulate their values, and order experience. Much more than frivolous media consumption, fandom designates a hermeneutic vector that participates in the broader cultural-political process through which competing values and interpretations struggle and ideas about what is essential, normal, moral, and true are established, reinforced, and challenged. As Ashley Hinck argues, fandom can inspire civic engagement and social activism, such as when Harry Potter fans advocate for fair trade or YouTube communities raise money for charity.[64] It can also manifest in harmful ways and lead to significant negative behaviors, particularly when fans feel betrayed or victimized by the media content they love.[65] In the contemporary digital environment, even anti-fandom is a significant cultural practice. According to Melissa Click, hate-watching, trolling, and the pleasure derived from expressing disdain in online spaces like X (formerly Twitter), Reddit, and Tumblr can shape identities and social interactions as much as their more positive behavioral counterparts.[66]

These emotional, performative, and political aspects of fandom also occur in conspiracy theory, where participants form identities and communities around shared interests. Take, for example, the #FreeBritney movement.[67] Naomi Smith and Clare Southerton argue that as a form of conspiracy theory, the movement is rooted not only in fear or paranoia but also in the pleasures of community engagement and close textual analysis.[68] The enjoyment derived from piecing together clues, interpreting Britney Spears's social media posts, and participating in the collective investigation fosters a deep sense of connection and community among the fans. These pleasures are similar to those found in traditional fandom, where the act of closely reading and discussing media content with others creates a shared experience and emotional investment.

The same holds for QAnon, where affective engagement and community building are central to its appeal. The dynamics that drive traditional fandoms—such as those around sports teams or TV shows—including practices like communal participation, affective bonds, and shared narratives, are at play in the QAnon movement.[69] Here, too, is a corresponding affective or attitudinal bifurcation. Traditional conspiracy theories (those emphasizing malevolence) map onto anti-fandom, where individuals express strong dislike or hatred for official versions of events, parapolitical or global systems of power, organizations of media and culture, and so on. In contrast, the pronoiac variety of conspiracist speculation (pop cultural esotericism) approximates the more traditional affirming fandoms—even in those instances where positive emotional attachments result in less-than-nice behavior.

Fan studies, however, provides the present study with something beyond a framework for understanding popular esotericism's affective valence and attachments. It also reveals points of contrast that highlight the unique facets of esoteric decryption. Esotericism is distinct from the more modern forms of hermeneutics that emerge from the fan studies tradition. The fan studies concept of "textual poaching" is a good case in point, as is, by extension, oppositional decoding. Introduced by Henry Jenkins in his seminal book *Textual Poachers: Television Fans and Participatory Culture,* textual poaching draws from the work of the French Jesuit scholar Michel de Certeau, who used the metaphor of poaching to describe how individuals appropriate and reinterpret cultural texts for their own purposes.[70] In the context of fan culture, textual poaching refers to the way in which fans engage with, interpret, and rework media texts (like TV shows, movies, or books) in ways that deviate from or challenge the intentions of the original creators. Fans "poach" content, taking elements they find meaningful and transforming them into something new—such as fan fiction, fan art, videos, or other creative works. Jenkins argues that this kind of fan activity is a form of resistance to the authority of producers and a means of democratizing culture by allowing audiences to participate actively in the creation of meaning rather than just passively consuming content.[71] Textual poaching is thus seen as a process that allows fans to assert their own interpretations and identities—to express their desires, fantasies, and social critiques—making fan communities spaces of creative and political engagement.

Stuart Hall's classic "encoding and decoding" formulation also emphasizes the active role of the audience in interpreting media content.[72] For Hall, audiences "decode" (interpret and make sense of) the meanings, values, and ideologies "encoded" or embedded by media producers in media content. Although audiences may interpret the messages in the way the producer intended, fully accepting the encoded meaning, they also may adopt a negotiated or oppositional position; that is, they may either adapt the encoded meaning to reflect their own experiences and interests—thereby leading to a modified understanding—or altogether reject the intended meaning and interpret the message in a contrary way, often criticizing the ideology or values embedded in the content. As with Jenkins's notion of textual poaching, Hall's theory highlights that meaning is not fixed and can vary depending on how the audience decodes the message. Both challenge the traditional notion of communication as a linear process in which the sender's intended message is directly received by the audience. Instead, they emphasize the complexity of media consumption, where audiences can resist or reinterpret dominant cultural narratives.

While in conversation with these theories, rhetorical esotericism ultimately constitutes a third, meta-hermeneutical position. Esoteric audiences do not oppose the encoded meaning; quite the opposite. According to Melzer, they oppose "liberation from the text as a whole, and certainly from its author's [or producer's] intentions."[73] Consequently, esoteric hermeneutics opposes oppositional and negotiated interpretations but also opposes what non-esoteric audiences incorrectly assume is the dominant-hegemonic position. As with poaching, esoteric readers may seize on textual elements they find meaningful and use them to create something new, asserting their own interpretation and identity in the process. They may even do so in creative, politically engaging ways. But this interpretive fan labor is always intended to be in the service of decrypting a text's "hidden" (and therefore "true") message. Bricolage may still be at play, but the piecing together is not equivalent to poaching because it is meant to be in keeping with the producer's intention, though this intention may be disguised.

Although the hermeneutic process of pronoiacally decoding secret, hidden messages bears a prima facie resemblance to textual poaching and counter-hegemonic modes of interpretation, we contend that contemporary esotericism constitutes a distinct political-cultural phenomenon. It does not decode so much as it sets out to *decrypt* what it assumes is a culturally provocative message encrypted within an anodyne exoteric structure of meaning, one that, if expressed unambiguously, would court persecution. As a point of contrast, an oppositional decoding of canonically straight characters, say, Captain Kirk and Spock, would reimagine them as romantically involved; a matching instance of textual poaching would be to take these characters and write them into a queer romance, perhaps borrowing elements from a fantasy romance narrative like *Twilight.* An esoteric approach, in contrast, would try to detect subtle stylistic or contextual clues suggesting that the producers of a movie like *Spider-Man: Across the Spider-Verse* (2023) wanted "careful readers" to decrypt Gwen Stacy/Spider-Woman as trans. According to that read, seemingly exoteric contradictions of Gwen's true identity would function simply as a discursive means of bypassing the censors of a transphobically punitive society and safely distributing a truth potentially inimical to common belief and opinion. Amateur esotericism thus represents a new critical lens through which to understand a species of pop cultural hermeneutics.

This book examines popular texts—or surfaces—that, to some, appear to invite exoteric decryption. This makes fan studies, in combination with the resources of rhetoric and esotericism, a suitable framework for understanding pronoiac conspiracy theory. QAnon, a movement to which we will return in a later chapter, became a global and ever-changing phenomenon because it replicated networked fan connection, not because it was a singular work by an individual or small group. As with QAnon, all our case studies involve popular media representations rather than dense philosophical tomes. Therefore, the esoteric fan readings highlighted in our analyses are a crucial part of the analyses. In our critiques of contemporary, popular forms of esoteric decoding, we identify what *fans* (not us, necessarily) find salient in a text for them to read it esoterically. In the parlance of rhetorical studies, we want to unpack a series of not-so-apparent invitations to esoteric decryption.

Academic esoteric readings have long been the domain of Straussians, who have written numerous books and articles on the hidden (and therefore "true") philosophical messages of what they regard as culturally significant works. Such works primarily consist of treatises by political philosophers such as Niccolo Machiavelli and Thomas Hobbes but also include some popular literary works, particularly Shakespeare's histories and tragedies. By changing the lens and zooming out from the world of periodicals and academic presses to that of fan cultures, we hope to bring to light a reticulate, multimodal world of amateur esoteric decryption. This world, which cuts its own methodological pathways, operates under the assumption that persecution does not belong to the dustbins of pre- or nonliberal modernity but constitutes a clear and present danger for various marginalized people and groups living in contemporary Western societies.

On that basis, and in conjunction with the wide-ranging communicative capacities of modern media technology, the world of esoteric fandom searches for secretly coded messages in the existing pop cultural landscape of which it is a part, messages that by virtue of their encryption are assumed to be carriers of suppressed political truths. Given the postconvergence phase of media development, as well as the anonymity afforded by networked digital information technology, the practice of amateur esotericism now outpaces, both in frequency and amplitude, its "legitimate" academic counterpart.[74] Through multiple nodes of mediological interaction, we show how the world of esoteric fandom takes advantage of a hyperfragmented media culture in which fans and self-styled media critics have virtually eclipsed the writings of professional critics—though not entirely, as we will see in our chapter on Straussian interpretations of Shakespeare. Esotericism, in other words, has gone viral, much to the chagrin of professional hermeneuticists.[75]

As a distinct species of amateur esotericism, esoteric fandom thus constitutes an important, understudied site for cultural criticism. It seems to be understudied because it has yet to be identified, theorized, or critiqued as such. This project aims to change that by applying a rhetorically inflected cultural studies approach to the diagrammatically byzantine worlds of esotericism, conspiracy theory, and fandom. With these methodological foundations in mind, our book articulates three major argumentative pathways. First, in postindustrial, telematic societies, esotericism functions primarily as an inventional and invitational hermeneutic rather than naming a purposeful quality infused into a text or work by an author. Second, fan cultures and media fandom operate as politically esoteric inflection points, whereby media texts are politically reimagined and then recirculated via a serpentine pipeline of multimodal interactivity and networked internet platforms. And finally, irrespective of authorial intent, some texts possess characteristics that invite or are seen to invite politically charged esoteric readings.

ESOTERIC COMPASS

The book's critical analysis is built around five case studies of esoteric fandom, ranging from fan interpretations of "old media" artifacts like Shakespearean drama and Disney animation to postdigital/internet ones like Taylor Swift, the *Dark Knight* trilogy, and the QAnon movement. Separated by time, subject matter, and media, these case studies examine how pop culture artifacts are decoded esoterically for recondite purposes. They elucidate new justifications and consequences of esoteric thinking that manifest in the pre- and postdigital contemporary era.

As Strauss and Straussians have averred (correctly, in this case), esoteric writing includes a deeply political element because it provides a means for safely engendering and maintaining a distributed, virtual community of like-minded dissidents within a hostile sociocultural environment. To take a twentieth-century example, in the Soviet Union, dissidents who may never have met face-to-face could be linked, like beads on an abacus, through a shared esoteric reading of a play, a novel, or a poem. Premodern philosophers, too, especially those whose ideas were perceived to violate common belief and opinion, were known to have written esoterically to reach and connect surreptitiously new students across different periods and cultures and to do so with a greatly reduced threat of persecution. For these and other dissenters in history, the prospect of composing illicit messages in a way that could escape community censors served as an inspirational, morale-boosting strategy.

In modern liberal democracies, where the threat of severe censorship has dissipated, esoteric writings can be decoded communally and in the open. Thanks to the recent emergence of digital-cultural interactivity and networked internet platforms, the easing of overt censorship has resulted in the proliferation of esoteric activity in a way that blurs together users or audiences and content producers. Given that the raison d'être of esoteric writing is to preserve secrecy, this development would appear to have obviated its political purpose, reducing it to the status of historical curiosity or pastime. Esotericism, however, can generate other discursive effects with political implications. For instance, the active process of deciphering esoteric messages can strengthen the subjective adherence to political content, as found in certain formal strategies like the enthymeme or narrative structure. Moreover, because esoteric messaging occupies a central rather than peripheral element in today's media culture, the collaborative decryption of messages tends to reinforce belief in the reality of persecution at the hands of powerful, secretive forces while instaurating the pronoiac belief that other, countervailing benevolent forces are at work.

We aim to identify and critique how certain stylistic, contextual, and creative-interactive elements of pop cultural texts invite esoteric interpretations, and to what political effect. To that end, this book will look to several distinct case studies involving close readings of popular texts undertaken by dedicated communities of esoterically minded fans. Rather than proposing alternate close readings, our cultural-rhetorical approach studies the dynamics of esoteric attraction to texts like *The Dark Knight Rises* and photos from former President Trump's Twitter/X feed. That is, the case studies read communities' readings of texts, exploring how, why, and to what ends they justify their esoteric interpretations in the face of more obvious exoteric interpretations.

The first and second chapters focus on esoteric queerness in fan communities devoted to Disney and to Taylor Swift. Chapter 1, "I Can Show You [a] World: Fans Queer Disney," looks at the history of queer Disney, focusing on select animated feature films from the company's Renaissance era (1989–1999), notably *The Little Mermaid* (1989), *Beauty and the Beast* (1991), and *Aladdin* (1992). It examines how critics and fans alike have read progressive messages about queerness into these and other of Disney's animated franchise films. Fan-favorite characters like Ariel and Belle, for example, are often read as intentional metaphors about escaping the strictures of heteronormativity—tropes allegedly embedded in the films by gay composer Howard Ashman. These pronoiacally queer readings are complicated because they overlap with, but are not identical to, the more paranoiacally queer readings of these films that issue from the Christian right. The chapter also discusses the potential risks that fans armed with esotericism pose to multimedia conglomerates that desire safe products with broad-based appeal. That risk is made more urgent from a political-economic perspective, given the ongoing process of media consolidation and the importance of global markets to media and entertainment companies like the Walt Disney Company.

Chapter 2, "You Can Want Who You Want: Taylor Swift as Gay Best Friend," examines the fan activity of the Gaylor community, a fandom of predominantly queer Swift fans who believe the singer-songwriter esoterically communicates her queerness to her most thoughtful, careful "readers." We look at this to demonstrate how esotericism can serve as a foundation for a particular type of parasocial relationship building. The Gaylor fandom draws on lyrics, music videos, fashion choices, album art, and many other kinds of signifiers to build a case that Swift is bisexual or lesbian. Like those involved in the QAnon movement, Gaylors take full advantage of digital spaces and social media platforms, most notably TikTok, to make myriad connections and elaborate deep, esoteric readings of their preferred star.

In the third chapter, "Where We Produce One, We Produce All: The Platform Conspiracism of QAnon," we explore claims that President Trump is the key to undermining a global cabal of baby-eating pedophiles. This chapter argues that there exists a tendency among QAnon followers to read and write esoterically, primarily in relation to President Trump, and to do so via the amateur "produsage" (from *producer* and *user*) made possible by a serpentine pipeline of digital-cultural interactivity and networked internet platforms. We examine Trump's speeches and tweets and how they are interpreted by Q, YouTube channels, self-published books, and message boards. Even though the QAnon movement centers (or initially centered) on Trump, we maintain that an esoteric hermeneutic can be comfortably cultivated in an ecosystem of produsage absent a central figure, emitter, or discourse.

The fourth chapter, "The Esoteric Hero the Dissident Right Needs: White Knighting the Batman," investigates how white nationalist and identitarian fan communities read the *Dark Knight* film series as a coded attack on liberal values by the secretly sympathetic writer-director Christopher Nolan. In a classic esoteric reading, white nationalists posit that super villains like Ra's al Ghul and Bane are giving voice to the true message of the trilogy—that liberal countries have become decadent and must be destroyed to give rise to "archeofuturist" ethnostates.[76] This chapter examines the white nationalists' criticisms of traditional media critics on both the left and the right in a way that helps to differentiate esoteric hermeneutics from more conventional professional critical readings.

The fifth chapter, "All That Glitters Is Gold: Straussianism as Rarefied Fandom," brings the discussion full circle by analyzing interpretations of

Shakespearean drama by self-proclaimed academic Straussians. It takes the lessons from the previous chapters and uses them to reframe applications of Strauss's philosophical hermeneutics in terms of rhetoric, audience reception, and fan studies. It argues that an equivalent cultural rhetoric connects professionally Straussian interpretations of canonical works to the amateur esoteric readings of pop cultural texts as detailed in the previous chapters. The takeaway is that if fans can be considered critics, then Straussian critics may also be accurately and productively thought of as fans.

The conclusion, "This Conclusion Is Not Esoteric," considers the sociohistorical implications of the growing practice of esoteric fandom, reflecting on how the esotericism expressed through digital systems of connectivity represents an overabundance of collective intelligence, such that, like an overactive immune system, it can address problems and puzzles whose existence is not falsifiable. It offers a summation of how our work critically expands on the fields of Straussian esotericism, conspiracy theory, and fan studies while predicting that esoteric movements like QAnon will proliferate and grow in importance as interactive, networked digital systems become more complex and intertwined in our daily lives. Absent a new set of tools, cultural critics could easily mischaracterize and thus misunderstand this new phenomenon.

1

I CAN SHOW YOU [A] WORLD

Fans Queer Disney

> I think that's what Ursula is all about. It's the hair and the makeup and the bustier and attitude, but those are also all fronts for what she is hiding. So it's definitely an ode to Divine.
>
> —Melissa McCarthy

We open with a case study on Disney's blockbuster animated musicals from the late 1980s and early 1990s, specifically *The Little Mermaid* (1989) and *Beauty and the Beast* (1991). We begin here partly in deference to linear chronology—these are the oldest case studies we will examine, marking a pivotal moment that straddles the mainstreaming of the internet and the seismic shifts it introduced to both conspiracy and fan culture. But there is another reason. These films are widely beloved, but they hold special significance for the queer community, many of whom have read them as speaking directly—though covertly—to their experience. Timeless classics, built on timeless fairy tales, perhaps even whispering a timeless philosophy of universal truths and justice. From a purely functional perspective, could anything be more esoterically Straussian? And yet the Straussians—those champions of reading between the lines—would likely dismiss these films with a refrain whose cultural significance they themselves might not even recognize: "They not like us, they not like us."[1]

We seek to blur the boundaries between fandom, conspiracy, and esotericism—boundaries often rigidly policed in academic discourse. This chapter begins by examining a Straussian disavowal of queer studies, queer readings of popular culture, and queerness itself. Pushing back against this imposed division, we draw on Straussian esotericism, as well as academic conspiracy theory and fan studies, to analyze the relationship among queer Disney fans, *The Little Mermaid, Beauty and the Beast,* and Disney as a cultural institution. In doing so, we establish a framework that recurs throughout our case studies, culminating in a final analysis of Straussian esotericism that challenges its presumed separation from both conspiracy and fandom. This approach uncovers new pathways for esoteric analysis rooted in aesthetics—or, as contemporary audiences might say, "vibes"—while simultaneously reframing esoteric decoders as fans and conspiracists.

DRAWING THE LINE(S)

In September 2020, a "Roundtable" episode of the *American Mind* podcast, from the Claremont Institute (one of the last bastions of academic Straussian thought), included a segment entitled "Leo Strauss and Queer Theory." In the episode, the hosts decry the "postmodernization" of the social sciences, by which they mean a fixation on quantifiable measurements as well as on racial and gender identity (such as "driving while Black" or "playing video games while trans"), then deride the recent decision of the American Political Science Association to give its Leo Strauss Award to a dissertation centered on lesbian feminist political strategies within the second-wave feminist movement.[2] The presenters dismiss the work as that of a "wokester" whose scholarship is fundamentally at odds with the kind of deep, philosophical questioning about the nature of truth and justice that Strauss pursued in his own work. The hosts broadly pan queer theory in general (and so-called postmodern theory even more generally) as an unserious, nonacademic undertaking—as fake research undeserving of the resources or attention conferred on it by the association and its award-granting bodies.

Dismissal of queer theory combined with a complete disinterest in examining the communication strategies of queer folk, however, is on the softer end of the Straussian reaction to queerness. In a *New York Times Book Review* containing multiple references to Strauss, Harry V. Jaffa, one of Strauss's most prominent disciples, indulged in some not-so-veiled swipes at queerness, writing, "The debunking both of Socratic skepticism ('the unexamined life is not worth living') and of biblical faith ('Fear of the Lord is the beginning of wisdom') has led to the crisis of the West, a chaos of moral relativism and philosophic nihilism in which every lifestyle, no matter how corrupt or degenerate, can be said to be as good as any other."[3] Jaffa's article, which appeared at a time when the gay marriage debate was capturing national headlines, leaves little doubt as to which "degenerate" lifestyles he had in mind. That room for doubt grows even smaller when one considers the review in connection with other of Jaffa's published remarks about homosexuality. As Nathan Robinson spells out in an essay for *Salon,* Jaffa consistently used the term *sodomites* to refer to homosexuals; he wrote a highly implausible dialogue between serial killer Ted Bundy and a potential female victim, in which Bundy justified rape and murder by claiming that society no longer considered sodomy a crime or immoral; and in a 1988 review of Allan Bloom's book *The Closing of the American Mind,* Jaffa controversially asserted that AIDS was a form of "retribution" for the acceptance of sodomy and lesbianism as recommended lifestyles.[4]

Although snubbing and outright censure are two of the more obvious reactionary responses to queerness, there are others. Peter Minowitz, for instance, offers a bizarre analogy between being gay in a heteronormative society and being a Straussian in the academy. The book's title, *Straussophobia,* captures the essence of that analogy while turning it into a neologism. The text itself is replete with appropriations of linguistic expressions originally intended to give voice to gay people and people of color, including claiming the phrase "coming out" as Straussian, describing the so-called institutional discrimination experienced by Straussians, and more. In Minowitz's hands, queerness and its limited social protections become a source of envy that motivates claims of Straussian entitlement. He writes, "Insofar as dominant sectors of U.S. society—political, corporate, legal, medical, and academic—are rapturous in celebrating diversity, Straussians too are entitled to grouse."[5]

Minowitz's treatment of queerness, which frames it as a competitor for institutional resources, "interacts"—oddly, perhaps—with those Straussian approaches that view it as only a force of societal and professional subversion. On the one hand, it forgoes the hypercritical language and sanctimonious tone of the Jaffa variety, striking what may even appear to be a note of sympathetic camaraderie (of a sorts). On the other hand, it also declines to consider whether and how the persecutory experience of queerness could translate into a source of esoteric communication. There is, however, another vantage point from which queerness (including queer theory) and Straussian hermeneutics form a more harmonious relationship.

Bloom, whose *Closing of the American Mind* served as an indictment of what Jaffa viewed as a waywardly permissive society, presents what is possibly an alternative Straussian model of queer reception. Alongside Jaffa, Bloom was one of Strauss's most esteemed students, and along with Jaffa and Camille Paglia is one of the most popular Straussian writers.[6] That reputation mostly stems from his *Closing of the American Mind.* On the surface, the monograph consists of a defense of the Western literary canon and its philosophical legacy, along with a de rigueur invective against the perceived ascendancy of postmodernism within university English departments. Originally published in 1987, it became an overnight bestseller and served as a cudgel wielded by conservative cultural warriors in the so-called culture war that the book itself, in part, helped ignite. Decades after its publication, it is still best remembered for sparking conversations and fueling controversies over such topics as history education in high schools and the efficacy of affirmative action and identity politics.[7] Standing in stark contrast to that legacy, however, are esoteric readings of the book by Eve Sedgwick (a student of Bloom's and founder of queer theory) and others, who attribute a purposefully homoerotic element to Bloom's call for a pedagogy dedicated to awakening in young men a desire for high culture.[8]

But how could it possibly be the case that a rarefied, homoerotic call to intellectual arms would be misconstrued as a rhetorical weapon in the cultural conservative's arsenal? There does not appear to be a simple, compelling answer. The best we can offer is the analogy offered by Blake Smith, writing for the *Tablet,* that "*Closing of the American Mind* was misrecognized by ordinary readers in something of the way that the Village People's ode to gay cruising, 'YMCA,' became the anthem of dorky straight people at sporting events."[9] If such misrecognition is actual and Bloom did hide a homoerotic pedagogy in his paean for conservative cultural values, then this maneuver would place him in contention for modernity's paragon of esotericism—and queer esotericism at that.

Beyond (or adjacent to) the possibility of a cryptic message of homoerotic mentorship embedded in Bloom's text, the relationship between queerness and queer theory prima facie provides fertile ground for esoteric communication. Recall that Strauss himself posited persecution as the rhetorical exigence of esotericism. Combine that raison d'être with the fact that most modern societies expend resources proscribing or disciplining queerness and it should come as no surprise, Paul Baker argues, that coded forms of communication enjoy a long, multifarious history within the queer world.[10] In the 1970s, for instance, gay men developed the "hankie code," using different colored handkerchiefs to signal their sexual proclivities to others in the know—a practice introduced to straight audiences in William Friedkin's controversial 1980 crime thriller *Cruising*, starring Al Pacino).[11] According to StormMiguel Florez's award-winning PBS documentary *The Whistle*, young lesbians living in New Mexico in the 1970s and 1980s used a particular type of whistle to signal their in-group status. In the central north African country of Burundi, where homosexuality is prohibited by law, lesbians make use of various symbols, like violets, to connect with one another while circumventing both state-run and "neighborly" surveillance.[12] These are but a few of the virtually countless examples of queer people availing themselves of esoteric means of communication to exploit the obliviousness of (exoterically communicative) straight majorities. Fear of queer persecution, in other words, facilitates not only esoterically rarefied academic texts but also a rhizomatic hinterland of equally untamed and indigenous inscrutability.

As extensive as these practices may be, queer esotericism encompasses purposes beyond that of individuals seeking personal connection. For example, suspicion has long surrounded the careers of many queer writers and creatives, built on an assumption that their public-facing works include homoerotic subtexts, similar to the Soviet-era belief that dissident playwrights, novelists, and filmmakers often smuggled into their works abstruse criticisms of the state. Alexander Doty, for instance, claims that queer directors such as George Cukor (*The Philadelphia Story; My Fair Lady*) and Dorothy Arzner (*The Wild Party; The Bride Wore Red*) incorporated many hidden references to queerness within their popular studio pictures, pointing to Arzner's *Christopher Strong* (1933) and *Dance, Girl, Dance* (1940) and Cukor's *Sylvia Scarlett* (1935) and *Camille* (1936) as typical examples. Doty writes, "We can say that directors—and certainly queer directors—who had particularly unspeakable ideological programs found it necessary to continue developing a repertoire of sly working-within-the-system expressive tactics even once they achieved stature within the industry."[13]

Lending apparent support to that claim is the statement by queer public intellectual Gore Vidal that he rewrote scenes in the biblical blockbuster *Ben-Hur* (1959) to imply a sexual relationship between the male protagonist, Judah Ben-Hur, and his male antagonist, Messala.[14] For a queer romance to be hidden within the largest-budgeted film at the time (more than $15 million), and one sporting *A Tale of the Christ* as its subtitle, meant that it could only "appear" esoterically, if at all. A more recent, though much less controversial, example of an artist disclosing an esoterically queer message comes from Lady Gaga, who in 2023 conclusively revealed that her worldwide chart-topping smash hit "Poker Face" is about having sex with men while thinking about women—with "poker face" being a sublimation of "poke her face," or, as she says more explicitly, "fuck her face."[15]

Interestingly, the *American Mind* podcast actually appears to endorse precisely these kinds of queer analyses in the same breath as it disparages queer theory writ large:

> This is an actually interesting critique that somebody could make of, say, for example, musical theater in America. If you really wanted to do a sustained study of this, like if you want to go into musical theater, note all the great musical theater in America is written by gays yearning to be able to express themselves when they can't. It's all about sublimating your homosexual desire into some heterosexual story about, like, I want this woman, I'm a man, that I want this woman that I can't have a liking to have because secretly you're a gay person. And that is why, like, so it's . . . such a disproportionate number of gay people have been successful in the American arts, is because, like, they were forbidden from expressing themselves directly. That's why the most ancient—one of the most interesting relationships with the *Maltese Falcon* is between Cairo and Willmar, the adult, like, you know, weird gay foreigner and the hired gun. Like, it's because it's sublimated, and once it's not sublimated, it comes out into the light. And it's, like, the blah, it's completely nothing.[16]

Despite the obvious intersection of Straussian esotericism and queer theory, Straussians, as evinced in their publications, do not seem particularly interested in parsing queer-coded messages; nor do queer theorists, for their part, appear especially keen on acknowledging any indebtedness to Straussian hermeneutics. The situation reads almost like a tacitly agreed-upon conspiracy of silence. A more likely—and less paranoid—interpretation is that the situation is characterized by reciprocal disinterest, with perhaps a dash of low-key antipathy, a predictable, albeit unfortunate, result of the mutually antagonistic orientations of queer theorists and Straussians, which tend to map onto the left–right divide. In a world of political polarization, the shared hermeneutic among queer theorists and Straussians, like the homoeroticism of *Ben-Hur*, is the affective kernel of a love that dares not speak its name.

While most queer encoding/decoding has occurred at the personal level ("How can I safely reveal my sexual identity to this person?") or the academic level ("Just why is Socrates leading young Phaedrus outside the city walls to talk about love?"), the phenomenon of queer esoteric reading has at times merged with fan studies to produce interpretive analyses of pop culture texts. Perhaps one of the most surprising of these involves stories produced by the dominant children's entertainment company of the twentieth and twenty-first centuries, the Walt Disney Company. These interpretive interventions suggest that, in the queer-hostile environment of the 1990s, Disney released films esoterically supportive of queerness, and that it continues to encode current movies with queer-friendly messages, even as Disney dominates many markets around the world that are openly hostile to queerness.

DISNEYDOM

Disney is currently an undisputed media powerhouse, one of a handful of large corporate conglomerates that dominates the global entertainment business. In 2019, as one of the "big five" movie studios (the others today include Warner Bros. Discovery, Universal, Sony, and Paramount), Disney accounted for nearly 40 percent of the U.S. box office market share, producing or distributing such tentpole blockbusters as *Frozen II* (2019), *The Lion King* (the 2019 computer-animated remake of 1994's traditionally animated film of the same name), and the second *Avengers* sequel, *Avengers: Endgame* (2019). For comparison, Disney's closest competitor at the time, Warner Bros. (then owned by telecom company AT&T), accounted for only 13.8 percent of the market share.[17]

Movies, however, represent only one division of the Walt Disney Company. It also owns Disney television channels, Disney stores, Disney radio stations, and—what tend to be the company's biggest cash cows—Disney parks and properties, including Walt Disney World Resort, Disneyland Resort, Disneyland Paris, Disney Cruise Line, and a host of other vacation-oriented properties.[18] A trailblazer in corporate convergence (the concentration of media ownership), Disney purchased Pixar Animation Studios in 2006, Marvel Comics in 2009, and to the tune of $4 billion, Lucasfilm in 2012, acquisitions that gave it control of a vast library of popular characters and franchises, which it extensively leveraged and synergistically promoted across its many divisions (films, themed environments, original television series, and more). Disney also owns Hulu, Starz+, ABC, National Geographic, ESPN (80 percent stake), 21st Century Fox, the Muppets, Vice Media (10 percent stake), and the venture capital firm Steamboat Ventures. In partnership with the Hearst Corporation, it holds 50 percent of the equity of A&E, the History Channel, and Lifetime.[19] Disney's corporate dominance is so prodigious that it has prompted calls for trust busting, not only in online communities but also in federal court, and its net worth of nearly $172 billion is larger than that of many countries.[20]

That much of Disney's recent growth is a function of twenty-first-century digital convergence may give the impression that the company has undergone a radical transformation, that it is not the same Disney that we remember from our childhoods or that our parents or grandparents remember from theirs. While not inaccurate, that impression runs the risk of occluding the socioeconomic fact that Disney, since its incorporation, has *always* been a dominant presence in the media landscape. In the film industry alone, Disney has been a major player ever since the establishment of the studio system and the beginning of Hollywood's Golden Age, from roughly the 1920s through the late 1940s. During that time, studios, including Disney, transformed a competitive market composed of many small firms into an oligopoly dominated by a handful of vertically integrated mega firms. Even during relatively slow-growth periods, the company can often point to immense gains, as it did in its 1999 report, which, while noting concern about a slower-than-expected expansion for the decade, still details an enormously successful entertainment empire: "We now have seven theme parks (with four more in the works), 27 hotels with 36,888 rooms, two cruise ships, 728 Disney Stores, one broadcast network, 10 TV stations, nine international Disney Channels, 42 radio stations, an Internet portal, five major Internet web sites, interests in nine U.S. cable networks."[21] What's more, the 1990s are included in what many refer to as the Disney Renaissance (1989–1999), a period of resurgence during which Walt Disney Feature Animation returned to producing critically and commercially successful animated films—films that went on to earn much greater profits than most of the Disney films of previous eras, including those of Disney's Golden Age (1937–1942).[22] This renaissance was itself but a piece of a longer-term surge in Disney share price, which from 1984 to 2014 rose an incredible 8,943 percent.[23]

Much of this recent growth derives from Disney's PG-rated fare, but the company has long dominated the G-rated market, producing blockbuster animated films such as *The Little Mermaid* and *Aladdin* (1992), as well as their straight-to-video sequels.[24] It is in fact such a G-ratings powerhouse that, as Lee Unkrich, the director of *Toy Story 3* (2010) and *Coco* (2017), recently observed, its shift in emphasis over the past two decades from G-rated to PG-rated films has coincided with a growing preference for the PG rating among studios, filmmakers, and audiences.[25]

Disney's clout with regard to children's and family movies in general deserves special attention. The average American has probably watched—and watched many, many times—the animated feature films that Disney released when they were children. The replay value of these films for children can be so high as to induce Disney fatigue in their parents, who find themselves captive audiences to the films (or, maybe worse, sequences of films) that their children watch or listen to over and over. The perception of parents' Disney fatigue is sufficiently real that it prompted the screenwriter and codirector of *Frozen* (2013), Jennifer Lee, to apologize for the catchiness of the film's songs: "A year ago, I'd meet people who, when they found out who I was, they'd say, 'Oh, we love the songs! We sing them all the time.' Now they're like, 'Yep, we're still listening to those songs.' . . . I've gone from 'Thank you' to 'Sorry'!"[26]

The massive popularity of these films among children obviously raises questions about what lessons the productions may be teaching to youth. This is true of almost any media content that appeals to children. What sets Disney apart in this regard is that most of its animated feature films are fables—stories featuring animals or inanimate objects as characters that are designed to convey a moral, to inculcate or reinforce values. Disney's fables, however, are not original stories but retellings of traditional fables from around the world; for example, *The Little Mermaid* is from Denmark, *Aladdin* originated in the Middle East, and *Mulan* (1998) comes from China.[27] These fables were intended to transmit and pass on from one generation to the next life lessons about correct behavior. While Disney often removes or revises the original moral content of these stories—for instance *Beauty and the Beast*'s (1991) message that young girls should accept arranged marriages to older men—there is little question that new morals emerge in their place.

There should be little surprise that a corporation serving as modernizing ventriloquists of the Brothers Grimm or Aesop—complete with theme parks, merchandise, and cruise lines—would attract critical attention vis-à-vis the moral lessons it imparts to its child audiences and patrons. A quick Google search reveals any number of articles criticizing Disney for the messages contained in its films for children. These disapprovals come from both the political left and the right. Mainstream liberals tend to take issue with the lack of agency attributed to female characters and the heteronormative depiction of marriage; conservatives, in contrast, point to the absence of strong parental figures as an attack on the traditional family. Mostly, however, these critical interpretations of Disney's animated features operate on either the explicit or the implicit, subtextual levels.

At the explicit level, for instance, *Mulan* (the story of a young woman in ancient China who disguises herself as a man to join the imperial Chinese army in order to fend off the invading Huns) contains an explicitly promotional message of gender equality—a message so unsubtle that even former Vice President Mike Pence criticized it as liberal propaganda.[28] Other criticisms focus on indirect messaging, such as Disney's implicit endorsement, mostly conveyed through characters' visual design, of unnatural and unhealthy body size, especially for girls. Critics reading at this level of meaning do not suggest that Disney actively seeks to teach children, for instance, that they should strive for unrealistic body types, but they argue that its films nevertheless have this effect on impressionable audiences.

In contrast to the explicit-implicit approaches to Disney's animated features stands the esoteric hermeneutic, that interpretive pathway that assumes a communicative strategy operating between the lines to encode its films with messages intended only for a limited audience of what Strauss describes as "thoughtful readers." Over the years, Disney has indeed attracted numerous esoteric readings. Its massive, long-standing influence and extended body of work seem almost to beckon an outré interest, especially given its archaeological location within a multilayered environment of superposed media strata. Although the pathways of esoteric potentiality are many, the most persistently actualized line relates to issues of human sexuality. In a rare instance of agreement between diametrically opposed discourse communities, accusations among some social conservatives that the company encourages sexual deviance in its animated feature films is echoed by queer people who also affirm, albeit in a different attitudinal register, a hidden pro-LGBTQ messaging at work. The rhetorical esotericism of some of Disney's most successful animated feature films (expressed through censorship, intertextuality, importance of and attention to detail, and the like) has invited individuals to seek out hidden messages, regardless of whether these messages were intentionally encoded in the text.

GAY DISNEY

Notwithstanding twenty-first-century controversies about gay characters in Disney movies (regardless of whether the queer status of those characters is alleged or confirmed), Disney's associations with queerness go back much further than the brouhaha surrounding, say, the *Frozen* franchise (beginning in 2013) or *Lightyear* (2022). According to Sean Griffin, these associations probably first emerged in the 1930s, roughly during the first decade or so of the Walt Disney Company (founded in 1923), when "Mickey Mouse" became a code phrase with which in-the-know queers could identify one another as members of the gay and lesbian community. In *Tinker Belles and Evil Queens,* Griffin traces the evolution of Disney's complex interaction with gay communities, offering queer interpretations of a variety of Disney's early animated projects. Films such as *Ferdinand the Bull* (1937), *The Reluctant Dragon* (1941), *The Three Caballeros* (1945), and others, he argues, commonly subverted gender stereotypes, featuring effeminate or sissy characters or behaviors, such as male-on-male kissing and cross-dressing, coded as queer.[29] Such interpretive inventiveness aside, Disney's early connection to the gay and lesbian community mostly consisted of one-way interactions whereby queer people either appropriated Disney-trademarked signifiers or read queerness into its films.

Disney itself, by and large, did not begin purposely embodying elements of queerness until the 1990s, when it acquired a well-deserved representation as a queer-friendly environment. Even then, its onscreen representation of the LGBTQ community was not pioneered by the company's animated, family-friendly divisions but by newly acquired subsidiaries like ABC and Miramax Films.[30] Disney purchased Miramax in 1993, the year following Miramax's promotion of *The Crying Game* (1992) and the year before its U.S. distribution of *Priest* (1994), two controversial milestones in the representation of queer sexuality.[31] In April 1997, Ellen DeGeneres's character Ellen Morgan became America's first openly lesbian character on television when she came out on the ABC sitcom *Ellen.*[32] Years later, in 2011, the transgender Chaz Bono debuted on season 13 of ABC's dance competition series *Dancing with the Stars.* Given today's levels of LGBTQ representation in pop culture, it may be difficult to perceive any of these episodes as particularly noteworthy, but each was regarded as a major event at its time and generated much in the way of public controversy.

These controversial milestones, however, were only one piece of Disney's burgeoning reputation as a queer-friendly company, albeit a significant one. Visibility of queerness in the realm of nineties-era film and television coincided with equally visible claims to ownership from the queer community itself. Perhaps the most rhetorically salient of these gestures involved the AIDS quilt celebrating the lives of people who had died of AIDS-related causes. Officially started in 1987 in San Francisco and displayed on Washington, DC's, National Mall in October of 1992, the memorial incorporated an array of Disney imagery, a gesture reflecting the acceptance of Disney properties, if not the company as whole, by members of the queer community.[33]

Less rhetorically charged but no less symbolic is Disney World Gay Days, a loosely organized weeklong annual event inaugurated on June 1, 1991, when between five hundred and three thousand queer individuals, their families, and supporters visited the Magic Kingdom Park at the Walt Disney Resort in Bay Lake, Florida.[34] The event has grown massively over time, a fact attested to not only by the numbers of attendees but also by the success of peripheral products such *Queens in the Kingdom,* a popular book offering itself as a guidebook to Disney theme parks and cruise lines for gay- and lesbian-discerning patrons.

During Disney's gay nineties, queerness was also gaining favor behind the scenes within the corporate structure and the workplace environment. Bucking virtually all hiring trends in global legal markets, Disney began employing openly gay people, like Andreas Deja (supervising animator for some of Disney's most memorable nineties characters), and in some instance even recruiting them, as in the case of lyricist Howard Ashman.[35] Several members of Disney's senior leadership, including Ashman, were openly gay. In a June 1994 article in *The Advocate,* the executive producer of *The Rescuers Down Under* (1990) and *The Lion King* (1994), Thomas Schumacher, a gay man, claimed that there were a lot of gay people at every level of Disney, describing the company as a very supportive environment.[36] *The Advocate* noted that even though there were not any openly gay or lesbian characters in Disney's animated films, the upper echelon of Disney was sensitive to LGBTQ issues.[37] That positive assessment may even have been an understatement. Walt Disney Feature Animation employed so many gay people at the time that when a straight male artist was fired, he threatened to sue the studio for sexual discrimination.[38] In 1995, a team of academics calling themselves The Project on Disney shared the following joke, allegedly common among Disney World employees, which captures the gay spirit of the times:

> Q: How many Disney straights does it take to screw in a lightbulb on Main Street?
>
> A: Both of them.[39]

Arguably the person who encapsulates Disney's increasingly queer-friendly reputation in the nineties is the late, openly gay playwright, lyricist, and stage director Ashman. Formerly the vice president of Disney's Hollywood Pictures, Ashman is best remembered for composing the lyrics for much of the music in *The Little Mermaid, Beauty and the Beast,* and *Aladdin* (though Tim Rice took over songwriting duties for *Aladdin* after Ashman's death in 1991 of HIV/AIDS). He is also ground zero for esoteric queer readings of these films.

Professionally hailing from the New York theater scene, Ashman was recruited by Disney to revitalize its struggling animation department.[40] Disney is today commonly associated with its hit animated feature films, but in the late 1980s Disney executives, including CEO Michael Eisner, were considering shuttering Walt Disney Animation Studios.[41] A string of eight mediocre animated films, retroactively lumped together under the unflattering monikers of the "dark ages" (1981–1988), had so shaken management's faith in the department that had been foundational to the start of the company that Disney Animation was relocated from the main studio to a cluster of trailers situated in an industrial park, itself adjacent to a bowling alley.[42]

The desperate situation at Disney Animation led the company to vest an unusual amount of creative control in Ashman. Beyond writing lyrics, he worked alongside Deja and other animators to design characters, proposed plot points to writers, and won a high-profile fight with his superiors to keep the song "Part of Your World" in *The Little Mermaid.* Roy Disney, former vice chairman of company and Walt Disney's nephew, said of Ashman, "I don't want to compare him to Walt, but on the other hand he had that kind of influence on everybody. It was a remarkable amount of influence. If Howard said it, you know, that was gospel."[43]

In hindsight, Disney's desperate measure would appear to be a calculated maneuver. *The Little Mermaid, Beauty and the Beast,* and *Aladdin* broke the nearly decade-long trend of poorly received animated features, each becoming a cultural classic, a critical hit, and a massive cash cow.[44] Ashman would go on to win an Oscar for the titular song "Beauty and the Beast," making him the first openly gay man to win an Oscar—and he was a remarkably visible, successful gay man at a time when most gay people were closeted.

It is entirely possible—perhaps even probable—that Ashman's sexuality had no intentional bearing on any aspect of the animated films with which he was professionally involved. But as with all the case studies we will be examining, it is also entirely possible that the signifying entities under consideration—in this, case the lyrical content of the films *Beauty and the Beast* or *The Little Mermaid*—are esoterically coded. Indeed, that ambiguity is the crux of esotericism's effectivity. Ashman, for his part, never publicly confirmed the esoteric status of his work at Disney Animation. What's more, those closest to Ashman, like his romantic partner, Bill Lauch, and sister, Sarah Gillespie, have never indicated that Howard confided his true artistic intentions to them or suggested that there were messages hidden between the lines of his songs, running parallel to any exoteric lyrical content. It is interesting to note that Lauch believes Ashman's films were trying to "imbue some point of view through a very subtle way," but even more interesting that this belief contradicts Gillespie, who says, "I don't think he put his personal life in anything he wrote or did."[45]

Nevertheless, the important question is why *The Little Mermaid* and *Beauty and the Beast* have been abiding conductors of esoteric desire. Our analysis of the esoteric fan theories surrounding these films will approach this question obliquely, first, through a consideration of the films' multivalent importance, and second, through an analysis of how certain queer fans draw on the hermeneutic resources of intertextuality and attention to detail to construct esoteric interpretations. Before that, however, a brief review of Disney's role in the history of censorship of LGBTQ representation in order.

PERSECUTION AND THE ART OF QUEER READINGS

While gender has always been a component of Disney animation (and animation in general), Disney has also participated in the long-standing censorship of LGBTQ content.[46] That involvement did not just go away in the 1990s but continued to shape content. That Disney would persist with suppressing or removing explicitly queer representations from its animated films is not surprising, even as the company broke barriers in other domains. First, despite gaining some cultural ground, queerness in the 1990s was still met with overwhelming opposition from the mainstream. The Defense of Marriage Act, for instance, was passed by large, veto-proof majorities in both the House and the Senate and was signed into law by Democratic President Bill Clinton on September 21, 1996. Intended to define and protect the institution of marriage, the act banned federal recognition of same-sex marriage by limiting the definition of marriage to the union of one man and one woman; it further allowed states to refuse to recognize same-sex marriages granted under the laws of other states. (Interestingly, the act was not repealed by Congress until 2022, even though the Supreme Court had ruled in 2015 that the fundamental right of same-sex couples to marry on the same terms and conditions as opposite-sex couples is guaranteed by both the Due Process Clause and the Equal Protection Clause of the Fourteenth Amendment to the United States Constitution.) Homosexuality itself was not nationally decriminalized until 2003, in the Supreme Court's landmark decision of *Lawrence v. Texas.* To add insult to injury—or rather to heap injury upon injury—legal scholars maintain that between 1970 and 2020 there were more than one hundred confirmed cases (and likely hundreds more) of defendants using the "gay panic defense," that is, a strategy of legal defense in which a straight person charged with a violent crime against a gay (or bisexual or trans) person claims that they lost control and reacted violently because of an unwanted sexual advance made upon them. This is used as an excuse or justification for defendants to evade punishment for the crime of murder, and it is successful even today with many jurors of a certain type.[47]

Even in the twenty-first century, the environment for pro-queer media entertainment is not altogether welcoming, though to be sure, in the United States, the corporate side of that environment has unquestionably become more accepting of queer issues and queer positivity. Disney, however, is not merely an American company but an American *multinational* mass media and entertainment conglomerate; its films are released in virtually every country on earth, and many of those countries staunchly oppose representations of queerness. Malaysia and Kuwait (plus one Alabaman drive-in theater), for instance, censored the Disney live-action/CGI remake of *Beauty and the Beast* (2017) over an allegedly "gay moment" that *USA Today* described as "much ado about nothing" and a "a blink-and-you'll-miss-it shot in the film's final seconds," where a male character dances with another male character (figure 2).[48] Disney's 2020 animated urban fantasy adventure film *Onward* included a brief reference to a female character's girlfriend (the sole queer reference in a movie with a runtime of one hour and forty-two minutes), which resulted in the film being banned in Kuwait, Oman, Qatar, and Saudi Arabia and censored in Russia.[49] China, Disney's most important foreign market, frequently boycotts or redacts media representations of queer relationships.[50]

This brief historical overview of Disney's complex, evolving connection to the LGBTQ community, combined with the persecutory social conditions aligned against affirmative representations of queerness (if not all representations of queerness), points to an interpretive environment conducive to the practice of esoteric hermeneutics in the Straussian mode. Incubating since at least the 1930s, that esoteric imaginary was finally able to gain purchase on the mainstream, at least along its edges, in the hyperliterate, increasingly pronoiac atmosphere of the 1990s. Further feeding that esoteric imagination, of course, were the numerous indications that Disney as a corporate entity was sympathetic to gay rights, particularly in light of Howard Ashman's role in revitalizing and shaping Disney Animation. These interpretive conditions

Figure 2. A brief image of two men dancing together in the 2017 Disney live-action remake of *Beauty and the Beast,* directed by Bill Condon.

achieved something close to perfect alignment in the early 1990s with *The Little Mermaid* and *Beauty and the Beast.*

Disney's original *Beauty and the Beast* is an animated musical romantic fantasy based on the 1740 fairy tale *La Belle et la Bête* by Gabrielle-Suzanne Barbot de Villeneuve and incorporating elements from a 1946 French film of the same name (marketed in America as *Beauty and the Beast*) directed by Jean Cocteau. In the Disney version, an enchantress transforms a cruel and selfish prince into a beast and his servants into household objects. The spell can only be broken if the prince learns to love another and be loved in return before the last petal of an enchanted rose falls; otherwise, he will remain a beast forever. His bestial nature causes the local villagers to fear and despise him and to shun the palatial grounds where he lives alone in a castle, save for his transformed servants—including a candelabra, a mantel clock, a teapot, a teacup, and others. Eventually the Beast is visited by Belle, the beautiful, book-loving daughter of a nearby eccentric inventor, en route to a fair to showcase her father's latest invention. Over the course of the story, Belle gradually falls in love with the Beast, despite his monstrous exterior, and the Beast simultaneously falls in love with her, thereby breaking the spell. It is easy to see from this bare-bones summary of the plot how it lines up with the film's reputation as a satisfying modern fable for children and their parents. Esotericism, however, tends to latch on to sources of popular satisfaction only as material to be excavated for their illicit, subtextual messages.

In the case of Disney's *Beauty and the Beast,* the first major esoteric salvo originated from a rather unlikely source, CBS's famed news anchor Dan Rather. In a 1992 broadcast commentary, Rather offered a reading of *Beauty and the Beast* that most viewers probably did not arrive at independently, positing that the character of the Beast was a metaphor for people living with HIV/AIDS. For Rather, the film's meaning lay in its hortatory purpose: to inculcate in audiences an attitude of acceptance toward those often viewed as monstrous, people with HIV/AIDS. He argued further that this message of basic human dignity was placed in the film by executive producer Ashman. In response to Disney's explicit denial of such a message, which Rather had earlier floated, Rather doubled down on his attribution of a hidden value, communicated to millions of viewers:

> But think what that legacy means if my interpretation is valid. Susan Sontag has said that every society picks an illness and assigns it meaning; people force diseases to say something about themselves. *Illness as Metaphor* [1978] is the title of her book, and it's a tidy phrase, too. In the nineteenth century, we were obsessed with tuberculosis (think of Greta Garbo in *Camille* [1936]), and for most of the twentieth century we were fascinated by cancer (think of Ali MacGraw in *Love Story* [1970]). So far, there hasn't been a drama about AIDS with that kind of mainstream success. Writers and producers try, but so far, we've seen only some movies-of-the-week and some art-house films: *An Early Frost* [1985] or *A Virus Knows No Morals* [1986]. *Longtime Companion* [1989] is as close to the mainstream as anybody's gotten without getting commercial.
>
> Say that the AIDS metaphor is just one way, a valid way, of looking at *Beauty and the Beast.* That means that millions of Americans, most of them children, are looking at a Person With AIDS with a new kind of compassion. We're crying when he's sad, cheering for him when he wins.[51]

This esoteric interpretation did not have much impact in 1992 but has since gained significant traction, in both academic and popular discourse as well as among people associated with Disney.

The shift probably began in the academic world. In 1995, in *Cinema Journal,* Cynthia Erb interpreted the film as possessing "gay subtextual meanings," which she ascribed to Ashman.[52] About a decade later, Sean Griffin offered what is probably the most comprehensive academic analysis of the film's hidden queer meanings, describing the film as "overtly homosexual," by which he means the queer message is intentional but not obviously exoteric.[53] Arriving a bit late in the game in the 2010s, popular media such as the *Artifice* and the *Atlantic* featured stories defending queer decodings of *Beauty and the Beast,* while the Disney+ documentary *Howard* (2018) explored the theory at some length through the lens of Ashman's biography.[54]

Disney employees with connections to the film have also subsequently acknowledged and defended the esoteric queer readings of the film. Dan Stevens, the director of Disney's 2017 live-action remake of the film, even went so far as to characterize the queer interpretation as an established fact.[55] Echoing Griffin's "overtly homosexual" interpretation, Don Hahn, producer of the original Disney *Beauty and the Beast* and writer/director of *Howard,* provides a slightly subtler reading based on his interpersonal knowledge of Ashman: "Howard was struggling with AIDS at the same time. ["The Mob Song"] was almost a metaphor for that. He was really dealing with a debilitating disease, in an era when it was stigmatised. And so, there were so many of those underpinnings to the movie that people may not have seen. And shouldn't have seen. It wasn't about the HIV epidemic at all. But if you study the man, and his struggles, and then look at his lyrics, you understand what he was going through."[56] From its release to the present day, some viewers have read *Beauty and the Beast* as a secret defense of tolerance toward homosexuality, which is a pattern similar to the one that surrounds Disney's *Little Mermaid.*

Loosely based on the 1837 Danish fairy tale of the same name by Hans Christian Andersen, Disney's *The Little Mermaid* centers on a headstrong sixteen-year-old mermaid named Ariel who is captivated by life on land. During one of her visits to the surface, which are forbidden by her controlling father, King Triton, Ariel falls in love with a human prince. In her desperation to be with him, she strikes a perilous bargain with the sea witch, Ursula: Ursula will transform Ariel into a human for three days' time in exchange for Ariel's voice. If Ariel can earn the prince's love ("true love's kiss") before time runs out, she will remain human permanently; otherwise, she will transform back into a mermaid and belong to Ursula. When plans go awry, King Triton is faced with making the ultimate sacrifice for his daughter.

While no celebrity commentator of Dan Rather's stature trumpeted an esoteric reading of the film, it has nevertheless given rise to numerous queer readings. As with *Beauty and the Beast,* the film's entire song score was composed by Ashman (in collaboration with Alan Menken), who, here too, serves as point of origin/justification for much of the esotericism. Queer readings of *The Little Mermaid,* however, generally do not involve mention of HIV/AIDS (Ashman was diagnosed in 1988) but mostly center on suggestions that Ariel's discomfort with her undersea, mermaid life is an allegory for queer people's oppression within and by a heteronormative patriarchal society. Leland Spencer, for example, conducted a transgender reading of the film and the original story in the journal *Communication Studies.*[57]

Despite the lack of digital archives documenting queer fan readings from 1989 through the 1990s, the *Huffington Post* has published many anecdotes of fans who at the time read the film esoterically in relation to Ashman. Representative of those accounts is that of fan Ben Eckersley, who is quoted as saying, "You can't help but wonder how much of Howard Ashman's own personal experiences became part of the lyrics.[58] YouTuber Jennifer Heaton also connects Ashman to themes in the film, which she identifies as being coded as queer, but she argues more specifically that Ariel's desire to transform herself into a human mirrors the trans experience of feeling uncomfortable in one's own physical body.[59] A *Los Angeles Times* retrospective of the film is even more nuanced, discussing what it characterizes as the long-standing recognition of the film's split exoteric/esoteric messaging before linking the esoteric message specifically to Ashman:

> The most direct reading of "The Little Mermaid"—about a 16-year-old princess who gives up everything including her voice for a chance at happily-ever-after with a prince she falls for at first sight—has long been recognized as painfully heteronormative and plenty problematic. *She's 16! She doesn't actually know the prince! She's 16!*
>
> But the story about a teen who feels like an outsider in her home falling in love with someone she isn't supposed to while she longs to feel accepted

> and belong somewhere she believes is beyond her reach has resonated with generations of queer fans. The queer subtext feels particularly poignant after understanding that LGBTQ artists like Ashman had a hand in bringing Ariel's story to life.[60]

These examples are only a sample of esoterically queer readings highlighting the theme of discomfort. Such interpretations are in fact relatively common and may be found in a variety of widely popular outlets like *Smithsonian Magazine*, the *Atlantic*, and the *Mary Sue*, often appearing well over a decade after the film's original release.[61]

Other esoteric readings of *The Little Mermaid* focus instead on themes of nonconformity and forbidden love, elements that have gained in cultural resonance since the film's release, in part because of the film's influence. These readings also tend to single out the sea witch Ursula, specifically, as the primary means by which the film signals its queerness. In the film, Ursula offers Ariel a chance to live on land at the risk of losing her soul. While on the surface this may not appear as an ideal form of queer representation, Straussians have long claimed that esoteric writers typically hide their true (but often objectionable) ideas by articulating them with antagonists, real or fictional.[62] Strauss himself argues that the esoteric effectiveness (or rhetorical esotericism) of certain taboo ideas rests on their seemingly intrinsic relationship to their villainous carriers, on the exoteric appearance that the ideas are themselves villain-dependent. This association, he argues, is so reliable that it explains why we find in "the greatest literature of the past so many interesting devils, madmen, beggars, sophists, drunkards, epicureans, and buffoons."[63]

In the case of *The Little Mermaid,* queer fan interpretations typically do not claim that Ursula conveys coded verbal arguments for queer liberation; they instead focus on character design, arguing that her appearance provides a visual representation of queerness. Instead of coming away from the film feeling sympathetic to any of Ursula's explicit statements or discursive maneuvers, this line of interpretation goes, viewers will more probably be attracted to the ways in which she visually communicates confidence—through fashion, gestures, hairstyle, and so on. Ursula, in other words, is regarded as embodying or visually connoting an extrinsic relation to extant (straight) culture that certain (queer) viewers, primed by their own discordant relation to heteropatriarchal normativity, will be inclined to read esoterically.

Figure 3. Ursula the sea witch in her drag queen glory, created by R. Clements and J. Musker (1989).

Shoring up the queer interpretation of Ursula's appearance is the fact that at the behest of Ashman, the character's creators, Ron Clements and John Musker (both straight-identifying men), modeled her visual design (figure 3) on the American actor and drag queen Divine, who is best known for his performances in John Waters's subversive independent comedies.[64] Queer audiences would probably be more familiar with Divine, and with other drag queens adopting a similar visual aesthetic, than their straight counterparts. One YouTuber, offering a queer decoding of the film, says of Ursula's big musical number, "Poor Unfortunate Souls," "It's *meant* to look like a drag performance, kids."[65]

Despite Ursula's unambiguous villain status, some queer fans read her features, movement, and attitude as signaling an acceptance of queer identity. Writing for *Smithsonian Magazine,* for instance, Michael Landis argues that the character's exteriority or performance represents "feminism, the fluidity of gender, and young Ariel's empowerment."[66] A piece published in *Gay Times Magazine* echoes and amplifies Landis's reading in a way that perfectly encapsulates a Straussian hermeneutic approach. Gabriella Geisinger writes, "Ursula became Schrödinger's villain. With the lid shut, she was simply the baddie. Lift it, and you find a depth of queer resistance."[67] Of course, the fact that Ursula "came out" looking as she does under Ashman's direction only provides further fuel for these esoteric claims.[68]

These readings run counter to the less generous exoteric possibilities that Ursula's aesthetic was poached in an act of uncompensated, uncredited cultural appropriation—or, more nefariously, that Disney chose Divine's image because its queerness would read as *grotesquely* villainous. To be sure, Hollywood boasts a long tradition of using queerness to signify evil. An article appearing in *Quail Bell Magazine* criticizing Disney's queer depiction of Ursula puts it this way:

> Based off the real-life drag queen, Divine, Ursula takes a step away from her male counterparts. She's curvy and fat, brazen and loud-mouthed, with a [*sic*] blood-red lips to match. Unlike Disney heroines, she is entirely disinterested in men, aggressive to a fault, and her temper is a force to be reckoned with.
>
> Why does Disney's blatant queer-coding of villains matter? Disney's use of queer-coding is almost always reserved for villains, and it creates the implicit equation that equates queerness with violence. This "otherness" becomes conflated with villainy, in which messages about being honest and kind are couple[d] with "don't be like *this.*" These cues associated with queerness are now lessons in how not to be. Whether it's Scar's effeminate nature or Ursula's brashness, children see these traits associated with villains and thus those traits become villainous.[69]

The *Los Angeles Times,* by contrast, offers a more esoteric view. Recognizing that Ursula exists in relation to the problematic tradition of coding only villains as queer, Tracy Brown argues that precisely this closeness serves more as camouflage: "She's easily one of the most charismatic characters in the movie, even if she is evil. And while the tendency to use queer stereotypes to project otherness onto a villain has long been a problematic feature of Hollywood movies, Ursula rings a bit different."[70] While hip straight folks, aware of Divine, may imagine Ursula as an extension of the grotesque roles he played in Water's films, queer viewers (many of them young) find in Ursula-Divine freedom and possibility.

The queer Straussian reading is bolstered by a few other notable examples, like that offered by Maddy Myers, who makes the following connection: "On Ariel's wedding day, Triton even uses his staff to paint a rainbow across the sky. The rainbow has long been a symbol of peace and of the bridging of two worlds (sunlight and rain), but it's also been a gay pride symbol since the 70s, long before Disney's *The Little Mermaid* came out."[71] What lends credence to Myers's interpretation is that, like other rhetorically esoteric texts, *The Little Mermaid* rewards close reading. Mickey Mouse, Donald Duck, and Kermit the Frog all are subtly visible in the crowd when Ariel's father, Triton, enters his kingdom. Prince Eric's palace has a painting of Prince Phillip and Princess Aurora from *Sleeping Beauty* (1959). The king and the grand duke from *Cinderella* (1950) appear at Ariel's wedding. The titular character in *The Incredible Mr. Limpet* (1964), a movie about a man who transforms into a fish and guides the U.S. Navy to Nazi submarines, appears when the crab Sebastian sings "Under the Sea." In one scene, Ariel sits on a rock in the same pose as the *Little Mermaid* statue in Copenhagen that serves as a tribute to the original Hans Christian Andersen mermaid tale.

Considered together, these examples paint a picture of a production team that takes minute, intertextual details seriously and for that reason may actively hide Easter eggs in their films, something that has become more commonplace today but was fairly atypical in the 1990s. What is more, it suggests a team of creatives that may want to signal to those "in the know"—those whom Strauss identifies as a text's true, "philosophically" driven readers—that there are indeed hidden images, messages, features just waiting to be discovered and decoded. At the very least, that impression—which bears explicit, visible, albeit fleeting, traces on the surface of the text—imbues esoteric interpretations of the film with a patina of believability, which makes it more believable that the film may have a hidden esoteric message.

The intertextual connection to the original Andersen mermaid story provides the last cypher in esoteric readings of the film. In Anderson's original nineteenth-century fairy tale, the Sea King's youngest daughter (called the Little Mermaid) falls in love with a terrestrial prince and makes a dangerous deal with the sea witch: In exchange for her human form, every step will feel as though the mermaid were treading upon sharp knives. The mermaid takes the deal, but in stark contrast to the Disney version, she is unable to convince the prince to marry her. She fails, in other words, to secure what the film calls "true love's kiss." As a result, the mermaid transforms into sea foam.

Some queer fans use this tale as an intertextual bridge between the film and Andersen's biography. Since Rictor Norton's edited collection, *My Dear Boy: Gay Love Letters Through the Centuries* (1998), many people have connected Andersen's "The Little Mermaid" to the author's unrequited romantic interest in Edvard Collin, such that the story of the mermaid's doomed love is read as an allegory for Andersen's own queer feelings.[72] In the hands of esoteric readers of Disney's *The Little Mermaid,* that allegorical function is preserved in the adaptation of the original fairy tale into a feature-length animated film. In the piece for the *Gay Times Magazine,* Gabriella Geisinger writes, "With all this knowledge at their fingertips, it's easy to see how Disney's John Musker, Ron Clements, and Howard Ashman were able to easily imbue Ariel with this same longing and eventual freedom—even if it is Disney-fied."[73] That hagiographic-intertextual relationship is so well established among some queer esoteric readers that in an article independently published on *Medium,* Chris Calfa expresses concern about whether the forthcoming 2023 live-action remake would maintain not only the original film's esoteric queerness but also that of Andersen's tale: "With everything going on [in] the world right now with all the politics against LGBTQ+ rising, this live-action remake is sort of coming at the best time possible. My main worry is it will lose what Hans Christian Andersen and Howard Ashman built for the character of Ariel that many queer people see in themselves."[74]

Underpinning these esoteric readings, whether explicitly stated or not, is the belief that queer individuals living in heteronormative patriarchal societies are primed to read between the lines:

> When a piece of fiction is written by a male queer creative and is meant to express said male queer creative's experience, to the point where the main character should be a queer man but instead features a hetero-leaning woman as the main character in order for the story to be accepted in mainstream heteronormativity, queer men, even before the internet, have a way of knowing when a story given this treatment is about them. *The Little Mermaid,* both the original story and the Disney adaptation, were no different. Queer men read Anderson's fairy tale and related with the main character—just as much

> as baby gay millennials, without even knowing how Howard Ashman and company added queerness to it, watch the Disney classic and absolutely fell in love with it.[75]

Queer culture's long history of secrecy in the face of oppression offers countless examples to help justify one's reading of *The Little Mermaid.* From the original queer text to the hankie codes, persecution and the necessary countermeasures have conditioned queer individuals to read between the lines.

QUEER VIBES

Because the 1990s lacked widespread internet use and much of the nineties internet is now lost to an unarchived past, it is challenging to trace esoteric readings of Disney with the same depth as our other case studies.[76] It does, however, provide a fascinating snapshot of the transition from individual esoteric readings offered by the likes of Rather and individual queer Disney fans to the internet-connected fan interpretations that retrospectively assess the films decades later. The focus on Ashman as a quasi-secret, behind-the-scenes auteur helps to contrast these esoteric readings with the more overt acts of textual poaching that appear in such expressive fan forms as slash fiction.[77] Fans who esoterically decode animated Disney films through a queer lens do not understand their interpretive activity as a repurposing of primary fan-objects; instead, they regard the films as being made for them, as conveying secret, hidden messages that fail to register with most viewers and with nonqueer fans. They do not need to repurpose what they believe is tailored to their interests and identity. If anything, these esoteric "decryptions" implicitly position Ashman as a textual poacher, as someone who hijacked a then failing division of a multibillion-dollar multinational company and secretly bent it to his will through a series of masterful encryptions.

Even after Ashman, a similar pattern of esoteric analyses continued to crop up around Disney Animation properties. Probably the most well-known instances of this involve the *Frozen* franchise, which was (and is) widely regarded as heavily queer-coded. In 2014, for example, the *Guardian* referred to "Let It Go," a hit song from the first *Frozen* installment, as an "LGBT anthem."[78] For *Frozen II, Vox* even ran a headline specifically referencing the film's esoteric nature: "Why Elsa from *Frozen* Is a Queer Icon—and Why Disney Won't

Embrace That Idea."[79] But queer fans also provided esoteric takes on other animated films, such as *Mulan,* elevating Captain Li Shang to a bisexual icon, and even nonanimated feature films like *High School Musical* (2006).[80] (There is a TikTok channel devoted almost exclusively to discussing the deliberate but subtextual queer coding at work in *High School Musical.*) In our digital era, the practice of approaching Disney properties through an esoteric lens has now expanded to include myriad cultural objects, as we will discuss more in the next chapter.

Despite the transition from a pre- to post-internet media ecology, these esoteric practices signal a departure from, and arguably an innovation of, classical philosophical esotericism. Traditionally, esoteric reading has been associated almost exclusively with the transmission of doctrine—particular ideas, verbally expressed through writing, that are forbidden and therefore must be communicated secretly, "between the lines." Even when examining the world of tragic drama in a search for esoteric messages, as with Shakespeare's plays, Straussian critics focus overwhelmingly on discursive texts rather than on extradiscursive features of dramatic performance such as acting, staging, costuming, or lighting.

While esoteric interpretations of animated Disney films do attempt to "uncover" in the film-as-parable the very general idea that queerness and queer people ought to be accepted, they also attend as much to the films' various aesthetic carriers of hidden messages as to the logographic/discursive ones. As we have seen, esoteric readings of Disney are as likely to revel in Ursula's queerness *not* as logical defense but as embodiment—in what the young folk today call "vibes"—as they are to celebrate the queer textual coding of Ariel's "Part of Your World." Characters like Ursula make queerness feel cool to fans who are receptive to that message (and who can read the rhetorical invitation in the first place). The purported messaging here relates to but fundamentally differs from something like Machiavelli hiding arguments against Christianity solely via textual and textual-stylistic choices.

2

YOU CAN WANT WHO YOU WANT

Taylor Swift as Gay Best Friend

Thank goodness we have Taylor Swift, otherwise I wonder if I'd be into QAnon.

—Anonymous Swiftie

On January 9, 2024, *Fox News* talking head Jesse Watters welcomed former FBI agent Stuart Kaplan onto his show, *Jesse Watters Primetime*, to speculate about how the Biden administration might exploit Taylor Swift's celebrity for propaganda purposes. (Spoiler alert: by attempting to indoctrinate the country's youth to vote Democrat.)[1] This speculation was the latter part of a segment in which Watters floated the idea, suggested earlier that day on X by former Trump administration State Department official Mike Benz, that Taylor Swift may very well be part of a CIA/NATO-led psychological operation (psyop) geared toward battling the online spread of "disinformation."[2] The basis for this idea, according to Watters (and Benz), was the recently surfaced 2019 footage of a presentation delivered at NATO's International Conference on Cyber Conflict by Alicia Marie Bargar, who at the time worked as a research engineer at Johns Hopkins Applied Physics Laboratory. The topic of her presentation was how (dis)information spreads through social media—somewhat ironic, given its subsequent conspiracist appropriation. To bolster his insinuation, Watters pandered to his conservative audience, pointing out that Joe Biden had recently confused Swift with Britney Spears and that Swift's boyfriend, the Kansas City Chiefs' tight end Travis Kelce, promotes vaccines for Pfizer, a rather persuasive association given conservatism's web of post-COVID conspiracist tropes.[3]

Accusations that Swift is a political psyop, however, are not novel. As *Forbes* magazine reports, "Swift has long been thought by relatively fringe elements to be a psy-op. After *Time* magazine named her person of the year near the end of 2023, chatter about how she would be 'weaponized' in the lead up to the 2024 presidential election got louder, with allegations that Swift fans are zombies who can't think for themselves."[4] As we have seen, such conspiracist allegations are not even peculiar to Swift's celebrity; with little modification, they could be applied to virtually any agential cut made by our media apparatuses, no matter how seemingly trivial or obscure the content of that cut. In fact, in our current post-Q, post-COVID, post–January 6 world, right-wing conspiracist speculation in particular has become especially mundane and predictable.

What is interesting and unusual about this particular right-wing conspiracist interpretation—of this specific iteration of the Swift-is-a-psyop trope—is its basis, which is not (this time) alleged inclusion in a satanic, child-murdering, exsanguinating cabal, a conspiracy of pharmaceutical companies to sell their products, or a plot to disenfranchise millions of voters. In this case, the cause for paranoid discursiveness appears to be popularity itself. The X account known as End Wokeness tweeted in December 2023, "Taylor Swift has a cult-like following that would drink poisoned Kool Aid [*sic*] for her. The media knows this and is feeding it." The account continues, "Music. Entertainment. Sports. Now they crowned her Person of the Year. The next step? Politics. If you don't think the regime has plans to weaponize her just in time for 2024, you clearly have not been paying attention." Likewise, Watters seems to think Swift's popularity is in itself a sign of some secret, dark forces controlling events behind the scenes. "Have you ever wondered why or how she blew up like this?" Watters wondered aloud, after running through some of Swift's accomplishments.[5]

This instance of twenty-first-century conspiracy thinking demonstrates, as much as any recent example could, the return of conspiracy theory as totalizing and absolutist, that pre-"postmodern" conspiracy theory regarded as mostly moribund by turn-of-the-century thinkers such as Jodi Dean, Timothy Melley, and Kathleen Stewart. More than that, it represents something bordering on the malefic, tropological purification or formalistic closure of conspiracy theorizing. In place of a particular content coming to function as the *stand-in* for the absent universal, à la Ernesto Laclau's theory of hegemony, with Swift we observe the universal as a black hole that metastasizes to any and all particular imaginations and agential cuts.[6]

In this way, her esoteric fandom operates as a rhetorical secret in Atilla Hallsby's sense, not simply as a concealed truth but as an absence that structures meaning, where what is missing—the confirmed, exoteric declaration of queerness—shapes the conspiratorial imagination more than any explicit revelation ever could.[7] What that universal may be, exactly, how it ought to be characterized, and so on, may be the grounds for hegemonic struggle (in this case a struggle on the right), but in the main it is hegemonized by what passes for capital-*L* Liberalism.[8] In this symbolic universe, conspicuity is itself grounds for suspecting the metastatic spread of Liberalism, simply by virtue of gravitational pull. What better inductor of the "liberal mind virus" than one of the most globally recognizable celebrities? In the parlance of right-wing online discourse, popularity on the order of Swift's would undoubtedly attract the "Eye of Soros."

However one may feel about this map of meaning-making—whereby what is popular is, by virtue of that popularity, suspect—it is coherent, and if it is not persuasive, then it is probably at least familiar. Indeed, misgivings about popularity extend both to generational and subcultural attitudes (to Generation X and hipsters, for instance) as well as to the biases of today's online populist right. Subtending that suspicion, and acting as its foil, is what we are characterizing as a pronoiac hermeneutics of esoteric fandom. For some of Taylor Swift's fans, Swift's popularity is indicative not of a furtive, creeping menace but of parasocial intimacy, encouragement, and above all, empathy. This idealization is perhaps especially pronounced in a subset of Swift's queer fans, and certain members of this group are as prone to speculating about what Swift's popularity secretly portends as are some of her right-wing detractors.

This more charitable mode of popularity-based conjecture, which, like the more paranoid-antagonistic one, does not shy away from self-assured coherent emplotment, can also lead to controversy. A good case in point is the *New York Times* article "Look What We Made Taylor Do," by opinion editor Anna Marks. In it, Marks insinuates not only that Taylor Swift is secretly gay but also that Swift has for years been secretly/not-so-secretly telling the public (or those with ears to hear and eyes to see) that she is in fact gay. Marks believes Swift chooses not to come out explicitly because "The difference between any person coming out and a celebrity doing so is the difference between a toy mallet and a sledgehammer." Extending that analogy, we would say that Swift may be more accurately compared not to a sledgehammer but to a hydraulic press.

SWIFT AS HYDRAULIC PRESS

Taylor Swift's professional music career is one of the most illustrious of any musician in the twenty-first century. Despite entering the music industry in the midst of radical technological change (the dark years of the 2000s and 2010s), Swift has established herself as one of the best-selling and wealthiest pop music stars of all time. For her 2008 sophomore album *Fearless*, twenty-one-year-old Swift became the youngest person to win the Grammy Award for Album of the Year.[9] That same album would also earn her the most simultaneous hits by a woman on *Billboard* magazine's Hot 100 chart.[10] Over the course of two decades as a professional singer-songwriter, Swift has released ten original studio albums, each of which has been certified platinum.[11] What's more, Swift's celebrity is not limited to English-speaking countries or even the Global North but resonates among diverse global populations. A 2021 YouGov poll of forty-two thousand people in thirty-eight countries and territories found that Swift was the seventh most admired woman, beating out Pakistani human rights defender Malala Yousafzai, Swedish environmental activist Greta Thunberg, and former chancellor of Germany Angela Merkel.[12]

Although she is unaffiliated with a major label, Swift's massive commercial success as a recording artist has meant that she wields unprecedented power in the music industry. In 2015, she could protest and successfully negotiate a deal with Apple Music ensuring that Apple paid royalty fees to artists for its three-month Apple Music trial period.[13] Three years later, in 2018, she repeated this feat when negotiating a multiyear record deal with Republic Records and Universal Music Group. The deal stipulated a unique condition: that any sale of Universal's Spotify shares would result in a distribution of money to their artists, nonrecoupable.[14] Swift is also a pioneer in terms of maintaining control of her own career. The same year she secured money for Universal Music Group's musicians, Swift left her first label, independent Big Machine Records. In her contract with the label, she did not retain ownership of her master recordings. So, in 2019, she revealed plans to rerecord her first six albums, resulting in new master versions to which she would enjoy exclusive proprietary rights.[15]

Swift's fans—commonly referred to and self-identified as "Swifties"—are legion and comprise a particularly devoted fan base. When, in 2018, Swift posted to Instagram an endorsement of Tennessee Democratic candidates Phil Bredesen and Jim Cooper, including a link to the nonpartisan voter registration website Vote.org, the website saw a massive single-day spike in Tennessee registrations.[16] Her tour for the 2022 album *Midnights* generated such fan interest that ticket sales crashed Ticketmaster. This incident would have been remarkable in and of itself, but the resulting fan backlash against Ticketmaster renewed calls to break up the company's virtual monopoly on ticket sales and distribution, eventually leading to bipartisan congressional hearings on Ticketmaster's business practices.[17] The hearings were full of allusions to Swift's music, even unfortunate puns. Richard Blumenthal, a Democrat from Connecticut, for instance, remarked, "May I suggest, respectfully, that Ticketmaster ought to look in the mirror and say, 'I'm the problem. It's me.'"[18]

The breadth of the Swifties' influence is so renowned that *Daily Show* host Trevor Noah joked in a 2023 interview with Swift that she should encourage her fans to lower the price of eggs, at a time when the price of eggs had dramatically increased by 70 percent over the previous year. Not long after the interview aired, one TikTok user took to the platform to share her surprise that the price of eggs had indeed fallen—by a significant 13 percent. In perfect pseudo-event logic, the TikTok video itself came to garner its own media coverage.[19]

Swift's prodigious cultural influence would not be possible, however, if it were not for the intense resonance her music creates in her many listeners. For Swifties, Swift's music provides an affective infrastructure through which they form intensely personal relationships to the star, with many of them integrating her music into all facets of their lives. In an op-ed for the *New York Times*, a prominent psychiatrist commented on Swift's profound impact on her patients' mental well-being:

> A few months ago, I started joking that half of the treatments in my psychiatric practice had become Taylor-based. Many of my patients are adolescent girls and young women, and they have leaned on Taylor Swift as a kind of big sister through the daily agonies of being a teenage girl: unsteady friendships,

> the 24-hour firing squad of the internet and, of course, the endless longing to feel seen and valued. At the end of a session exploring these struggles, I've appreciated having her to keep my patients company the rest of the week.[20]

For many of Swift's ardent fans, Swift's music has become a shared way of making sense of the world, articulating values, and ordering experiences. Many fans find themselves forming a deep parasocial relationship with Taylor Swift, where they feel personally affected, for example, by whom the singer chooses to date.[21]

That parasociality is not unique to Swift's relationship with her fans. Many media celebrities are positioned by fans or followers as the foci of a one-sided, unreciprocated sense of intimacy, in which a fan or follower comes to feel that they know the celebrity as a friend. The difference is that many, if not most, media celebrities attract such one-sided intimate relationships by doing nothing more than being famous. Swift, in contrast, appears to invite parasocial relationships by taking active steps to display her personal life to her fans and by affirming their belief (or fantasy) that they—as individuals—are an important part of her life. Anonymous Swiftie itsthenugget posted on Reddit in 2023 that Swift encourages the forming of parasocial relationships by sharing her journals with fans, writing messages such as "I need you guys very much for my well-being."

Swift's use of "Easter eggs" (messages hidden in media by their creators) is another way she courts parasociality among her core fans. Puzzling over hidden messages, alone or cooperatively, nourishes the sense among fans that they are being granted a quasi exclusive backstage pass to Swift's inner world. As Amelia Morris argues, Easter eggs construct a "digital bedroom" for older fans, reminiscent of their childhood bedrooms, where fans can embrace "wistful dreaming" and experience "embracing intense emotions."[22] This culture of Easter eggs is not a mere sideshow to Swift's media celebrity. It provides the favored interpretive lens through which Gaylors seek to identify and decode Swift's queer-affirming messages.

SAM SAM SAM SAM SAM SAM

Of all our case studies, Taylor Swift comes closest to providing fans with an esoteric smoking gun. In a popular YouTube video posted to the Vietnameserun channel Swifties Land—which claims, in all caps, "WE'RE NOT FANS, WE'RE SWIFTIES!!!"—Swift playfully hints at an esoteric dimension to her music, stating, "I love to communicate via Easter eggs. I think the best messages are cryptic ones."[23]

This video was not Swift's first quasi admission of esoteric writing. Her penchant for coded communication goes back to her earliest recordings and is well known among hardcore fans. For instance, her seven-time-platinum self-titled debut studio album featured randomly placed capital letters within the lyrics in the CD booklet, spelling secret messages that reveal hidden meanings in the songs. When asked by the *Washington Post* about the origin of the liner notes game—the earliest sign of her later, much more intricate puzzles—Swift responded, "When I was 15 and putting together my first album, I wanted to recreate the experience I used to have for my fans in a reimagined approach. I decided to encode the lyrics with hidden messages using capital letters"[24] The liner notes for the ninth track, written by Swift when she was sixteen, encode a message with "misplaced" capital letters: "Sam Sam Sam Sam Sam Sam." Evidence arose years later on social media that "Sam" refers to Sam Armstrong, an unfaithful high school boyfriend of Swift.[25]

A host of other hidden communications have either been confirmed by Swift or been proven true by later events. For the song "Betty," Swift corroborated a fan theory that she "named all the characters in this story after my friends' kids."[26] Fans figured out that one of the songwriting credits for the album *Folklore,* "William Bowery," was actually a pen name for Swift's then-boyfriend, British actor-songwriter Joe Alwyn. They deduced that identity because Swift and Alwyn first met at New York's Bowery Hotel and Alwyn's grandfather was named William Bowery.[27] Swifties also spotted an Easter egg in Swift's social media post announcing the release of her studio album *Fearless (Taylor's Version).*[28] Here again Swift capitalized certain letters to encode a message, this time a release date, a move that some fans obviously remembered from her early-album era.[29]

Culturally, Swifts penchant for Easter eggs and hidden messages stands out for its public nature. Going against the tendency of esoteric writing to disguise both individual messages and the fact of message concealment, Swift's brand of pop cultural esotericism is relatively well known outside her devoted fan base and even occasionally attracts mainstream attention (or what passes for mainstream attention today). *CBS News,* for example, published an online

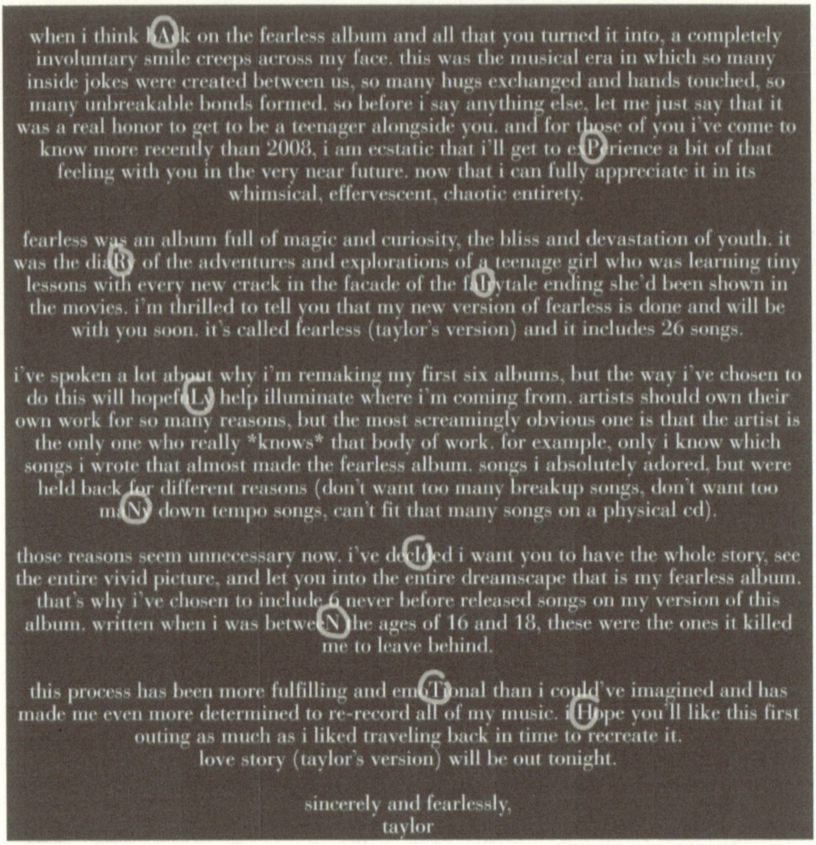

when i think bAck on the fearless album and all that you turned it into, a completely involuntary smile creeps across my face. this was the musical era in which so many inside jokes were created between us, so many hugs exchanged and hands touched, so many unbreakable bonds formed. so before i say anything else, let me just say that it was a real honor to get to be a teenager alongside you. and for those of you i've come to know more recently than 2008, i am ecstatic that i'll get to exPerience a bit of that feeling with you in the very near future. now that i can fully appreciate it in its whimsical, effervescent, chaotic entirety.

fearless was an album full of magic and curiosity, the bliss and devastation of youth. it was the diaRy of the adventures and explorations of a teenage girl who was learning tiny lessons with every new crack in the facade of the faIrytale ending she'd been shown in the movies. i'm thrilled to tell you that my new version of fearless is done and will be with you soon. it's called fearless (taylor's version) and it includes 26 songs.

i've spoken a lot about why i'm remaking my first six albums, but the way i've chosen to do this will hopefuLy help illuminate where i'm coming from. artists should own their own work for so many reasons, but the most screamingly obvious one is that the artist is the only one who really *knows* that body of work. for example, only i know which songs i wrote that almost made the fearless album. songs i absolutely adored, but were held back for different reasons (don't want too many breakup songs, don't want too maNy down tempo songs, can't fit that many songs on a physical cd).

those reasons seem unnecessary now. i've decIded i want you to have the whole story, see the entire vivid picture, and let you into the entire dreamscape that is my fearless album. that's why i've chosen to include 6 never before released songs on my version of this album. written when i was betweeN the ages of 16 and 18, these were the ones it killed me to leave behind.

this process has been more fulfilling and emoTional than i could've imagined and has made me even more determined to re-record all of my music. i Hope you'll like this first outing as much as i liked traveling back in time to recreate it.
love story (taylor's version) will be out tonight.

sincerely and fearlessly,
taylor

Figure 4. Taylor Swift post with coded messages that reveal the release date of her next album. Instagram, taylorswift, February 11, 2021.

article pairing Swift's songs to ex-boyfriends; late-night host Jimmy Fallon performed a bit on the *Tonight Show* about secret messages in Swift's music, confident that his general audience could follow; and even the notably unhip *Today* website published an in-depth analysis of messages embedded in Swift's songs, liner notes, and music videos.[30]

Communication via coded messages has thus become an established part of Swift's brand or star image, a composite image of how she lives and what she thinks, constructed from representations of her that circulate through the culture in a variety of media.[31] In Swift's case, her star image—or Swift as polysemic text—creates not only the sense of a publicly available private life but also ever-increasing long-term engagement on the part of fans—not unlike the elaborate achievement systems of massively multiplayer online role-playing games or multiplayer online battle arenas. Like these video games—or even machine gambling in Las Vegas—the star image of Taylor Swift is almost "addictive by design."[32]

To help ensure such habit formation, Swift goes out of her way to provide methods of decoding. In one YouTube video, she outlines a non-exhaustive list of some of the ways in which she has encoded hidden messages. According to Swift, her practices of encryption range beyond the lyrical and textual to include signifiers as diverse as set design in her music videos and graffiti. Nail polish foreshadows the color tones of a forthcoming album, an offhand mention of the band Panic! At the Disco discloses a musical collaboration, the use of palm trees symbolizes rebirth and new beginnings, and on and on.[33] The video serves as just one example, albeit a densely packed composite example, of Swift's active encouragement of her fans' obsessive reading of all the texts she produces, of her borderline behavioralist approach to fan engagement. As she baldly stated in an interview with *Entertainment Weekly,* Swift has trained her fans to behave that way.[34]

In less pathological terms, Swift's practice of coded messaging serves to unite her fandom, enabling her music to foster media events in an era of narrowcasting and disaster marathoning.[35] Although many of her messages are not able to capitalize on "liveness"—the ability to see and hear what is happening far away from us—they do allow large segments of the population to unite in a series of shared vibrations. Her encryptions glue fans' senses to an ongoing puzzle or mystery, bringing them together as they share in a common set of affects. As Swift wrote to the *Washington Post,* color coding, numerology, word searches, elaborate hints, Easter eggs, and the like are all intended to turn "new music into an event" for her fans, "to entertain them in playful, mischievous, clever way."[36] They help to calibrate an interactive spectacle, thereby compensating, in part, for social media's hypermodulating effect, which tends to isolate us in asynchronous bubbles, as well as for the incessantly looped broadcasts of terrorist attacks, wars, floods, hurricanes, and other crises.

These and other examples should leave little doubt that Swift intentionally codes a variety of mass and masspersonal communications to connect with her fans and increase their engagement with Swift's star image.[37] To that end, she provides a set of techniques, in almost an unofficial handbook style, to help ensure that, when presented with, say, a hit single, Instagram post, or fashion choice, dedicated fans will receive messages that remain undetected by more casual audiences. This instructive or propaedeutic aspect of Swift's communications strategy is crucial to esoteric "writing" and to our case that Swift is purposefully engaging at least some of her fan base on an esoteric level—or at the very least, giving highly engaged fans reason to believe she is doing so.

That attention to detail invites the logographic assumption (essential to esoteric hermeneutics) that Swift does not make mistakes—that everything she publicly communicates is intentional, existing as part of a code within a code. And yet, as we have seen, esotericism, according to the Straussian tradition, is not merely the sending of coded messages, not simply amateur spycraft. If it were, then all coded messages could conceivably qualify as esoteric, from literary allusions and tropes to simple substitution cyphers—even, potentially, computer programming, digitization, or any semiological process involving symbolic signs. The specific difference separating esoteric communication from all other interpretive acts is the presence of a rhetorical exigence, specifically one centered around both the fear of societal persecution for holding certain "abnormal" or "antisocial" beliefs and the accompanying need to circumvent that hostility while simultaneously continuing to communicate unpopular messages.

Nevertheless, none of these examples would seem to position Swift as an esoteric figure. Hidden clues about the color palette of a future album cover may entertain dedicated fans, but there are no strong societal norms (that we know of) requiring secrecy to avoid persecution related to the use of pastels.

COMPULSORY HETEROSEXUALITY AS PERSECUTION

Proper esotericism, according to Strauss, necessarily presupposes censorship, an ever-present societal force (or deeply felt belief in one) that demands for certain unpopular ideas silence or evasive messaging. Ancient, medieval, and even early modern philosophers feared execution à la the death of Socrates. Soviet dissidents feared what Aleksandr Solzhenitsyn famously called the "gulag archipelago." The Walt Disney Company feared (and still fears) loss of revenue in hostile market environments, both international and domestic.

QAnon maintained that conservative Americans, and even the former President Donald Trump, had something to fear in the form of a "globalist" and "deep state" conspiracy, involving everything and everyone from lowly FBI office drones to A-list Hollywood celebrities.

Among this veritable who's who of esoteric senders, where or how could one reasonably situate Taylor Swift? On the one hand, Swift has a lot to lose if it were to come to light that she harbors impolitic beliefs, opinions, or values. In monetary terms alone, she enjoyed an estimated net worth of $1.1 billion in 2024. (In 2015, she made an astounding $1 million a day.)[38] On the other hand, as detailed in the previous section, none among the variety of Swift's coded messages appears designed to avoid persecution. Indeed, given the content of the coded messages, there does not appear a compelling reason to fear persecution in the first place.

There is, however, an important contextual factor that makes up part of Swift's overall media ecology: Gaylors—a distinct online fan community whose members argue that Swift is gay based on a cluster of distinct yet overlapping suppositions about Swift's sexuality (bi, pan, queer, fluid?), her purported romantic partners, and crucially, symbolic clues discovered within her music and in the interstices of her star image.[39] Writing for *Jezebel,* Caitlin Cruz points out that rumors of Swift's nonheteronormativity have followed her since her 2006 self-titled debut album was certified platinum seven times, "as an undercurrent beneath mainstream celebrity media that spent over a decade fascinated by her real—and sometimes PR-appearing—relationships with men."[40] From a Gaylor fan perspective, Swift makes use of coded language to avoid a potential homophobic backlash that would cost her millions of dollars in fan revenue and irreparably damage her star image.

But the question is whether the potential of a homophobic backlash constitutes a real and pressing persecutory risk for someone of Swift's celebrity, especially given present ascendant attitudes toward homosexuality and gender identity? Without downplaying the persistence of antihomosexual bias, one could reasonably suggest that Swift lives at a time when many openly gay celebrities appear to be living relatively comfortable lives without experiencing major cultural demotion or blacklisting. More importantly, if Swift is concerned about backlash, then that concern is almost glaringly absent in many of her public actions and statements. She has, for instance, publicly aligned herself with LGBTQ causes; performed at the historic Stonewall Inn, the site of a gay riot that launched the modern American queer movement; and in 2019 created a petition in favor of the Equality Act, a congressional bill (HR 5) that, if passed, would amend the Civil Rights Act of 1964 to prohibit discrimination on the basis of sex, sexual orientation, and gender identity in employment, housing, public accommodations, education, federally funded programs, credit, and jury service.[41] Her music video for the song "You Need to Calm Down" featured many queer celebrities, such as Laverne Cox, Chester Lockhart, and Billy Porter and explicitly targeted homophobia. And in 2018 she criticized the Republican Senate candidate Marsha Blackburn (Tennessee), with Swift stating that she wished she (Swift) had come out against Trump during his 2016 run, even as her advisers warned her that doing so could cause a backlash.

These public actions and statements would seem to suggest that if Swift is queer then she is not overly concerned about any potential backlash against disclosing her sexual orientation. Moreover, a properly handled coming out would probably even mitigate adverse reaction to her public positions on queerness. The use of queer imagery in the music video for 2019's "You Need to Calm Down" predictably angered conservative-leaning fans, but it also sparked outrage among members of the queer community.[42] Spencer Kornhaber, for the *Atlantic,* argues that Swift problematically draws a false equivalence between the nasty tweets she receives and the dangerous forms of persecution faced by members of the LGBTQ community.[43] He writes, "The entire song, indeed, subsumes queerness into Swift's narratives. Its breathtaking argument: that famous people are persecuted in a way meaningfully comparable to queer people."

The *Atlantic,* however, was by no means alone in pointing out Swift's misstep. *Esquire* published an article by Dave Holmes titled "No Shade, but There's a Wrong Way to Make a Gay Anthem," while the satirical newspaper the *Onion* threw plenty of shade with its article "Taylor Swift Inspires Teen to Come Out as Straight Woman Needing to Be at Center of Gay Rights Narrative."[44] With publicity like this, one could convincingly argue that Swift's position as a "gay ally" opens her up to more criticism from all sides of the political spectrum than would an embrace of a queer identity.

Gaylors consistently offer a different perspective, maintaining that coming out would deeply damage Swift's image in ways that would have significantly negative, material repercussions on the entertainer's career. In support of this belief, TikTok Gaylor fan Swiftieplanntika pointed to the intensely negative reaction to a *Rolling Stone* article that broached the possibility that Swift could be queer as proof that anything other than an esoteric coming out would provoke a massively adverse response among her fan base. She compared the number of retweets to quote-tweets and took a quick survey of the responses to make the case that the fan response to the Gaylor thesis is overwhelmingly hostile. In a since-deleted TikTok video, she also detailed the abuse that she alleges she faced from Swift's fans who did not appreciate her defense of the Gaylor theory. In a TikTok video posted by another Gaylor user, Criesinevermore, included video footage in which lesbian country music artist and activist Chely Wright discussed the difficulties of being openly queer in the music industry. The posting of the video by a Gaylor fan suggests that Swift's refusal to come out may be, in part, a defensive reaction to the tribulations of her friend Wright and others like her whose careers have been hindered by their openly queer identities.

According to some Gaylors, the potential loss of revenue is only one of the motivating factors behind Swift's decision to remain closeted, and not the primary one. As one fan, TikTok username sapphicka, suggests, Swift is "more accolade-motivated than necessarily profit-motivated." Even if Swift were not materially to notice the loss of tens of millions of dollars in revenue, alienating fans could jeopardize her ability to break records and win awards based on indexes like chart placement and sales. Swift, after all, currently holds the "honor" of being the only female to break into the top ten highest-paid musicians list in 2021, securing the precarious number ten spot at that.[45] The argument advanced is that while Swift may not notice the loss of even millions of dollars, the loss of metric-related accolades would sting.

In terms of identification, persecution based on sexual orientation can function as a powerful cathexis for Gaylors vis-à-vis Swift. It is likely that many queer Gaylors have had personal encounters with that kind of hostility and ill-treatment. Those experiences make credible the idea that Swift would face negative consequences for coming out, despite her superstar status. As we have seen, Marks uses the contrastive analogy between a toy mallet and a sledgehammer to indicate the asymmetrical difficulties faced by celebrities who come out compared to those of the average person.[46]

That asymmetry, however, does not diminish the difficulties faced by queer noncelebrities in a world of what can appear as compulsory heterosexuality. Fear of persecution may in fact be one of the reasons why Gaylors, who are often queer, tend to converge in online spaces—why the term *Gaylor* refers to a distinct online community—which allows geographically remote fans to connect safely from all over the world. Complicated algorithms funnel Gaylor content based on social media users' demographic information and interests, which means they may not even have to seek it out. When properly moderated, these spaces allow Gaylors the ability to exclude hateful rhetoric and create safe spaces in which to discuss Gaylor theories and just be queer in peace.

GAY-LORE

Gaylors have no shortage of online spaces they may call home. Some of them are even quite popular. The Reddit community r/Gaylor_Swift, for instance, boasted more than twenty-eight thousand members in 2024, which places it among the top 4 percent most popular Reddit communities. X (formerly Twitter) also sees a good amount of pro-Gaylor traffic, with one particular post by redsapphic detailing Gaylor theories racking up more than ninety thousand views since 2023. Many theories originated on the social networking site Tumblr, but with one exception, all the fan theories examined below were posted to TikTok. The algorithmic nature of the short-form video hosting service means that if a user expresses interest in a certain subject matter, such as by watching or liking a video, then TikTok's compilation of rules and data will decide what the user wants to see on the platform and make suggestions accordingly. In our experience, our "interest" in Gaylor video content resulted in a deluge of related-video suggestions.

As is the case on other social media platforms, content producers attempt to secure user engagement for their videos by linking them to similar content via hashtags, such as "#Gaylor." They also frequently reference videos by other, similarly interested content creators, a self-marketing strategy that helps sustain the niche attention economy in which their own videos circulate. Such references may occur verbally, in the videos themselves, but more often creators will link to related content, typically in the title or description of their own videos, or even include and comment on segments of other videos.[47] With these techno-cultural conditions in mind, our examination of the Gaylor esotericism begins with the most classically textual element of Swift's oeuvre: her lyrics.

Unsurprisingly, Gaylors present much of Swift's lyrical content as self-evidently and independently queer. One TikTok user, Annika, identifies an array of examples in the song "Seven" from the 2020 album *Folklore:* "And we can be pirates / Then you won't have to cry / Or hide in the closet." Another go-to song in Gaylors' arguments about queer lyrical content is "Maroon," from *Midnights* (2022). In it Swift sings, "The lips I used to call home / so scarlet, it was maroon." Gaylors point to this as a clear reference to lipstick, which would imply a female romantic partner. Anticipating heteronormative counterinterpretations, one TikTok Gaylor, frozenarrow73, indignantly proclaims, "There is no heterosexual explanation."

Many but not all Gaylor TikTok videos operate at this level. They identify lyrics that on the very surface seem to invite queer interpretations because, they argue, those surfaces are encoded as queer. Unsurprisingly, this also applies to liner notes, given Swift's explicit acknowledgment of having previously hidden encoded messages in her albums' liner notes. In the liner notes to *Red* (2012), Swift included the coded words *Hyiannis Port.* Gaylors such as whatiwillsay argue that these words designate a location—Hyannis Port, a small Massachusetts beach town, where Swift is known to have vacationed and where Gaylors claim she was romancing her muse, Dianna Agron, for the love song "Everything Has Changed." The misspelling of Hyannis Port, Gaylors argue, is intended to evoke Dianna Agron, with both *Hyiannis* and *Dianna* containing the string of letters I-A-N-N-A. For Gaylors, that mirroring, combined with the fact that Swift spent a significant amount of time with Agron at Hyannis Port immediately prior to writing "Everything Has Changed," signal purpose rather than coincidence.

Some of those surfaces are visual rather than textual, or both. In an article published on the open platform *Medium* entitled "Why 'Gaylor' Believers Like Me Think Taylor Swift Is Bisexual," Stephanie Leguichard analyzes the music video for "You Need to Calm Down," in which Swift's hair is dyed the colors of the bisexual pride flag (pink and royal blue). Leguichard comments, "Let's just say I don't blame Gaylor believers for interpreting this as foolproof evidence of her bisexuality."

This statement is itself worthy of comment. Although not esoteric, it displays a rhetorical savvy not uncommon among the Gaylor community and perhaps even comparable to that which Gaylors attribute to Swift. Leguichard, a Gaylor who refrains from identifying as such in the article, positions herself as an objective cultural observer testifying to the virtual infallibility of Gaylor interpretations. In a similarly deft move, the TikTok poster river_witch7 begins a stitch with a TikTok from user rainbowhistoryclass about the history of Marie Antoinette, which argues that rumors about Antoinette's homosexual proclivities served to unite lesbians of eighteenth-century France, enabling them to fantasize their existence as a community from positions of social isolation. river_witch7's TikTok then cuts to Swift's video for "Bejeweled" (from *Midnights*), which shows Swift adorned in an outfit resembling something the queen of France might have worn at the end of the ancien régime. The clear implication, as confirmed in the video's many comments, is that Swift dressed as Antoinette to signal her queerness.

Other Gaylors, however, go beyond (or below) a linear transmission model of sending/receiving encoded/decoded messages, charting a more properly Straussian course. Their interpretive efforts do not stop at the superficial, exoteric level of overt lyrical content but extend to perceived lyrical "mistakes," which they regard as signs of a potentially deeper, hidden, and therefore true meaning. One commonly referenced example of a pregnant mistake occurs in "The Very First Night," from *Red (Taylor's Version)* (2021). In this song about a past romance, Swift reminisces about privately shared moments between romantic partners:

> 'Cause they don't know about the night in the hotel
> They weren't ridin' in the car when we both fell
> Didn't read the note on the Polaroid picture
> They don't know how much I miss you

As even casual listeners may notice, the words ending the first couplet (*hotel* and *fell*) rhyme, whereas those ending the following couplet (*picture* and *you*) do not. However, while casual listeners may be inclined to regard this formalistic jolt as a compositional error, chalking it up to lazy songwriting or editorial oversight, Gaylor kales_o points out that *picture*, the word ending the first half of the second couplet, does rhyme with *her*. *Her*, Gaylors argue, would be as symbolically appropriate as the word that actually appears in the song lyrics (*you*) but would have the benefit of fulfilling a classical rhyme scheme. *Her* would therefore be a superior aesthetic choice, and the obviously better choice at that, an aesthetic judgment that Gaylors unproblematically ascribe to Swift, arguing that the word is made present through its conspicuous absence, if only one has the ears to hear. For Gaylors, "errors" such as these are compelling examples of Swift esoterically communicating with a clued-in audience that can reach below the exoteric surface to grasp the true meaning. And that meaning, disguised in ambiguity but visible to her *true* fans, is that Swift is unambiguously queer.

Some Gaylors complicate their esoteric readings of Swift's lyrics by way of intertextual analysis, frequently reading a particular song in the context of Swift's collected body of work, which includes music videos as well as sound recordings. For example, in the music video for the second single from 2019's *Lover,* "You Need to Calm Down," Swift is shown sunbathing with her friends while an angry (presumably) homophobic mob protests. Accompanying images of the angry crowd are the lyrics "Shade doesn't make anyone less gay." The standard interpretation is that Swift is using *shade* informally as slang, to mean a subtle, sneering expression of contempt for or disgust with someone.[48] This definition implies that the animosity will not make anyone less queer. Over against that reading, user degraceful suggests assuming the dictionary meaning of the word *shade,* by which she means a metaphoric use signifying either a position of relative obscurity or a shadow or area of darkness. Doing so, she argues, reveals a very different interpretation of line, which is the intended meaning (hidden in plain sight): being hidden (closeted) does not make someone less gay.

To justify her preferred reading, degraceful references another song, "Paris," which is something of a deep cut since it appeared on *Midnights (3am Edition)* (2022) rather than on the standard edition. Here, Swift explicitly clarifies the meaning of her use of the word *shade:*

> Sit quiet by my side in the shade
> And not the kind that's thrown
> I mean the kind under where a tree has grown

Swift's in-lyric explication of *shade* would seem to provide retroactive, intertextual support for degraceful's interpretation of the word in the earlier "You Need to Calm Down," an appearance that Gaylors readily embrace as truth. The need to clarify in one instance suggests that the unclarified *shade* is meant to be read with the other definition. From this perspective, the obscurity of "Paris" relative to "You Need to Calm Down" lends additional intertextual support because it positions "You Need to Calm Down" as a cypher and "Paris" as the key.

Gaylors also make connections between the imagery in Swift's videos, specifically color, and other queer texts. For example, one Gaylor connects the red imagery in "You Need to Calm Down" with the film *To Wong Foo, Thanks for Everything! Julie Newmar* (1995), one of the few mainstream movies of the 1990s to feature gay characters (albeit gay characters who were coded as asexual). river_witch7 draws similar visual connections between the house represented in the music video for the "Lover" (from *Lover*, 2019) and 1999's satirical teen romantic comedy *But I'm a Cheerleader*, a film about a lesbian high schooler forced to attend a gay conversion camp. river_witch7 argues that both the film and Swift's video use the color yellow to symbolize the closeted metaphor. In the video, Swift's closet is full of only yellow clothing, despite her wearing an array of colored clothing throughout the video. river_witch7 points out that Swift only wears yellow in the video when her character is in the fishbowl with her lover, which she argues represents "the fishbowl of celebrity, you know, everyone looking at you."

Some intertextual analysis goes further than Swift's collected body of work, referencing paratexts, like tabloid and entertainment news, which play a role in determining Swift's star image. After referencing a celebrity-news article focusing on the amount of time Swift and singer/actress Zoë Kravitz spent together in quarantine during the COVID-19 pandemic, one Gaylor (heyitsmoog) points out that Zoë recorded a song that refers to a summer romance, called "Kid," while Swift's song "Illicit Affairs" (from *Folklore*) includes the lyric "Don't call me kid." According to heyitsmoog, the inter- or paratextual meaning of *kid* is so obvious that "it's not even a rabbit hole, it's like a straight down hole." She concludes the video by reminding viewers that "Taylor doesn't do anything by accident."

Swift has already primed her fans to hunt for Easter eggs and deeper meaning, so the Gaylor project makes much more sense within the context of Swiftie fandom. As one Gaylor says, "If you are a self-described Taylor Swift fan who knows her catalog like the back of your hand and still does not believe that she is gay or is at least not open to the idea that she is gay, you are doing such a disservice to her genius and her lyrical prowess." Like Donald

Trump vis-à-vis QAnon followers or Christopher Nolan's *Dark Knight* trilogy with respect to white nationalists, the Taylor Swift adored by Gaylors is a Taylor Swift who is in complete control of her messages and her messaging; there are no accidents, only purposeful communiques, and if there is channel "noise," then it too possesses significance.

These hermeneutic maneuvers with regard to the text of Swift's artistic output may seem to be in line with standard esoteric reading practices, but for Gaylors anything originating with Swift can legitimately be considered material for hidden meaning. For instance, Swift posted a link to a song by the unknown artist Niceboy Ed. A Google search for the band name includes a link to the academic essay "High School Crack-Up," in the essay collection *Margaret Mead Made Me Gay.* The essay focuses on performative heteronormativity, and the Gaylors make the case that Swift's "shout-out" to Niceboy Ed is a two-step-removed signal of her own compliance with the believable yet illusory performance of heteronormativity. In reference to this essay popping up in Google searches, lethbyathousandkates claims, "I am here to tell you that there is no possible way this is a coincidence." According to the Gaylor Reddit community, this too is a sign of Swift's between-the-lines (and liner notes) queerness

In another instance of accidental overselling, Gaylors point to the Taylor Swift documentary *Miss Americana* (2020). While discussing plans for a music video with her collaborator Brendon Urie, Swift at one point says, "Then there's me: it's like dancers, cats, gay pride, people in country western boots and I start riding a unicorn. Everything that makes me me."[49] Gaylors such as frozenarrow73 have seized upon this phrasing as being highly odd for a straight person. Would even the staunchest ally claim that gay pride is fundamental to who they are? Possible, but nowhere near probable.

Gaylors generally adopt a counterintuitive interpretive ethos, reflexively decoding evidence that prima facie appears to confirm Swift's heterosexuality as secret codes signaling the opposite. One Gaylor references a news article describing Swift as "famously straight." At first glance, this would seem to contradict the Gaylor thesis. This Gaylor, however, offers the following rebuttal: "We still live in a world where straightness is created as default, so if somebody is famously straight . . . the lady doth protest too much methinks. Like, let's think for a second, about why a person, how a person would even become famously straight in the current world that we live at, if they weren't trying to shove that narrative down our throats for some reason." While strange, this fits with Melzer's idea that emphatic statements of opposition may in face esoterically signal support.[50]

In another case of assuming the opposite of what is explicitly conveyed, Swift claimed in a since-deleted Instagram post that she got the name of her song "Lavender Haze" (from *Midnights*) from an episode of *Mad Men* about protagonist Don Draper's love for his future wife. Despite Swift's explicit statement that this fictional but heterosexual pairing was the inspiration for her use of the term, Gaylors pushed back. They claimed that "lavender haze" and its connotations precede *Mad Men* in such cultural artifacts as a 1976 scholarly sociology article about lesbianism as well as in the song "Do You," from *Perfectly Clear* (2008) by American singer-songwriter Jewel, which Gaylors such as anniemaladapted also read through a queer lens. They are argue that these reference points—or their interpretation of a reference point—are the more likely inspirations for Swift's use of the phrase "lavender haze," despite Swift's explicit pronouncements stating otherwise. Gaylor lissajostewart summarizes this interpretive attitude by simply stating, "Lavender is a well-known queer color."

This collection of Gaylor readings is in no way meant to be exhaustive. In fact, it omits some of the most compelling pieces of evidence put forth by Gaylors, including an analysis of a Swift *Saturday Night Live* skit, a photograph in which Swift allegedly replaced one of her eyes with one of Karlie Kloss's, and a performance in which Swift seemingly fingers the air. A popular meme circulating among Gaylors superimposes a number of theses on the image of an iceberg, the idea being that Swift's queer signaling exists on a spectrum of ever-deeper esoteric coding (figure 5).

While many Gaylors claim that the queer coding is so obvious as to be irrefutable, TikTok Gaylor sapphicka makes the case that Swift deploys a more nuanced, sophisticated form of esotericism. In her view, Swift regularly crafts an exoteric message for the masses while embedding within it an esoteric message that likely only queer fans will receive:

> When people say the invisible stream is about her relationship with Joe Alwyn, they are correct because that is one of many narratives that she in-

Figure 5. The Gaylor Iceberg depicts the layers of the Gaylor conspiracy. Instagram, yeahbutstillpod, September 30, 2022.

> tentionally wove into that song. When people like myself say that invisible string is actually a gay anthem, we are also correct, because knowing just how surgically and precisely Taylor crafts her songs means knowing that the inclusion of all of the colors of the rainbow and then conveniently dropping all of the bi pride flag colors in one line towards the very end could have never been done by accident.

Presumably, the attribution of such genius to American pop star would make Strauss and his followers bristle. Typically, esoteric writing is seen as the purview of a canonical (male) mind, someone on the order of a Machiavelli, Plato, or Shakespeare. Of course, this raises the question which is signifier and which signified, the cause and the effect, the esotericism or the celebrity. But Gaylors, in justifying their deep readings, point both to Swift's artistic genius and the fact that she has a huge marketing team—professionals whose job it is to review all her actions and public communications and to look for references that they or she would not want associated with her star image—and that this team, so Gaylors argue, approved of Swift's many queer Easter eggs. Gaylors, in other words, deploy their own critique of Swift's alleged esotericism, claiming that she should boast an even greater esoteric prowess given the enormous public relations apparatus she has at her disposal.

This idea of esotericism by committee even undercuts one of the most compelling arguments against all esoteric readings, regardless of the source, namely that the "esoteric elements" are really just unintentional coincidences. According to sapphicka:

> Particularly someone like Taylor Swift, who has cultivated an entire brand off of the idea that she's including Easter eggs and little clues and all of her public facing communication. . . . The idea that her and her team would just decide to completely check out of public discourse surrounding her in this album right now, when all of these gay TikToks are blowing up, gay articles are being written about her . . . is so laughably ridiculous to me.

For such Gaylors, it is credible to believe that a lone, independent artist could occasionally and accidentally include queer references in their work or public statements. Swift, however, is a different story, despite her "independent" status.

Her messages are subjected to what is essentially a thorough vetting process. With so many professionals checking her work, it becomes difficult to believe that so many of queer references would have circulated without her knowledge and consent.

Gaylors also draw on the history of queer flagging in their defense of reading Swift esoterically. The idea that Swift (a genius) and her marketing team (well-paid professionals) would be ignorant of the history of queer flagging is presented as impossible. However, even if Swift and her team were somehow ignorant of this history, Gaylors argue that Swift has close personal and professional relationships with many queer people, any one of whom would surely let her know at one point or another. The idea that Swift is straight and knows about the coded nature of her speech is presented as equally implausible because her queer friends would not stand for it. As 2003unbearable says in a video, "Taylor Swift does not have close personal relationships with this many queer people, for her to be intentionally misleading our community. If Taylor Swift was not gay, or bi, or whatever member of the LGBT community and she was simply dropping, Gaylor Easter eggs everywhere as a marketing ploy, she would not have the love and support privately and personally of this many gay people." In this way, the Gaylor ecosystem functions as a smooth-functioning decryption machine/assemblage, making esoteric arguments at every level—through sign, lyric, appearance, promotion, fashion, and so on, and even through contextual factors like the decisions of Swift's marketing team. The Gaylors truly have a mastery of invention. Whether this is the canon of rhetoric or flights of fantasy is not for us to decide.

The obsessive all-consuming nature of the Gaylor sleuthing has drawn comparisons to conspiracy theories, specifically to QAnon. Interestingly, many Gaylors do not immediately reject the analogy. In an article in *Gawker*, perhaps the most prominent exploration of the Gaylor phenomenon, a fan referred to only as Annika said, "It's not a perfect comparison because Gaylors, first of all, aren't evil. . . . And second of all, we're right. But it does scratch that same social itch of being in a community where everyone has the same, you know, niche knowledge and speaks the same coded language and are in on a little secret that the general public doesn't know about." She recognizes that Gaylor and QAnon structurally operate in a similar manner.

Likewise, Gaylor thesianrigby claims on TikTok,

> If Taylor Swift and Karlie Kloss do not come out as gay together during the midnight album premiere, I'm going to check myself into a mental hospital, and not because I'll be devastated, which I will be, but because it's gone too far, the conspiracy theory. It's become my reality, it's truly my reality. . . . I'm sure there's not a lot of overlap between QAnon and the Gaylor Swift community, but it's like a crazy political conspiracy theory where they believe just really, like genuinely believe really insane shit, just because they kind of talk to each other into it. And like, you just can't pull them out of that reality. And I always, like, look at those people and I'm, like, [I] just feel bad for you, like you are completely lacking . . . the ability to see the real reality and, like, use logical reasoning. But that's literally me.

These Gaylors see the connections between what they do and the pronoia of QAnon. The big difference isn't about rhetorical method or structure but about content.

WELCOME TO THE SECRET CLUB

Reading the history of philosophical esotericism, Melzer identifies pedagogy and politics as two categories of compelling reasons to communicate between the lines. As we have seen, political esotericism seeks to build covert support for revolution against some problematic aspect of the status quo; in contrast, pedagogical esotericism strives to establish barriers so that only the most deserving individuals may access a text's true hidden message. Both varieties are framed in terms of authorial intent, but they also may easily (and justifiably) be read in terms of function. A text read in a politically esoteric way still functions rhetorically. There is no objectively esoteric text, only texts that invite, say, a politically esoteric readerly position and seem, from that perspective, designed to escape censorship, regardless of the author's (or authors') intent.

The rhetorically esoteric aspects of Plato's dialogues—and insomuch as there are esoteric aspects in the dialogues, they're *all* rhetorically esoteric—have invited Straussian interpretations for decades, enabling the formation of a clique of professional hermeneuticists capable of surmounting the steep, craggy walls of pedagogical esotericism. Whether Straussians are engaged in an elaborate decryption program akin to cracking the Enigma cypher or an elevated elaboration of the informal Texas sharpshooter fallacy is irrelevant to the result—a club of academic thinkers bound by shared reading practices.

Gaylors highlight another functional purpose of esotericism, which does not exclude that of the Straussians: rhetorical in-grouping. It is the esotericism of the password to the childhood clubhouse, of the coded and intricately folded note passed in the cafeteria or study hall. Esoteric decoding can also engender, maintain, and strengthen bonds and identity. That may even be its primary (architectonic) rhetorical function. One anonymous Gaylor, posting on the Gaylor subreddit r/Gaylor_Swift in 2024, put it this way: "I hate how addicted I am to this subreddit, and how parasocial I have become with Taylor Swift since discovering it. I think it's because this is the closest thing I have to an active queer community, given where I live." Other Gaylors attend "Camp Gaylor," a hybrid modality event where Gaylors gather in person as well digitally to discuss esoteric readings of Swift's discography. At camp, one particularly self-aware Gaylor claimed, "I actually would prefer she didn't [come out] because I think it's more fun this way."[51]

What little Gaylor research exists supports the claim that Gaylor theories produce identity-forming effects. Leah Dajches and Jennifer Stevens Aubrey, for instance, find that Gaylors' beliefs facilitate acceptance of queer identity, in both others and themselves.[52] These findings join other works about the psycho-emotional and communal benefits of queer media readings and their ability to cultivate positive mental health effects such as reduced anxiety.[53] Common sense would also bear this out: Swift's Easter eggs represent acceptance from one of the most influential and recognizable celebrities in the world while providing access to a global community of queer folks sharing similar interests.

Of course, the Gaylors are not alone in benefiting from the identity-forming and identity-sustaining aspects of esotericism. Such features and their advantages are also apparent among QAnon believers. Participant observers not only pore over hundreds of hours of content but also sport QAnon-branded clothing and receive QAnon-themed tattoos. (In the next chapter, we will consider connections between these ideologically disparate pronoiac communities.) Less obviously, we hear the pride in the voice of noted Leo Strauss student Harvey Mansfield when he recounts stories of decoding Machiavelli's mysteries with his mentor, and we see it in the cliquish nature of the

Straussians as a whole—despite their sometimes inimical division into East Coast and West Coast rivals, like some parody of the infamous hip-hop rivalry of the 1990s. Pronoiac conspiracy theories appear to foster bonds among adherents and sustain group cohesion, regardless of the fan-object. The collaborative nature of pronoiac/benevolent conspiracy theorizing also works to strengthen these in-group connections—in almost autopoietic fashion—even bolstering conspiracy theories not typically viewed as pronoiac, as in the case of QAnon.

3

WHERE WE PRODUCE ONE, WE PRODUCE ALL

The Platform Conspiracism of QAnon

> Hey. Nobody has any trouble believing in the internet, right, which really is magic. So what's the problem believing in a virtual private network for Santa's business? It results in real toys, real presents, delivered by Christmas morning, what's the difference?
>
> —Thomas Pynchon, *Bleeding Edge*

Hillary Clinton and Katy Perry drink the blood of murdered children to live forever, Barack Obama and Tom Hanks participate in the sex trafficking and molestation of children, and a cabal of Satan worshipers controls global events from behind the scenes. Do not worry, though, because President Trump and his military allies are working secretly to unmask this elite coven of cannibalistic, child-murdering pedophiles and to make sure that they are carted off to Guantánamo and hanged for their crimes. This was the central, animating idea behind the QAnon conspiracy theory, and it makes other political conspiracy theories appear almost quaint in comparison, both in terms of content and extension.[1] The scope of QAnon is in fact so extensive that it easily assimilated less far-reaching (but no less right-wing) conspiracy theories, as it assimilated the notion of a so-called COVID-19 plandemic.

As outlandish as QAnon or any other fringe conspiracy theory may sound, there is a common grammar to the rhetoric of conspiracy that lends it a certain coherence. Perhaps the most important text in the critical analysis of conspiracy theories is historian Richard Hofstadter's famed essay "The Paranoid Style in American Politics."[2] In it he outlines five features that distinguish conspiracy theories as a rhetorical genre, each of which is conspicuously present in the QAnon conspiracy theory: totalizing narrative, conspiracy as the explanation of historical events, public figures as villains, a call for an apocalyptic response, and large amounts of evidence that nevertheless demand of the audience a huge logical leap. Subsequent critical writings about conspiracy theories tend to take Hofstadter as a point of departure and have come to identify other tropes common to conspiracist discourse, many of which are also found in QAnon.[3]

Nevertheless, as illuminative and original as this critical approach may be, its ability to offer generalizable statements about all conspiracy theories means that it is at a disadvantage when it comes to isolating and analyzing those features that distinguish any particular theory. This is especially the case given the technologically augmented and accelerated world of late-stage capitalism, in which, according to Fredric Jameson, it is impossible to think the totality of the world system. As the technology of contemporary society "becomes more—and more visibly—complex," Jameson argues, conspiracy not only proliferates but also "must of necessity become more bizarre, intricate, and violent to accommodate it." Conspiracy, from this perspective, is thus an inevitable outgrowth of the total logic of late capitalism—a degraded figure, to be sure, but also a last-ditch attempt "to represent the latter's system, whose failure is marked by its slippage into theme and content."[4]

For that reason, this chapter departs from the critical practice of attempting to classify tenets common to all conspiracy theories and instead focuses on a prominent, unusual, but heretofore unelaborated discursive feature of QAnon that provides a compelling explanation for QAnon's ability to differentiate itself from a digital expanse of rival conspiracies. That distinguishing trait is the tendency among QAnon followers to read and write esoterically, primarily in relation to President Trump, and to do so within a serpentine pipeline of digital-cultural interactivity and networked internet platforms. Esoteric writing is by no means exclusive to QAnon, but what sets this phenomenon apart is its fusion of traditional conspiracy thinking with esotericism, a convergence now occurring through the mechanisms of social media. This is not to say that any contributor to QAnon is versed in the history of esoteric writing, only that QAnon as a discourse appears to rely heavily on a communicative strategy of encoding and decoding that bears strong resemblance to an esoteric hermeneutic, but played out across social media.

Whereas Hofstadter's paranoid style provided a paradigm for analyzing conspiracy theories in general, this chapter maintains that the conservative political philosopher Leo Strauss furnishes an additional method for critically analyzing the idiosyncrasies of QAnon. According to Strauss, philosophers in the ancient and early modern world commonly wrote and read a work's true message "between the lines."[5] Although it is disguised within a superstructural exoteric message, an obscure, esoteric meaning of a text remains decipherable to all thoughtful readers in all times and places, as it is often conveyed obliquely by any number of rhetorical strategies and compositional techniques—obscure references, irony or paradox, hyperbole, deliberate self-contradictions, or even dubious brazenness. When these and other compositional errors appear in the works of great philosophers, "thoughtful . . . careful readers," Strauss argues, ought to at least consider the possibility that such apparent mistakes may be exoteric signs indicative of an esoteric philosophical meaning.[6]

With that methodological observation in mind, we note that QAnon performs distinctly, even if accidentally, Straussian readings of public texts, identifying a variety of esoteric messages in the public pronouncements of President Trump, but with the splayed intent of publicizing rather than concealing their true, hidden messages. The medium on and through which this communicative practice takes place, however, is not incidental but plays a constitutive role in shaping and prolonging the discourse. The interactive dimension of social media results in an invitation to esotericism, at once enabling and encouraging followers to become esoteric content producers in their own right.

In addition, then, to drawing on the esoteric hermeneutics of Strauss, our examination makes use of contemporary fan studies, particularly Axel Bruns's notion that networked internet platforms have worked to blur the line between users and content producers through the activity of what he calls "produsage."[7] QAnon's invitation has resulted in an entire ecosystem of amateur internet produsage that includes at least dozens of YouTube channels and

Reddit threads, any number of which may boast thousands of members who are devoted to the task of actively decoding hidden messages intended for the faithful while cryptically encoding and distributing some of their own.[8] QAnon, on this read, comes to cut a paradoxical figure, transforming a compositional method designed to preserve knowledge for a coterie of brilliant philosophers into the basis for a mass movement that occupies the populist fringes of right-wing political discourse. It is a movement that appears set to outlive both Trump's presidency and QAnon, who has not posted since the 2020 United States presidential election.

THE MYTHICAL BEGINNINGS OF QANON

Insofar as the QAnon conspiracy theory admits of a beginning, we can place its origins in a post that first appeared on the message board 4chan, the birthplace of the notorious Gamergate controversy.[9] The post was uploaded by an anonymous person (or persons) using the online handle "Q"—whence the *Q* in QAnon. Q, which is shorthand for "Q clearance" or "Q access authorization," is a reference to the Department of Energy security clearance required to access top secret restricted data, formerly restricted data, and national security information, as well as secret restricted data. What is believed to be Q's initial post was styled in the manner of other alleged insider accounts, such as FBIAnon, HLIAnon (high-level insider), and CIAAnon, according to which the poster implicitly or overtly claims to be a high-ranking government official who is breaking both professional protocol and the law to leak critical information to the public. QAnon's first posts offered 4chan users a portentous take on the near future:

> Q Post 2017-10-28
> >>147005381 HRC extradition already in motion effective yesterday with several countries in case of cross border run. Passport approved to be flagged effective 10/30 @ 12:01am. Expect massive riots organized in defiance and others fleeing the US to occur. US M's [Marines] will conduct the operation while NG [National Guard] activated. Proof check: Locate a NG member and ask if activated for duty 10/30 across most major cities.
> [Q reference post:]

>>146981635 Hillary Clinton will be arrested between 7:45 AM–8:30 AM EST on Monday—the morning on Oct 30, 2017.[10]

The posts essentially maintained that two days later the U.S. military, in conjunction with the National Guard, would arrest Hillary Clinton for some unspecified crime. It would seem that the falsity or unreliability of such a prediction was easily demonstrated, since Clinton was in fact not arrested on October 30. Q argues, however, that the U.S. government is effectively owned and operated by a clandestine, international network of powerful, wealthy, and predatory elites whose tentacular, globe-spanning reach extends from the Vatican and the European Union to pharmaceutical companies, entertainment industries, nongovernmental organizations, and beyond.

This secret cabal is thus thought to control the entire political apparatus of the United States (and of other countries) through the strategic placement of key nodal agents like Hillary Clinton, Nancy Pelosi, and Barack Obama and the deployment of unelected bureaucrats operating within the organs of the deep state. While such an interpretive lens may strike many as highly peculiar, if not utterly bizarre, it is not unique to twenty-first-century message boards; rather, it traces its roots to the hypothesis, first popularized during the Cold War by New World Order conspiracism, that a secretive power elite with a globalist agenda is conspiring to bring about a totalitarian one-world government.[11] In this narrative of contemporaneity—if not of history as such—many of the world's large-scale tragedies are the desired outcomes of carefully orchestrated strategies of domination and oppression, from famines and population displacement to war, economic turmoil, and now, according to QAnon, a global child sex trafficking ring.[12] Emphasis on the latter outrage is perhaps one of QAnon's more distinguishing traits vis-à-vis the wide-ranging field of New World Order conspiracism, though it, too, is not without precedent. Indeed, the religiously inflected characterization of the cabal as Satan-worshipping pedophiles invokes the moral panic of satanic ritual abuse (often referred to as the "satanic panic") that originated in the United States in the 1980s and by the late 1990s had spread throughout many parts of the world.[13]

Enter Donald Trump, whose presidency, according to Q's interpretation, amounts to a successful recruitment strategy spearheaded by anonymous "patriotic" insurgents in a bid to undermine the cabal and return peace to the globe. Whereas emphasis on the activities of a purportedly elite-run, satanic pedophilia ring is a highly visible feature of the QAnon universe, it is perhaps the persona of Donald Trump that most distinguishes QAnon as a unique brand of twenty-first-century right-wing conspiracism. On the second day of posting (post 4), Q announced, "Don't fool yourself into thinking Obama, Soros, Roth's [the Rothschild family], Clinton's etc have more power present day than POTUS [President of the United States]. Operation Mockingbird Patriots are in control. Sit back and enjoy the show."

This "operation," which Q would later come to refer to as "The Plan," consists of an intricate and convoluted series of strategically linked events involving double agents, moles, mass arrests, and military tribunals. As indicated in this second post, President Trump is believed to embody the center or organizational principle of this grand design, to such an extent that Q and Q's supporters have more or less come to treat it as Trump's master plan. In support of that view—of the existence of The Plan as well as Trump's role in it—Q supporters point to a number of international events that they believe evince a singular, Trump-directed counterinsurgency or counterconspiracy.

As a social media phenomenon, Q, by rights, should have fizzled out, as had so many other allegedly government-leaking "anon" accounts, yet through the chance logic of virality the inverse occurred. Insofar as such rapid circulation can be causally charted, it would appear that in this case the spread began once Q's posts were brought to the attention of YouTube personality Tracy Diaz. Diaz was a relatively obscure content provider at the time, but her popularization of Q's posts simultaneously worked to the benefit of her own channel and internet celebrity, securing her well over one hundred thousand YouTube subscribers and viewership in the millions.[14] Soon thereafter, QAnon groups active on 4chan began migrating to the more mainstream discussion and social news aggregation website Reddit, and from there to the even more mainstream social networking service Facebook, where they were able to interface with an older, more diverse demographic. Then, in March 2019, a book of QAnon essays, published under the pseudonym WWG1WGA (shorthand for the rallying cry "Where we go one, we go all"), was listed as among the top fifteen of all books sold on Amazon.[15]

At that point, QAnon had effectively metastasized throughout the cultural imagination: In July 2020, the head of the New York Police Department's second-largest police union gave a television interview while seated in front of a mug clearly bearing QAnon imagery and slogans; that November, QAnon supporter Marjorie Taylor Greene won the Republican House primary for Georgia's 14th Congressional District. Also that August, *NBC News* reported that an internal investigation by Facebook had uncovered thousands of groups and pages supporting the QAnon conspiracy theory, with millions of members and followers.[16]

In response to these reports, and worried about the possibility that Democrats and their constituents would dismiss QAnon as a fringe group of conspiracy-minded zealots, *New York Times* columnist Kevin Roose wrote an article comparing the rise of QAnon with the emergence of the Tea Party movement in 2009.[17] The psychopolitical vectors that today would present QAnon as a potent grassroots force in right-wing politics resonate with the media environment of 2009, in which sympathetic media outlets covered the Tea Party rallies and portrayed the movement as an emerging strain of populist politics—a protest movement born of frustration with a corrupt, unaccountable elite. "Then, to everyone's surprise," Roose adds, "its supporters started winning elections," and the movement "proceeded to become a major, enduring force in American conservatism." Recent polling would seem to bear out Roose's observations. Based on the polling data of 1,368 U.S. adults, a September 2020 *Daily Kos/Civiqs* poll reported that 33 percent of Republicans believed that the QAnon conspiracy theory is mostly true, while another 23 percent said that some parts of the QAnon theory are true.[18]

Despite the historical and media-technical specificity of the QAnon phenomenon, in many ways it figures as a palimpsest of right-wing, New World Order conspiracist discourse: an interpretive strategy, guided by a storehouse of imagistic tropes, that uncovers hidden meaning and motive in the reverberations and repetitions between events. From black helicopters, chemtrails, and medical breakthrough suppression to false flag operations, Manchurian candidates, and weaponized weather technologies, the overwhelming majority of modern right-wing political conspiracy theories portray state governments or state-run agencies as either independently motivated bad actors—manipulating events in secret and in ways contrary to common belief and opinion—or instruments in the thrall of criminal transnational organizations such as the Illuminati, the Freemasons, the Knights Templar, and the like.

What is much less common, and thus distinguishes QAnon as a conspiracist framework of a right-wing variety, is the nearly reverential, quasi fatalistic pose it adopts with respect to the state and symbols of state power, the president in particular. One is almost tempted to view QAnon as enacting some version of Jean Baudrillard's fatal strategies, whereby the subject no longer believes itself to be more clever than the object and instead supposes the object—in this case, Trump as metonymic symbol of the nation state—"to be more shrewd, more cynical, more brilliant than the subject."[19] Likewise, Calum Matheson argues that QAnon is distinct from traditional conspiracy theories, which tend to position the government as the enemy, because it casts Donald Trump as a heroic figure fighting against shadowy elites. He interprets this as a "metastatic relation"—an epistemological operator whereby conspiracy adherents attach to Trump and his narratives to fill gaps in their understanding of the world.[20]

Such a posture is qualitatively different from those relatively rare but nevertheless disastrous occasions when government actors have deployed conspiracy theories against targets labeled "enemies of the state," such as the Nazi accusations of a Jewish plan for global domination or the Rwandan Coalition for the Defence of the Republic's propaganda campaign alleging, in "mirror politics" fashion, that the Tutsis had fabricated events of ethnic crisis. In cases such as these, state governments, acting conspiratorially, position themselves as a bulwark against evil, secretive forces of chaos. QAnon, in contrast, while discursively pro-government, is not officially acknowledged by the U.S. government, and what is more, it appears to originate outside the scope of the state apparatus. In venerating that heteronomous relationship, QAnon effectively inverts the conspiracist–conspiracy dynamic, replacing the "banal strategies" of ordinary right-wing conspiracism, according to which the conspiracist subject believes itself to be more masterful and sovereign than the conspirator, with the more fatal strategy that recognizes the supremacy of the conspirator, in this instance a counterconspirator, and therefore takes the conspirator's side and surrenders to its strategies, tactics, and rules.[21] There is of course a religious dimension at work here as well. Like the Pythian priestesses of ancient Greece, the high priests of QAnon receive and make available to initiates what they consider to be enigmatic prophecies from a virtually omniscient source; invention precedes the transmission of the original message, leaving only the discovery and decryption of meaning for the QAnon priests, priestesses, and initiates.

BEYOND REVELATORY TRANSMISSIONS

As the top-level hierophant, Q purportedly receives his or her or their transmissions from a privileged position within the Trump administration. The handle "Q" itself refers to the idea that the entity behind the label enjoys access to knowledge denied to high-ranking civil servants and average citizens alike. As a politico-rhetorical phenomenon, however, QAnon does not owe its success to mere disclosure, that is, to insider delivery of top secret information. That model, most likely spearheaded by the hacktivist "trickster" collective Anonymous—a decentralized, international activist movement—describes the method of previous "priestly" anons, such as HLIAnon or CIAAnon, who gained notoriety among certain niche segments of conspiracist discourse communities.[22] FBIAnon, for instance, claimed that the Clinton Foundation would soon be brought down in a massive money laundering scandal. In an interactive question-and-answer interview on the subreddit r/IAmA (or AMA, short for "ask me anything"), FBIAnon asked, "What reason have we to believe you?," answering with, "None. It's better that way."

For this and similar anons, and despite the infrequent semblance of interactivity, communication mostly proceeds according to the unidirectional, sender–receiver model as formalized in the Shannon-Weaver model, whereby information is transmitted from a source to a receiver by means of a technical channel.[23] Recipients either receive or fail to receive a message; they either believe or disbelieve the content. Feedback from receiver to sender, while not absent from the model, is nevertheless "meaningless." It only functions to make sure that the message has been received, that it has not been interrupted by physical noise. Whether the message accomplishes a particular rhetorical end or elicits a desired cognitive-attitudinal effect is a matter of indifference.

From the very outset, the communicative method of QAnon departed from this sender–receiver model. Indeed, Q's first post begins with a "proof check": "Locate a NG member and ask if activated for duty 10/30 across most major cities." In other words, Q requests that the audience ask a member of the U.S. National Guard if he or she has been activated for duty (presumably to aid in the arrest of Hillary Clinton). The proof check is not simply a matter of verifying, via amateur internet sleuthing, a purported fact—much less a matter of confirming whether a message has been received through a channel. Rather, it functions rhetorically as an inexplicit performative, as a call to become actively involved in a participatory network of actual or potential counterconspirators.

Of a piece with that interactivity is the stated incompleteness of the missives. In the sixth post, for example, Q writes, "Some of us come here to drop crumbs, just crumbs," a suggestion of partiality that simultaneously invites others to follow Q's example. Many of Q's early posts, in fact, speak primarily in the "breadcrumb" language of suggestive illocutionary directives. Here, for instance, Q poses twenty-one questions in a relatively short post (post 78):

> What was POTUS' last Tweet (prior to)?
> To who was it addressed?
> When was POTUS' Twitter taken down?
> Why is this relevant?
> What was POTUS' last Tweet (prior to)?
> Who was it addressed to specifically?
> When was POTUS' Twitter taken down?
> Has this ever happened before?
> Why now?
> Coincidence?
> How many times did the attack occur (secondary clean up)?
> What is the purpose of tracking?
> What is the purpose of disruption?
> Why did POTUS have military guards (uniform) while in HI?
> Why is this relevant?
> Do military guards (uniform) typically assist the USSS?
> Why is this relevant?
> What flying object was recently shot down?
> Why is this relevant?
> How precise is geo tracking (non-public c-level pro)?
> Why is this relevant?

Anonymous Q supporters Pamphlet and Radix liken Q's posts to the Socratic method, to "letting the person think for themselves and answer the questions on their own, rather than providing the answers for them in the beginning."[24] That comparison, however, while perhaps flattering, is not quite accurate, as the Socratic method is deductive rather than, say, abductive, and relies on a pedagogical method in which the hierarchical relationship between teacher and student is rather pronounced.

A more apt description can be located not in classical antiquity but in contemporary fan studies, the analysis of textual interpretations carried out by especially dedicated, loyal, and emotionally committed viewers who form part of media fandom.[25] QAnon supporters/followers are indeed fans; they do not merely enjoy Q's posts but also take them up as challenges, as puzzles to solve, sharing them with other fans and thereby helping to engender and cultivate what appears to be a participatory, grassroots community. When QAnon members stormed the Capitol on January 6, 2021, they engaged in all types of fan behavior, like taking souvenirs and wearing elaborate costumes.[26]

Despite its analog manifestations, QAnon fandom is deeply enabled by digital technologies that give rise to networked internet platforms such as Facebook, Twitter, comment threads, and the like. QAnon itself, in fact, would not be possible as a social media phenomenon without digital media and networked audiences. These same technologies, however, by making audiences more visible as well as more creative-interactive, work to dissolve fans into new forms of digital-cultural production so that they are no longer "merely" devoted fans. Bruns refers to this transformation of fandom as amateur produsage, a new phase of media creation and distribution in which internet users and content producers blur together via the activity of the "produser," who may be a blogger, a meme maker, or a digital artist/photographer.[27] The effectiveness of Q's posts can thus be confirmed by pointing out that Q and Q's fans dissolved, mutually and simultaneously, into the produser known throughout the world as QAnon. The question of whether the participatory culture represented by the collective handle "QAnon" could be considered a method of reasoning and online discussion in order to discover the truth or is instead a cynical joke that has transmogrified into a global phenomenon is ultimately less relevant than its status as a conspiracy theory produser.

Although Q's call for the creative-active participation of audiences functions as a means of capturing attention, the way in which internet platforms such as 4chan figure produsage simultaneously fills a particular "need" in the online ecosystem of the 2010s. As Marshall McLuhan famously implied with his aphorism "The medium is the message," the medium motivates the content by requiring the manufacture of new content with which to fill that medium.[28] What is noteworthy about Q in this regard is that Q's response to the demands of interactive computer-mediated virtual communities—the technological interpellation of internet users/followers as QAnon produsers—established within the field of online conspiracist discourse, and conspiracist discourse more generally, what Thomas Kuhn called a paradigm. Conceived of in the context of the history of science, in which the word refers to the set of concepts and practices that define, at any given period, a scientific field of inquiry, paradigms possess two essential characteristics: "Their achievement was sufficiently unprecedented to attract an enduring group of adherents away from competing modes of [intellectual or practical] activity. Simultaneously, it was sufficiently open-ended to leave all sorts of problems for the refined group of practitioners to solve."[29]

Q's method of posing invitational directives certainly fulfills the second criterion. It offers readers a variety of "rabbit holes," or labyrinthine puzzles, to follow while simultaneously tailoring them in such way that they appear solvable. Ultimately, this technique is what enabled Q to attract the subjective adherence necessary to win over new converts, thereby fulfilling Kuhn's first requirement of a paradigm. As one follower put it, "Following Q is like working a 50,000-piece puzzle. It's slow, but intriguing and fun—as we wait for clues and put pieces together."[30] While FBIAnon and other high-clearance anons limited themselves to promising to provide direct revelation, Q actively encouraged followers to make the jump to produsage and to become fellow creator-distributors. In contrast, while there was some speculation about the veracity of FBIAnon's claims, and paratextual sites kept a record of those claims, their lack of ambiguity did not leave much room for fans to become content produsers.

Solving Q's riddles, however, not only made possible a new paradigm of conspiracist produsage but also created an opportunity for social media celebrity and monetization. That opportunity extends to the world of analog media as well. Over a relatively short period of time, a host of books have been written by Q followers, each work purporting to offer insight into what Q is trying to do.[31] Nevertheless, although Q may have begun with enticing breadcrumb posts, the real innovation of Q was the introduction of a specific hermeneutic principle: to approach both Q's posts and the wider political world, especially that of Donald Trump, as consisting of so many esoterically coded meanings; to see the politico-media landscape as a repository of deeper, hidden messages whose true meanings only register between the lines and below exoteric surfaces and can be deciphered only by the priestly Q and QAnon initiates.

PRODUSING ESOTERICISM: THE INTERACTIVE HERMENEUTICS OF QANON

While the produsage enacted by QAnon is different in kind from the Socratic method, it understands its interpretive method as performing an evangelic form of truth-seeking, where the word *evangelic* functions in the original Greek sense of the word as "noticing" or "revealing."[32] Through a fundamental *in*-sight, QAnon understands itself as engaged in a practice of invention and discovery that catches sight of relationships, of similitude, among things and through it surpasses both what lies before us in sensory awareness and what comes to us by way of mass-mediated belief and opinion. While Q post 3, "Many in our govt worship Satan," may strike non–Q supporters as preposterous or cynical, within the structure of QAnon's discourse that utterance amounts to the revelation of a hidden, subterranean truth.

Such esotericism is rhetorically useful in that it exploits a sense of initiatory mystery to increase subjective adherence and a sense of camaraderie. At the same time, Q cautions that for reasons of self-protection QAnon participants must use esotericism as a guide for intragroup communication. Insofar as esotericism is recommend both as evangelic insight and as a means of escaping detection, it functions indirectly to redouble produsers' feelings of commitment and identification, effectively demonstrating the high-risk, perilous nature of their endeavor. That sense of danger, of what Hélène Cixous describes as the pleasure and thrill of the hunt, appears in very early posts such as "Not everything can be publicly disclosed because so much ties back to foreign heads of state. Much will be revealed, we want transparency but not at a cost we can't recover from" (post 27).[33]

Notwithstanding the practical necessity of composing and circulating coded messages, we as academic critics should not discount the bodily or affective impact of the belief that an array of ever-alert internet spies is working around the clock and in the digital interstices to intercept and decode one's messages. As Jenny Rice reminds us, evidence only has an impact because there is a body to impact, which is to say that the thrill of esoteric produsage is likely not incidental but central to how certain audiences read those messages.[34] Esotericism gains in affectivity the less distal it becomes, and few things are as effective at removing distance as anticipation and fear.

After making multiple references to Alice in Wonderland, Q writes, "You'll soon understand the meaning behind Alice '&' Wonderland. Everything has meaning" (post 78). This is why we say that QAnon's amateur produsage is at the same time an amateur version of esoteric hermeneutics as articulated by the mid-twentieth-century German American political philosopher Leo Strauss. For Strauss, esoteric writing is made necessary by the fact that some truths are dangerous, and for many reasons, chief among them the likelihood that those who are seen as harming the majority through the disclosure of censored truths are more likely, in turn, to be harmed by the majority, or by their guardians:

> Persecution . . . gives rise to a peculiar technique of writing, and therewith to a peculiar type of literature, in which the truth about all crucial things is presented exclusively between the lines. That literature is addressed, not to all readers, but to trustworthy and intelligent readers only. It has all the advantages of private communication without having its greatest disadvantage—that it reaches only the writer's acquaintances. It has all the advantages of public communication, without having its greatest disadvantages—capital punishment for the author.[35]

The premise of QAnon hinges on the notion of persecution, which serves as the rationale for Q's anonymity and their method of cryptic communication. Q claims to speak in code to safeguard their plan, although this approach paradoxically undermines operational security by using a cypher so rudimentary that adherents can readily decode it—thereby exposing sensitive information rather than protecting it.

Q's followers are conditioned through various means to embrace the necessity of secrecy, a mediological imperative, given that conspiracy theories often struggle for mainstream acceptance unless framed within a fictional narrative. The media's refusal to engage with Q then serves, in their eyes, as further evidence of a coordinated effort to suppress the truth. As a right-wing conspiracy theory, QAnon attracts individuals enculturated in a belief that their views are subject to various forms of censorship. Conservatives in general have long derided what they view as the exclusion and denigration of their views by a culture industry that is owned and operated by out-of-touch "coastal elites," citing as evidence, for example, the alleged commonplace use within the industry of the derogatory term *flyover country* to refer to Middle America. The social and professional ostracism of certain public figures who maintain right-of-center views only reinforces conservatives' feeling of marginalization and in the 2010s led conservative internet culture to appropriate the terms *cancel culture* or *call-out culture* to describe this practice.

In 2020, as knowledge of Q and QAnon began to seep into the mainstream, social media sites like Reddit and Facebook did indeed begin purging QAnon groups, seemingly confirming the forbidden nature of Q's messages.[36] Such low-stakes censorship (low-stakes, that is, when compared to the life-and-death implications of forbidden speech in ancient Greece or Soviet Russia) understandably motivates the search for some form of communicative concealment that could allow conservatively like-minded but geographically disparate persons to hide their messages in plain sight. And this is exactly what esotericism offers QAnon produsers: The thrill entailed by this secretive online investigative work intensifies the desire for continued participation while simultaneously promoting a degree of laxity. Q's most public-facing adherents never seem to acknowledge the fundamental contradiction that Q codes the message to safeguard the movement but then they publicly decode it.

Esotericism is thus not merely an incidental aspect of QAnon; it is a defining characteristic that runs consistently throughout Q's posts. It is a feature, not a bug. Q explicitly encourages followers to "read between the lines," reinforcing the idea that messages are deliberately encoded. In post 736, Q states, "Double meanings work well against sniffers," implying that coded language is a strategic tool for evading detection. At the same time, Q frequently claims that "disinformation is real and disinformation is necessary," a probable allusion to the importance of reading his/her/its/their own posts as abstrusely coded messages (see, for instance, post 158). A number of QAnon produsers have heeded the call, treating virtually every element of these posts as a po-

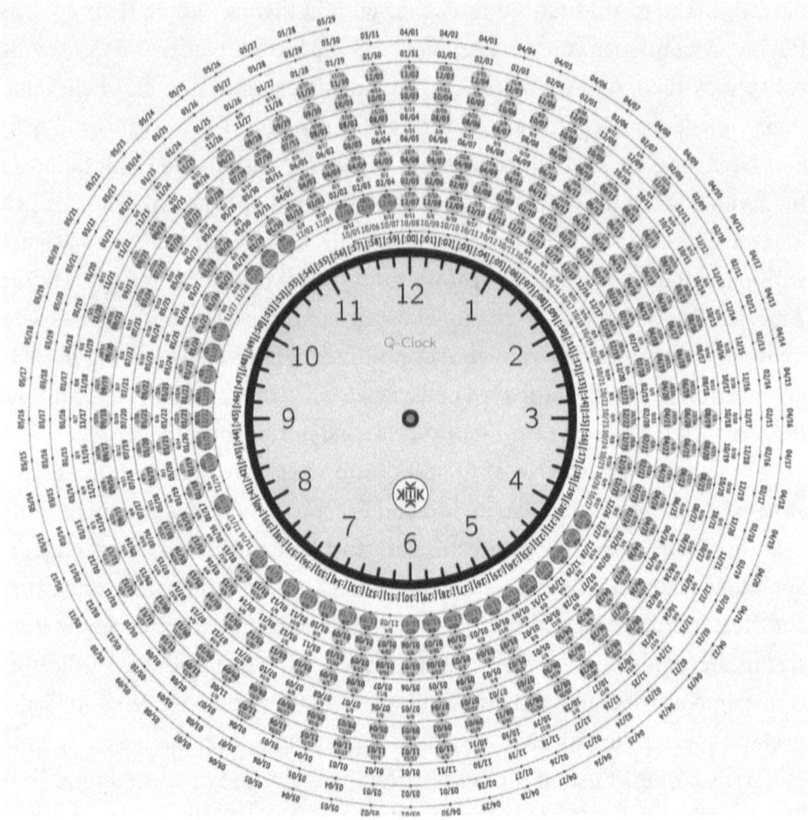

Figure 6. The Q clock offers an elaborate formula for finding meaning in the dates of Q posts. "How to Read the Q Clock," *QNN*, March 11, 2019.

tential Easter egg, from the analysis of individual words to an elaborate system of inferring hidden meaning from the date and time of a given post, as determined by the "Q clock" (figure 6).

By September 5, 2020, Q had amassed well over four thousand posts. That number, however, is not as significant when considered in the context of the exhaustive kind of resource analysis that Q encourages among Q supporters, especially given that many of the posts are relatively short messages.

On November 2, 2017, a mere five days after the initial posts, Q had suggested that QAnon produsers begin applying an esoteric hermeneutic to President Trump, whose speeches, photos ops, tweets, policy statements, and so on were immediately taken up as revealing/concealing hidden layers of meaning. In terms of the emergence of QAnon as a social media phenomenon, this is probably the closest we can get to a precise moment or specific text in which Q crossed the threshold separating internet users (Q followers) from content producer (Q as online oracle). In post 38, Q wrote:

> Four carriers & escorts in the pacific? Why is that relevant? To prevent other state actors from attempting to harm us during this transition? Russia / China? Or conversely all for NK [North Korea]? Or all three. Think logically about the timing of everything happening. Note increased military movement. Note NG [national guard] deployments starting tomorrow. Note false flags. Follow Huma. Prepare messages of reassurance based on what was dropped here to spread on different platforms. The calm before the storm.

The closing line—"The calm before the storm"—is perhaps the most intriguing and hermeneutically generative element of the post. It is an oblique reference to a minor news story from earlier that October, when, during an unscheduled press meeting at a dinner thrown for military commanders and their spouses, Trump gestured to his dinner guests and said, "You guys know what this represents? Maybe it's the calm before the storm." Trump was asked for clarification on what storm he was referencing but only restated, "Could be the calm before the storm." In the following days, the administration continued to stonewall when pressed about "the storm." When asked whether Trump was being purposely vague, Press Secretary Sarah Huckabee Sanders said, "If you're asking, is the president trying to do that? Absolutely. I mean, I don't think that's a secret."[37]

Given the context, Q's allusion contains two suggestions: First, that the coming storm refers to an imminent crackdown on the Clinton family and their associates; and second, that by publicly alluding to a clampdown, Trump is esoterically prognosticating to an initiated readership, to those "thoughtful . . . careful readers" who can read between and across lines, ferreting out and arriving at an appreciative, critical understanding of a text's true political message.[38] In the days following Q's post, "Calm before the storm" became something of a meme and in-group signifier among QAnon produsers, eventually making its appearance on various consumerist paraphernalia, such as T-shirts, coffee mugs, baseball caps, and the like.

Since that initial clarion call to adopt an esoteric approach to Trump's voluminous, multimodal communiqués, and under the oracular guidance of Q, QAnon produsers have by and large done just that. As General Michael Flynn writes in the first chapter of the best-selling book *Q Anon: An Invitation to the Great Awakening,* Q "is dropping crumbs for us Anons to decipher, what is essentially, direct communication from the President."[39] While instances of QAnon produsers esoterically interpreting Trump are too numerous to itemize, a few representative anecdotes are in order. For example, at a rally on July 31, 2018, Trump said,

> You know, I told the story the other day, I was probably in Washington in my entire life seventeen times. True, seventeen times. I don't think I ever stayed overnight. You know what I'm getting at, right? And we have a great cabinet now, a couple of little changes. But we have a great cabinet. We have—Mike Pompeo, our Secretary of State. So many great people. And we're really getting—we have just incredible people. But I made some choices that I wouldn't have made. But I'm riding down Pennsylvania Avenue. Again, I've only been here about seventeen times. And probably seven of those times was to check out the hotel I'm building on Pennsylvania Avenue and then I hop on the plane and I go back. So I've been there seventeen times, never stayed there at night. I don't believe. And then I'm riding down in this beautiful car, picked up at the airport by Secret Service, holding the hand of our great first lady.[40]

In response, QAnon produsers highlight what they consider Trump's odd and conspicuous use of the number seventeen, as opposed to, say, a multiple of five, arguing that the repetition signals something other than Trump's self-proclaimed outsider status. The revealed meaning, they maintain, consists in the inference that since Q is the seventeenth letter of the modern English alphabet, Trump is sending a coded message validating QAnon. Similarly, QAnon produsers interpreted a photograph posted to Trump's Twitter account (November 8, 2017) as containing another coded message. The photograph depicts Trump and his advisers positioned around a conference table, giving the thumbs-up gesture (figure 7). According to the QAnon decryption, the individual thumbs are placed in such way so as to form the letter Q.

Figure 7. A photo tweeted by Trump. Individuals have argued that the thumbs up make a Q, as depicted here. realDonaldTrump, Twitter, November 8, 2017.

Another watershed moment for QAnon began in April 2018, when an anonymous poster asked Q to prove its insider connection to Trump by having the president include the term *tip-top* in his State of the Union address. Although Trump did not use the phrase in his State of the Union, about two months later, at the White House Easter egg roll, he stated that the White House Historical Association and Melania keep the White House in "tip-top shape," adding, "We call it sometimes tippy-top shape." QAnon produsers immediately picked up on the use of *tip-top* (and *tippy-top*), but they also inferred a hidden meaning from the fact that while he was intoning the secret word, Trump was standing next to a person dressed in a giant Easter Bunny costume. The rabbit, they argued, was an allusion to the White Rabbit of *Alice's Adventures in Wonderland* and thus, given Q's frequent references to Lewis Carroll's novel, a symbolically coded message to QAnon. After Trump's comments, Q post 991 said, "It was requested. Did you listen today?"

Among QAnon produsers, the *tip-top* example is frequently cited as a turning point. Lori Colley, a major Q follower and YouTuber, wrote, "Everyone who follows Q had one: a day when you knew, that you knew, that you knew, that Q wasn't a hoax. When you were sure that Q wasn't a hoax or a LARP (live-action role-play), or a too-good-to-be-true conspiracy theory. My day came when Trump used the words 'tip-top, tippy top' in April 2018."[41]

Notwithstanding the esoteric significance of Trump to QAnon's political hermeneutics, QAnon's produsage esotericism extends beyond Trump to include purported allies and enemies of the president. Q, for instance, writes that, "Their need for symbolism will be their downfall" (post 184), an oblique but esoterically intelligible reference to Trump's pedophilic enemies within the deep state. Since that posting, Q's followers have sought to unpack the symbolism of Trump's alleged foes. Colley, for instance, invokes Pizzagate to accuse John Podesta of using occult symbols and code to cover up his participation in a satanic pedophile ring.[42] SerialBrain2 recommends using the psychoanalytic notion of projection as an additional means to esoterically decrypt the messages of Trump's critics, writing, "They blame people for what they themselves do." As an example, he points to popular accusations that Vladimir Putin is in possession of sensitive information that, if made public, could damage Trump. While appearing to accept the premise that Putin does possess damaging information on someone, SerialBrain2 appeals to the interpretive logic of projection to argue that the information at Putin's disposal pertains not to Trump but to Trump's political enemies.[43] Colley makes a similar argument about former CIA director John Brennan: When Brennan claims that Trump will face American justice, it is actually Brennan whose head is on the chopping block, so to speak, as he runs the risk of serving time in the Guantanamo Bay prison.[44]

Beyond these and other visible traces of an esoteric hermeneutic, QAnon produsers and QAnon detractors alike have noted QAnon's predilection for a quasi-Delphic approach to interpretation. Pamphlet and Radix, two of the personae who helped bring Q to fame, explicitly point out the esoteric elements of QAnon produsage: "There is also a historical intersection between the occult and esoteric, and narratives nested within other narratives. From symbolism and art used to communicate a hidden meaning, to theater and performance art, to use of cyphers and allegory."[45]

Let us assume, for the moment, that the mainstream and commonsense opinion of QAnon is, in fact, the correct one: Trump is *not* actually communicating esoterically about a secret ring of high-level Satan-worshipping government officials who run a pedophile ring. (Obviously, we do not think such an assumption would stress the limits of casuistic stretching. If anything, merely stating the assumption qua assumption runs the risk of appearing uncritically sympathetic toward an extremist conspiracy theory.) If this negation is true—and, for the record, we believe that it is—then the pressing issue becomes how Q managed to cultivate a large and devoted group of produsers committed to approaching Trump through an esoteric lens. If the phenomenon is a hoax, then could Q have turned any person or any text into a cypher that provided the foundation for a mass movement?

Even if QAnon is not a hoax—that is, even if QAnon creator-distributors believe in the reality of the world they are producing—Q posts appear to many intelligent people as little more than an instance of mass apophenia, or the tendency to perceive meaningful connections between unrelated things. Certainly, American society has dismissed many other "decodings" as mere conspiracy theory fodder, confining them to the margins rather than transposing them to the center of public consciousness, where they can attract the subjective adherence of a broad swath of the American public. It is our contention that part of the reason why Q's esoteric hermeneutic has obtained its current place within the cultural imagination is that Trump's multimediated and paratextually elaborated persona shares important characteristics with traditional esoteric texts. Q-created content was able to cross the virality threshold to become QAnon produsage in part because the image or text of Trump *appears* to be esoterically coded.

INVITING A NEW HERMENEUTIC

In his comprehensive study on philosophical esotericism, Arthur Melzer provides a set of heuristics for identifying esoteric texts. He asserts that one of the primary methods for recognizing and initiating an esoteric reading is to search for authorial clues: "Since the author certainly desires that the intelligent reader be able to penetrate his veils, it makes sense that he might endeavor to provide him some subtle guidance. Thus, it is very important to be on the lookout for such clues, especially whenever the author speaks about writing in general or his own writings in particular."[46] Melzer's analysis is particularly useful in that it details the historical efforts of various philosophers to apply an esoteric hermeneutic to the works of their predecessors, including Aristotle, Machiavelli, Montaigne, and Plato, among others.

Melzer's analysis of esoteric texts emphasizes how authors provide subtle guidance for discerning readers—clues embedded within their writing to signal a deeper, hidden meaning. This interpretive strategy does not simply hinge on what is said but on how messages are structured to obscure their true significance. While Melzer does not claim expertise in psychoanalytic theory, his explication of philosophical esotericism resonates with Jacques Lacan's "schema L," a diagram introduced to formalize the structure of intersubjective communication, emphasizing how meaning is not directly transmitted between subjects but is mediated through the Symbolic order, particularly the Big Other (*l'Autre*).[47] According to Christian Lundberg's reading of schema L, meaning is always routed through the Big Other (the locus of language and the symbolic order, where meaning is structured), rendering communication inherently incomplete and requiring interpretation to fill in the gaps.

QAnon followers operate in this very space of interpretive necessity, treating ambiguity as an intentional design rather than an obstacle to understanding. They exemplify this esoteric practice by treating Trump's pronouncements as laden with hidden messages requiring decryption. His apparent contradictions are reinterpreted as deliberate cues for "careful readers." In terms of schema L, meaning is sustained through what Lundberg calls an "economy of tropes," where "the sign [interpretation] is the result of artificial . . . tropological connection—and . . . as a result, the sign [interpretation] is a site of affective investment rather than stable reference.[48] Instead of revealing a singular hidden truth, from this perspective, QAnon thrives on a perpetual unknowing in which the search for meaning itself becomes the movement's central dynamic.

This participatory model of interpretation reflects what we might call "platform conspiracism"—a shift in esoteric hermeneutics from selective, controlled readerships to an open-ended, digital ecology in which every receiver becomes a producer. Trump's deliberate opacity—from vague proclamations to refusals to disclose personal or policy details—thus works to foster a discursive technical environment where plugged-in, perpetually online followers are conditioned to read between the lines. The driving force of QAnon's rhetorical culture is thus the interpretive process itself rather than any definitive revelation; it reinforces belief through the act of interpretation rather than traditional modalities of proof. In this sense, QAnon is not merely a conspiracy theory; it is an esoteric mode of engagement shaped by the failures and excesses of digital discourse.

To be sure, Trump as a businessman-cum-celebrity-cum-politician does not make the grade as a philosopher, much less as a great one. To our knowledge, he has not publicly issued any statement that could be compared to the philosophical utterances of, say, a Maimonides, a Montesquieu, or a Jean-Jacques Rousseau. At the same time, Trump has cultivated a large body of content that to some popular audiences, QAnon produsers in particular, *seems* to call for a hermeneutics of suspicion. More importantly, Trump has on many occasions indicated that it is inappropriate to speak facts or to speak them clearly. For example, in 2016, during an NBC-hosted commander in chief forum, Trump refused to specify his plan to defeat ISIS, saying, "I don't want to broadcast to the enemy exactly what my plan is."[49] Even after taking office, he refused to divulge his allegedly secret plan.[50]

This opacity—which Trump encodes as strategic—has in fact become a defining feature of the Trump administration. After the U.S. military deployed the GBU-43/B Massive Ordnance Air Blast against ISIS forces in Afghanistan, Trump refused to say whether he had ordered the attack or it was an operation initiated within the military chain of command. "Strategic ambiguity" in the realm of foreign affairs is not, however, limited to the administration's dealings with ISIS. Writing for the *National Review,* Jerry Hendrix praised Trump's inscrutability in foreign policy, claiming that "North Korea, for the first time in a generation, has opened talks with South Korea. China has increased its pressure on the Kim regime, and NATO members are spending more on their own defense."[51]

Lack of transparency is also applied defensively to Trump's very persona. For instance, despite repeated pledges during both the 2016 and 2020 presidential campaigns, Trump has yet to release his tax returns.[52] Hence, while Trump's cryptic remark about an imminent "storm" helped give rise to QAnon produsage—indeed, could be construed as its efficient cause—QAnon's esoteric approach to Trump was conditioned and to a certain extent legitimated by a reticulated communications strategy seemingly designed to give absolute priority to keeping motives, personal information, and the true meaning of messages hidden.

Contributing to that esoteric ecology is Trump's abusive description of traditional newsgathering and reporting practices as "fake news." Oftentimes leveled at specific news organizations such as CNN and the *New York Times,* and occasionally at individual journalists such as CNN's Jim Acosta, Trump's overstated, bald criticism of the news media can also appear to take as its object the relation of news organizations to society as a whole—the unwritten sociopolitical and cultural guidelines these organizations follow and the implicit ideological assumptions they make.[53] To select just one example, in a 2018 speech to a veterans association he said, "What you're seeing and what you're reading is not what's happening."[54] On one level, such statements can be read as simplistic, ideologically driven indictments of corporate news media; on another level, they invite "thoughtful, careful readers" to see through the news media's distorted representation of reality and locate a deeper, truer reality anterior to and hidden beneath what Baudrillard refers to as "the order of sorcery."[55] Trump's self-ascribed Delphic ability—as well as his encouragement of others to cultivate their own esoteric third eye—is not limited to seeing behind the artifices of the news media, nor does it originate with Trump's assumption of the office of the president.

The strategic ambiguity that created the legitimating conditions for QAnon's esotericism has been bolstered by what the literary critic Kenneth Burke describes as processes of identification, symbolic-persuasive acts whereby two or more people are both "joined and separate, at once a distinct substance and consubstantial with one another."[56] People identify with one another insofar as they assume or are persuaded to believe that they share common interests. While it is unlikely that Trump intended what is in all probability an off-the-cuff remark like "tippy-top shape" as a secretly coded message, he has given QAnon produsers reason to believe that "they" (Trump and QAnon participants) are substantially one, that through him the separatist identities represented by "QAnon" form a corporate, inclusive "we." Indeed, as a *Media Matters for America* investigation claims, "As of August 20, 2020, President Donald Trump has amplified accounts promoting the QAnon conspiracy theory at least 216 times via at least 129 individual accounts."[57]

Basically, Trump parlays ambiguity into consubstantiality by retweeting memes and quotations by influential QAnon produsers. This has the effect of raising individual QAnon profiles, to be sure, but more importantly, the retweeting can be (and has been) read as a tacit endorsement, albeit an ambiguous one. But here, too, that ambiguity is interpreted as strategy. For instance, in *QAnon: An Invitation to the Great Awakening,* SpaceShot76 and RedPill78 write, "There have been countless mainstream articles, well into the hundreds, that have gone out of their way to try and discredit Q. However not one pundit will actually ask President Trump the one question we all want them to ask, 'President Trump do you know anything about this person or entity that is Q Anon?'"[58] In 2020, after noted QAnon produser Marjorie Taylor Greene won her Republican primary for a House Congressional seat, a reporter asked Trump what he thought about QAnon.[59] While he dodged the question at the time, a few days later he responded to a similar question by saying, "I don't know much about the movement other than I understand they like me very much." He continued, "I've heard these are people who love our country."[60]

AN EXTREMELY STABLE GENIUS

Esoteric works are special, and they are special in a way not possible for the merely exoteric. Esoteric writings, in contrast to their exoteric counterparts, require the author to speak to multiple audiences at the same time and through a single text. What is more, the strictures of esotericism demand that the author speak to those multiple audiences in such a way that only one of them is aware of the multiplicity of meanings being conveyed. As per the thinking of Strauss and Melzer, this rarefied method of composition effectively renders any genuine instance of esoteric writing a work of "rare genius." For that reason, many of the possible techniques for communicating esoterically are not commonly perceived as indicating esoteric intent. Melzer, for instance, claims that contradictions, poorly argued points, key points hidden either in the body of a text or in a footnote (rather than included in the introduction or the conclusion), disregard for ideas relevant to one's argument, lack of clarity, and equivocation are all tactics of esoteric writing. Consult any English composition teacher or textbook and they will tell you that these are all examples of bad writing. They are "mistakes," things someone would not and should not do on purpose.

Over against standard readerly and writerly conventions, an esoteric approach operates under the assumption that errors are intentional, albeit oblique, gestures indicative of hidden meanings. Rather than assuming that errors are simply "errors," an esoteric reader, Melzer argues, should "provisionally adopt, as a working hypothesis or heuristic device, the assumption that the author is essentially omniscient: correct in all the major aspects of his thinking and also in perfect control of all the major aspects of his writing."[61]

Such a view of authorial control is entirely out of step with post-Enlightenment approaches to textual interpretation and harks back to premodern, religious hermeneutics. As the political theorist Bernard Yack points out, Islamic and Jewish rationalists in the medieval period were pushed to read and write esoterically because of their religious studies: "Since God cannot, by definition, make mistakes, any inconsistencies or misrepresentations that we find in scripture must therefore serve a purpose, such as concealing some deeper truths from weaker minds."[62] Like a medieval rationalist approaching a divinely inspired text, the esoteric reader must attribute a virtual omniscience to the esoteric writer.

This partly explains why so few texts, whether scholarly or popular, are read esoterically. In post-Enlightenment modernity, readers tend not to view the writer as a godlike genius; the "errors" in contemporary works are not regarded as keys to unlocking hidden meanings but rather are assumed to be errors, plain and simple. As with divine revelation, true genius would seem to be relegated to a premodern or early modern past—to canonical, mythical figures like Machiavelli, Plato, and Shakespeare. This is the type of writer an esoteric reader could imagine planting elaborate "errors" as signs of a greater meaning. In these cases, the error hypothesis is more convincing to the esoterically sensitive than the prospect of genuine mistakes. Perhaps some contemporary writer, either established or unknown, has written a masterful esoteric work. It is unlikely to be received as such. Only someone already perceived as a genius will get the benefit of the doubt with regard to esotericism.

Given the status conferral at work within institutions of power, the president—or whoever occupies the office of the president—is far more likely than the average person (whether writer or celebrity) to receive the benefit of the esoteric doubt. The American public in particular is especially prone to viewing the executive office as significantly more powerful than is the case. As Gene Healy points out, "Few Americans find anything amiss in the notion that it is the president's duty to solve all large national problems and to unite us all in the service of a higher calling. The vision of the president as national guardian and redeemer is so ubiquitous it goes unnoticed."[63]

Even when despised by constituents, in fact, the sitting president often benefits from the ascription of inordinate power and cunning. Critics of George W. Bush's presidency maintained that Bush did not foolishly stumble into Iraq—that he did not merely cave to pressure from his advisers and secretaries, many of whom were holdovers from his father's administration—but rather planned the war to make money for Halliburton Company. (Some critics on the fringe pushed these allegations even further, going so far as to accuse Bush of engineering the September 11, 2001, attacks as a false flag operation). During Obama's presidency, critics argued that the president was planning to seize all American guns in a secret operation to undermine the Second Amendment. Others alleged that Obama's Affordable Care Act contained a clause allowing for the forced euthanasia of the elderly and infirm. As these and many other cases demonstrate, the power associated with the office of the president is a superconductor of conspiracist speculation. The compossibility of conspiracy and esotericism, their considerable overlap, ensures that it is ripe for reading between the lines.

Even when compared to other American presidents, Trump provides the perfect storm for the attribution of cunning. Unlike other contemporary presidents, he regularly issues statements that appear to be mistakes while simultaneously presenting himself as a genius. In fact, Trump—the celebrity turned politician—references his own intelligence more than any politician in recent memory, perhaps ever, describing himself in a tweet as "an extremely stable genius!" Consider the following self-descriptions: "Is Donald Trump an Intellectual? Trust me, I'm like a smart person"; "I went to the best schools, I'm like a very smart person"; "I have a very good brain."[64]

Axios compiled a list of quotes comprising all the subjects about which Trump claims he knows more than anyone. The list includes campaign finance, TV ratings, ISIS, social media, the courts, lawsuits, politicians, the visa system, trade, U.S. government, renewable energy, taxes, debt, money, infrastructure, borders, Democrats, construction, the economy, technology, drones, and Senator Cory Booker.[65] Articles from *Axios,* CNN, the *Los Angeles Times, Vox,* and the *Washington Post* also have noted that Trump rarely if ever apologizes.[66] Trump refuses to back down and apologize even when presented with very clear evidence that he was incorrect, like when the administration claimed that Trump's inauguration was more attended than Obama's.[67] He is, however, prone to fake apologies, like this one from 2013 posted at realDonaldTrump on Twitter: "Sorry losers and haters, but my I.Q. is one of the highest—and you all know it! Please don't feel so stupid or insecure, it's not your fault." The lack of a record of apologies allows one to read Trump as mistake-free; the "mistakes" are more likely read as part of a master plan.

When Trump does make a mistake, he will typically double down rather than admit wrongdoing, as when he referenced the "calm before the storm." In another example, Trump tweeted "Despite the constant negative press covfefe." Rather than ignore the tweet or admit an error for including a made-up word, Trump tweeted six hours after the original tweet, "Who can figure out the true meaning of 'covfefe'??? Enjoy!"[68] Press secretary Sean Spicer was then asked about the tweet, which resulted in this exchange.

> Reporter: Do you think people should be concerned that the president posted somewhat of an incoherent tweet last night, and that it then stayed up for hours?
>
> Spicer: Uh, no.
>
> Reporter: Why did it stay up so long? Is no one watching this?
>
> Spicer: No, I think the president and a small group of people knew exactly what he meant.[69]

Spicer covers the mistake by all but explicitly saying the tweet was esoteric. It is little wonder, then, that Colley argues, "Trump purposely tweets misspellings as codes."[70]

THE KING IS DEAD, LONG LIVE THE KING!

QAnon is a totalizing discourse, Manichean and revisionist—like most major conspiracy theories—but it is also strangely democratic and egalitarian (proof that these principles are not intrinsically good). A true believer in UFOs, for instance, can go his or her entire life without having an actual firsthand UFO experience, but the esoteric produsage of QAnon means that Q's followers will always be able to find hidden messages, if only they look hard enough. This paradoxical opening up of the esoteric has allowed a hundred flowers to bloom in the form of countless books, blogs, YouTube channels, and internet threads, each one delving into an official photo, tweet, or speech by Trump. In Q's corner of the digital world, sacred knowledge is not hoarded but given freely and with the knowledge that, like George Bataille's metaphor of a solar anus that endlessly extretes energy, there is always more esoteric wisdom to uncover.[71] In that regard, QAnon is anti-elitist and antimonopolistic—a modern-day medium for haruspicy whose democratic ethos makes it an apparently good fit for the national populism that animates the produsage. That fit, however, was placed under pressure by 2020's changing of the guard and the election of Joe Biden as the forty-sixth president of the United States.

Published on the heels of Trump's defeat in the 2020 presidential election, a *New York Times* headline proclaimed, "Shocked by Trump's Loss, QAnon Struggles to Keep the Faith."[72] But it was only weeks after election day that pro-Trump protesters, many of whom openly identified as part of the QAnon movement, stormed the United States Capitol in a failed attempt to overturn Trump's electoral defeat.[73] This hours-long violent attack, which included acts of vandalism and looting, is significant for any number of reasons, not least of which is the light it shed on the contingency of heretofore peaceful transfers of power. In terms of the esoteric produsage of QAnon, it appeared to be the moment when Trump abandoned the last vestiges of plausible deniability and, by encouraging the occupation of the Capitol, exoterically endorsed the Q movement. (In any event, this was the case the Democrats made during the subsequent impeachment proceedings.)

That moment, however, was short-lived. The QAnon produsers eventually returned to their deep readings of various political statements and began issuing claims to the effect that Trump would be inaugurated on March 4, a theory so outlandish that even Trump and his surrogates never suggested it openly.[74] These developments, which were strangely responsive to and recalcitrant against the ebbs and flows of partisan politics, are particularly noteworthy because they occurred in the near absence of Q, who largely disappeared after the 2020 election.[75] What this suggests is that an esoteric hermeneutic can be comfortably cultivated in an ecosystem of produsage absent a central figure, emitter, or discourse. It is even easy to imagine QAnon, as a phenomenon, far outlasting Trump and Trumpism.

The transition of QAnon from internet backwater to major political force in just a few short years would not have been possible without the combined mediatory effects of esoteric hermeneutics and internet produsage. At the same time, because these rhetorical modalities make available a new set of topoi for an era of digital mediation, we should not be surprised if others seize upon this commonplace for diverse political purposes. Building upon Fredric Jameson's remarks about cognitive mapping in a technologically complex world, James Bridle argues that what self-confirming groups such as QAnon reveal is that our ability to describe the world is a product of the tools at our disposal: "We're all looking at the same world and seeing radically different things. And we have built ourselves a system that reinforces that effect, an automated populism that gives people what they want, all of the time."[76] As a decentralized, interactive, and in some ways anonymous means for grasping a network of power and control that is difficult for our minds and imaginations to grasp, esoteric produsage is potentially attractive to people and groups of all political stripes, but perhaps especially to those whose anti-elitism entails—for better or worse, accurately or inaccurately—fear of persecution.

4

THE ESOTERIC HERO THE DISSIDENT RIGHT NEEDS

White Knighting the Batman

> everyone who makes "batman just beats up poor mentally ill people" jokes would loose their shit if they learned about the court of owls
>
> —SewageCrow on Twitter

There have always been comic book characters espousing views that seem, to varying degrees, to align with white racial politics. Examples include Captain America's archnemesis, Red Skull; Peacemaker's father, White Dragon; and more questionably, fan-favorite Rorschach from *Watchmen* (1987), to name only a few. When one thinks of white nationalist characters in comics, presumably few would identify them as the moral centers of those make-believe worlds. With respect to the Batman universe, however, some prominent white nationalists do just that. Specifically, they lay claim to director Christopher Nolan's Batman films as something of a pop cultural ambassador, arguing that a careful reading of the *Dark Knight* trilogy (2005–2012) reveals messages (and characters) sympathetic to their political worldview. On a recent podcast with other members of the "dissident" far right, Richard Spencer said, "My conclusion is that Nolan—and I don't mean this as a criticism—is a kind of statist, almost fascist-like thinker, and he's presenting this under the guise of a mainstream popular comic book movie."[1]

But how does that happen? How is it possible that an enormously successful mainstream American film franchise based on an even more popular American comic book character could attract what in the cultural imagination amounts to a cult Nazi following? One possible answer is that the texts themselves exhibit semiotic patterns that align with white identity politics, though this answer is not convincing. It asks us to ignore or minimize the popular and critical reception of the film series (and its title character) as well as the kinds of economic decision-making that guide the motion picture industry. More importantly, it neglects the decisive factor of viewer interpretation and the complexities of interaction between polysemic encoding and ideological decoding. A better question, which promises a more compelling answer, is how or why does *this* particular fan community watch the *Dark Knight* trilogy and come away with the message that it does?" Or more specifically, how do white nationalists watching movies about a bat-inspired caped crusader decipher an overtly political message—and a politically fringe message at that—that escapes not only other fan groups and professional movie reviewers but also scholarly critics?

Critics working within the multidisciplinary field of media and cultural studies have devoted significant scholarly attention to understanding the construction of meaning within and across superhero media, particularly Batman-related media. Over the past decade and a half, this interpretive work has increasingly involved the study of fans, fan cultures, and fan activities, and for good reason. As Ashley Hinck reminds us, the fandoms cultivated by comics, movies, books, and so on can lead to "public engagement that emerges from [and blends with] a commitment to a fan-object."[2] Hinck refers to this type of investment as "fan-based citizenship," but we could just as easily flip the subject and predicate, as Hannah Mueller does, and call it the politics of fandom.[3]

On the surface, that interpretive lens is sufficiently capacious to include the critical examination of any number of political commitments and ideologies, no matter how outré or niche they may appear to fan studies scholars. Yet academic studies of the politics of fandom have tended to focus on the participatory, cocreative activities of left-leaning fans, often to the exclusion of their right-leaning counterparts. In the introduction to a recent special issue of *Television & New Media,* Mel Stanfill writes, "Fan studies frequently sees fandom as fundamentally progressive."[4] The issue itself, Stanfill argues, represents a concerted effort to help redress that imbalance.

To that end, contributors take stock of various instances of reactionary cathexis—for example, anger directed at professional Black athletes such as Lebron James and Colin Kaepernick, or in the case of Gamergate, outrage over the increased inclusion of women and racial or ethnic minority groups in video games.[5] Other scholarly attempts to map what Stanfill describes as "the reactionary in the fan and the fan in the reactionary" include interpretive analyses of conservative political commentators.[6] Adjacent to these engagements are efforts such as those by Paul Elliott Johnson, whose rhetorical analysis of *Breaking Bad* (2008–2013), in part, explores Walter White's resonance among conservative Americans, and Anastasia Salter, who explores the phenomenon of fans who elevate the DC Comics character Harley Quinn, despite her connection to problematic representations of interpersonal violence.[7]

Apart from selecting an uncommon topic of analysis, these studies fundamentally differ in their approach compared to broad swaths of fan studies literature. Instead of focusing on how fans poach or appropriate texts, they primarily concern themselves either with fan backlash—specifically, backlash against the inclusion of progressive ideas in a popular culture thought to be politically neutral—or with conservatism as a form of fandom itself, independent of other forms of pop culture media—such as the "Make America Great Again" slogan as a pop culture phenomenon. On net, there is not much academic literature exploring conservative or right-wing fans' in-depth readings of pop culture texts.

This tendency is not without justification. There is a paucity of popular media that embraces overtly right-wing views, by which we mean conservative or reactionary views that espouse some form of anti-egalitarianism. That is perhaps why some police officers and military personnel have embraced the insignia of the violent fictional antihero the Punisher (Francis "Frank" Castle), despite the creator's public rejection of the appropriation.[8] In order to enjoy popular media, the right, and especially racialist factions of the dissident right, have had to make do with readerly tactics such as textual poaching and oppositional, against-the-grain readings.

Certain white nationalists, however, claim that there is no need to resort to such counterhegemonic participatory practices in the case of Christopher

Nolan's Batman films. The *Dark Knight* trilogy, they argue, is in fact esoterically coded so as to communicate to elect viewers, and only the elect, a message of white nationalist revolution. We imagine that this interpretation will strike many as highly idiosyncratic, though since their inception, superhero comics have sometimes been accused of promoting fascism, a charge repeated by academics as well as comic luminaries like Alan Moore.[9]

Despite these recriminations, critics have generally come up short in being able to point to concrete examples of self-identified fascists who embrace a comic book character, much less a comic series, as their own. Even if a comic series or comic-based storyline did implicitly embrace a fascist trope (say, that of the Übermensch or a paramilitary vanguard devoted to a cult of personality), it would in all likelihood situate that trope in opposition to the racialist politics of white nationalism. It is just as unlikely that most viewers would interpret the series as in any way fascist or sympathetic to fascism.

Nevertheless, from the perspective of dissident rightists—particularly white nationalists associated with Greg Johnson's website and publisher Counter-Currents—the rejoinder that millions of viewers miss the true coded message of fascism is entirely beside the point. In their view, the masses probably don't "get it" because they were never intended to understand it. They may even argue that the narrative was designed to prevent most audiences from being able to discern the true message animating the story. The true message would not be so obvious as to be embodied in the protagonist's words and actions; more likely it would be hidden between the lines and perhaps even give voice by the villains.

Per the rationale of esoteric hermeneutics, eyebrow-raising dismissals only serve to confirm the existence and efficacy of the very persecutory conditions that make esoteric writing and reading a practical necessity. Our aim in this chapter is to make sense of this interpretive phenomenon. After contextualizing the *Dark Knight* trilogy as one of the most successful movie franchises of its era and of all time, we will analyze white nationalist readings of the trilogy, highlighting the creative, politically charged, and at times counterintuitive use of esoteric hermeneutics. We then provide a framework for understanding the type of reading that white nationalists perform when engaging the series, comparing it to the philosophical practice of esoteric reading and situating it in relation to alternative interpretive practices like oppositional readings and textual poaching, before concluding by explaining how this form of interpretive practice aligns with other trends in esoteric fandom.

This chapter focuses primarily on the book *Dark Right: Batman Viewed from the Right,* a collection of essays commissioned and distributed through the website and publishing house Counter-Currents by self-identified white ethnonationalists. The Southern Poverty Law Center refers to Counter-Currents as "an epicenter of 'academic' white nationalism," by which it means a practice of white nationalism that deliberately takes on a more formal and academic style as opposed to hyperbolic, epithet-laden venues like the *Daily Stormer.*[10] The Counter-Currents website (from which many of the essays appearing in *Dark Right* originated) receives a shocking 130,000 unique visitors per month, a strong indicator of its privileged status within the global white nationalist/identitarian ecosystem.

The detailed, idiosyncratic interpretations contained in *Dark Right* serve as both an exemplar and a likely point of origin of far-right readings of the trilogy. What's more, combined with individual contributors' apparent appreciation of the films, the collection would seem to fit with Jenkins's broad definition of fans as "individuals who maintain a passionate connection to popular media, assert their identity through their engagement with and mastery over its contents, and experience social affiliation around shared tastes and preferences."[11] Appearances notwithstanding, it is more probable that the contributors to *Dark Right* are less fans of the trilogy than partisans who strategically deploy extant Batman fandom for their own politico-rhetorical ends—poaching the poachers, so to speak, in a mimicry of fan culture. Insofar as that mimicry is potentially misrecognized as the genuine article it can function as a form of strategic ambiguity, creating an interface or conduit between Batman fans and white ethnonationalist partisans that otherwise may not have existed.

POPULAR READINGS OF A POPULAR FRANCHISE

The *Dark Knight* trilogy began with the 2005 film *Batman Begins* and became a commercial and critical success. The films made an enormous amount of money at the box office, with *The Dark Knight* being the fourth-highest grossing movie at the time. Reviewing *Batman Begins,* the renowned movie critic

Roger Ebert wrote, "I said this is the Batman movie I've been waiting for; more correctly, this is the movie I did not realize I was waiting for, because I didn't realize that more emphasis on story and character and less emphasis on high-tech action was just what was needed. The movie works dramatically in addition to being an entertainment. There's something to it."[12] Rotten Tomatoes, a review-aggregation website for film and television, calculates high percentages of positive reviews for each of the three films, with *Batman Begins, The Dark Knight* (2008), and *The Dark Knight Rises* (2012) measuring approval scores of 84 percent, 94 percent, and 87 percent, respectively.[13]

The success of the series, combined with the already existing fan cultures surrounding the DC character, virtually assured the generation of a significant body of commentary, much of which attached political significance to the films, individually and as a whole. This was especially true of the final film in the trilogy, *The Dark Knight Rises,* which, relative to previous installments, contained the most overt allusions to real-world politics. While pundits on both the left and the right produced many popular-press articles speculating about the film's underlying politics, there was never consensus about its political import, even among political tribes.

Some on the liberal right saw the film as little more than an attack on conservatism. The popular conservative talk radio host Rush Limbaugh, for instance, claimed that the name of the film's antagonist, Bane, was designed to create a negative association for then-Republican presidential nominee Mitt Romney, whose former employer was Bain Capital, an American private investment firm based in Boston, Massachusetts, and specializing in private equity, venture capital, and impact investing, among other things. "A lot of brain-dead people . . . [are] gonna hear 'Bane' in the movie, and they're gonna associate Bain," Limbaugh claimed, arguing further, "The thought is that when they start paying attention to the campaign later in the year, and Obama and the Democrats keep talking about Bain, Romney and Bain, that these people will think back to the Batman movie."[14] Perhaps not the most sophisticated rhetorical analysis, but as the *Atlantic* reported, that apparently did not prevent it from being echoed by Republican pollster Frank Luntz and conservative commentator Jed Babbin.[15]

Other conservatives, however, offered very different, even antithetical interpretations. In a *Wall Street Journal* editorial, Andrew Klavan wrote that *The Dark Knight* was "at some level a paean of praise to the fortitude and moral courage that has been shown by George W. Bush in this time of terror and war."[16] Ben Shapiro, writing at the time for *Breitbart,* said of the film that it was "probably the most conservative film of all time."[17] In his review, Shapiro points to ten things that he believes evince a conservative ethos. Some of those things are rather odd—for instance, his connection of the film's fusion reactor with the failed solar company Solyndra—but some are rather substantive, like his argument that Bane's parroting of liberal shibboleths functions as a criticism of Occupy Wall Street. John Nolte, also reviewing the film for *Breitbart,* made similar arguments, which he broadcast in the subtitle of his review, "Nolan Slaps Obama with a Masterpiece."[18]

Left liberals and progressives were also of two minds about the film. Some, like former Clinton aide Christopher Lehane, followed conservatives in seeing connotative significance between the homophones *Bane* and *Bain.*[19] Following suit, the *Daily Kos* provided a template for readers to make memes connecting the two.[20] These approaches to the film, like those of Limbaugh and company, were almost bracingly superficial—though, to be fair, many were publicized before the film's release date. However, reviews by leftists published after actually having seen the film tended to read into it a much more conservative messaging. The politically progressive/liberal website *Salon,* for instance, ran an article by executive editor Andrew O'Hehir that plainly stated, "It's no exaggeration to say that the 'Dark Knight' universe is fascistic (and I'm not name-calling or claiming that Nolan has Nazi sympathies). It's simply a fact." In O'Hehir's view, the film presents "a vision of human history understood as a struggle between superior individual wills, a tale of symbolic heroism and sacrifice set against the hopeless corruption of society." He then goes on to articulate Batman's use of deceptive tactics in light of the esoteric philosophy of Leo Strauss, whom he describes as a "neocon founding father."[21] Along similar lines, the award-winning journalist Matt Taibbi described *The Dark Knight Rises* as "a Hitlerian whack-off fantasy about an unfairly maligned billionaire who sneaks out at night in bondage masks and Kevlar underpants and uses secret military technology to beat the living shit out of the Occupy movement."[22] And in a since-deleted tweet, blogger and journalist Matt Yglesias called *The Dark Knight Rises* a "balls-out insanely rightwing movie."

In contrast to these readings, the esoteric interpretation of the *Dark Knight* trilogy eschews left-liberal and conservative viewpoints, favoring instead an antiliberal traditionalist or dissident right-wing perspective. The dissident right broadly rejects the liberal foundations against which left liberals and conservatives are seen as mere variations. From that perspective, both camps are equally committed to the abstract, universal principles of liberal modernity, differing only in terms of the rank ordering of these principles; whereas left liberals privilege equality, conservatives (or conservative liberals) prize freedom. Skeptical of modern democracy and all the liberal aspirations that underlie it, the dissident right broadly advocates for a universal type of civilization. Such a civilization is characterized by the recognition of a metaphysical order as well as the presence and authority of elites that derive from this higher plane the principles and values necessary to found a well-articulated social organization, to open paths to transcendent knowledge, and to give life true meaning. An important component of this civilizational ideal is racial homogeneity. Thus, at the extreme, the dissident right advocates for ethnonationalism, emphasizing above all the "health" and security of future white ethnostates. While it is unclear how many Americans hold this worldview, what is clear it is that most global media conglomerates do not. To find its views expressed in a mainstream movie franchise like the Batman trilogy requires a determined effort to read between the lines.[23] And that is exactly what some right-wing fans do.

ESOTERIC BATMAN

Given these heterodox beliefs and values, it should come as no surprise that the dissident right counterposes its interpretations of the *Dark Knight* series to those of mainstream conservative liberals, often underscoring the oppositional nature of their readings in a manner quite unflattering to their conservative foes. Representative of this "shots fired" approach is the white nationalist essayist Gregory Hood, who ascribes conservatives' poor filmic interpretations to an intellectual deficiency, arguing that "what passes for the American Right is not intellectually capable of understanding [*The Dark Knight Rises*]."[24] For Hood and like-minded right-wing critics of conservatism, "normie" conservative are too ideologically committed to liberalism as a framework to pick up on the antimodern, antiliberal traditionalism that constitutes the trilogy's core message.

Although these critics do not exhibit much familiarity with mainstream literary or cultural studies themselves, this line of attack effectively charges mainstream conservatives with laboring under what the literary critic Kenneth Burke refers to as a "trained incapacity," a "state of affairs whereby one's very abilities can function as blindnesses."[25] From that perspective, the professional political enculturation of mainstream conservatives has so built their scheme of orientation that they can only interpret cultural artifacts in a dichotomous fashion, either as instances of left-liberal/progressive propaganda or as vindications of the bourgeois social order consisting of free-market capitalism, limited government, middle-class virtues, and so on.

Special ire is directed at mainstream conservative readings of the films, with Gregory Hood and Luke Gordon writing, "Conservatives misinterpret the movie because they lack the ability to comprehend anything deeper than corporate profiteering dressed up in platitudes like 'free markets' or a 'shining city on a hill.' Higher ideas like Traditionalism or the nature of man, society, and power might as well be a foreign language to the Last Men pining for the second coming of Ronald Reagan."[26] Instead of approaching the trilogy through a liberal conservative or progressive framework, the dissident right tends to see it as consistent with, indeed expressive of, their own worldview. This resemblance, they argue, is most pronounced in the third installment of the series, *The Dark Knight Rises.* Writing under the pseudonym Trevor Lynch, Greg Johnson describes it as an "extremely Right wing, authoritarian, fascistic movie," while Gregory Hood and Luke Gordon refer to it as the "most subversive and overtly right-wing movie to be made in many years."[27]

The film certainly proliferated within the (mostly online) white nationalist ecosystem. White nationalists and other dissident right-wing communities—identified generically at the time as the "alt-right"—would quote Bane or make Bane-related memes. Quotations from the revolutionary/terrorist appeared, for instance, in the white separatist writings of the Traditionalist Worker Party (dissolved by 2018) and the commentary and message board website the *Daily Stormer.* A member of the notorious imageboard website 4chan dressed as the bit character "CIA Agent" from *The Dark Knight Rises* to disrupt Shia LaBeouf and Jaden Smith's anti-Trump streaming project.[28] Armed white supremacists quoted Bane in a viral video uploaded shortly before three white men in masks opened fire on a Black Lives Matter protest in Minneapolis.[29]

In an era of digitally networked interactivity, however, what is peripheral has an uncanny ability of finding its way to the center, as Marshall McLuhan observed in the 1960s vis-à-vis electronic media.[30] Writing for the feminist website *Jezebel,* Gabrielle Bluestone accused Trump of plagiarizing Bane in his inaugural address.[31] One does not need to commit to the principle of logographic necessity to appreciate the remarkable parallels between Bane's words and Trump's. Despite the widespread fan uptake among radical conservatives, the short memes never provide an explanation for what about the trilogy appeals to white supremacists.

If these critics are correct in their political analysis and the *Dark Knight* trilogy is radically conservative, then an equally interesting question is how a movie series boasting an uncompromisingly fascistic message achieved such critical, commercial, and cultural success. The most probable and consistent answer—regardless of whether the specific term is referenced—is that the movies are esoterically coded. Whereas the exoteric, surface-level mishmash of various political ideologies leaves something for everyone to latch on to, the true hidden message is one of traditionalism, authoritarianism, and fascism, so much so, in fact, that the *Dark Knight* films are ones that run-of-the-mill "conservatives are attracted to" even if they "will never truly understand."[32]

While these readings can be quite nuanced and are explored in more detail in the following pages, in broad strokes the overarching esoteric interpretation is as follows: Gotham City, the home of Batman, represents America—or any liberal, market-oriented democracy. It is hopelessly corrupt, dirty, mismanaged, and overrun by crime both organized and chaotic. The League of Shadows—an ancient, martial secret society that acts as a catalyst for the restructuring of decadent civilizations around the globe—recognizes that Gotham cannot be redeemed and so plans to destroy it in the hope that a better, more noble community can emerge in its place. It has successfully carried out such missions many times before, as its leader, Ra's al Ghul, tells a young Bruce Wayne in *Batman Begins:* "The League of Shadows has been a check against human corruption for thousands of years. We sacked Rome. Loaded trade ships with plague rats. Burned London to the ground. Every time a civilization reaches the pinnacle of its decadence, we return to restore the balance."

While Wayne acknowledges Gotham's systemic problems, he ultimately rejects the world-revolutionary spirit of the League of Shadows (as well as its edict that killing is often a necessary evil). Instead of revolutionary action, he takes up the vigilante identity of "Batman" as a means of saving the city from itself and restoring justice. At the level of exoteric encoding, the League of Shadows and its members are positioned as the villains; they represent obstacles to Batman's goal of restorative justice and are thus in the wrong. Against that interpretation, the antiliberal right argues that, like the villains of so many other esoteric texts, the League of Shadows functions as the narrative's voice of reason, speaking the hidden truth of the films. Although Batman does triumph at the end of the first installment, his victory over the League of Shadows is not a clear victory for liberal reformism. Rather, in this view, Batman represents the intervention of Nietzsche's Übermensch—an exceptionally virtuous, self-overcoming individual—to save Gotham from its own decadence and subvert its entropic decline, a situation that cannot be sustained over the long term. Despite the esoteric encryption, the dissident right maintains that this message only becomes more incontrovertible as the trilogy unfolds.

In *The Dark Knight*, organized crime and other forms of corruption once again run rampant in Gotham, despite Batman's continued efforts to shore up the fabric of civil society. Impressed by the idealism of the new district attorney, Harvey Dent, Wayne hopes that Dent, in coordination with Lieutenant Jim Gordon of the Gotham City Police Department, can replace the extrajudicial justice that has been necessary to keep Gotham from falling into chaos. This plan fails spectacularly with the appearance of the Joker, whose wanton, violent criminality centers on Dent and results in the moral and physical transformation of Dent from law-upholding prosecutor to the vengeful, spree-killing villain Two-Face.

With the loss of Dent as a beacon for hope, Gotham's need for a Batman-like figure reasserts itself and Batman, in concert with Lieutenant Gordon, decides that the news of Dent's fall would be too demoralizing to publicize. As Gordon explains, "The Joker won. Harvey's prosecution, everything he fought for . . . undone. Whatever chance you gave us at fixing our city dies with Harvey's reputation. We bet it all on him. The Joker took the best of us and tore him down. People will lose hope." Batman insists that Gotham's citizens should never know about Dent's devolution, and Gordon and Batman concoct a story that Batman was responsible for Dent's death. This noble lie functions to preserve the myth that reforms from within the system can ultimately save Gotham. That such a myth is necessary, however, underscores Gotham's politico-existential need for a superhero, and this exigence, the radical right argues, renders the film fascistic. As Hood and Gordon explain, "The idea of

Figure 8. Gordon smashes the Bat-Signal to preserve the lie. *The Dark Knight* (2008).

a superhero can be inherently 'fascist'—a superhero is a being of pure will and great power who is held to a different standard so he can impose that will on the larger society. A superhero saves society from itself. . . . Democracy can only be saved by people who don't really believe in democracy."[33]

Among the three films, the final installment, *The Dark Knight Rises,* has attracted the most attention from dissident right-wing critics. According to such critics, the film provides the master key for grasping the trilogy as a whole. The film introduces a new villain, Bane, a masked terrorist/revolutionary and former member of the League of Shadows. In short order, Bane seizes control of Gotham, destroying its bridges, instituting martial law, releasing violent criminals from Blackgate Penitentiary, and exiling and killing its elite. At each step of the way, Bane publicly and explicitly justifies his actions in terms of left-wing populist and egalitarian ideals that could have been lifted from the Occupy Wall Street protest movement of 2011–2012.

This left-liberal/progressive messaging, however, is merely a cover. Bane, it turns out, remains an active member of the League of Shadows. After physically crippling Batman and imprisoning him abroad, Bane converts a fusion reactor core into a decaying neutron bomb with the aim of accelerating the collapse that the League of Shadows predicts is inevitable. While the League appears to have been vindicated, by the end of the film a healed Batman escapes from prison and returns to Gotham, defeating Bane and restoring some semblance of order to the city. Bruce Wayne, however, is no longer interested in being Batman. He retires, leaving a young police officer to potentially fill his shoes. In effect, the dissident right argues, the extraordinary effort of unique individuals can stave off societal corruption, but perhaps not forever. Or as Hood and Luke Gordon put it:

> Despite the happy ending of Bruce Wayne and Selina Kyle palling around in Florence, the ultimate message of the film, and the trilogy, is far too dark for ever-optimistic American conservatives to internalize. Gotham only functions when it is built on lies. Lacking both an aristocracy capable of leading, and a populace capable of being lead [*sic*], Gotham reverts to brutal authoritarianism in order to bring about order. . . .
>
> The nature of the people themselves ultimately never changes. When left to their own devices, the people allow radical psychopaths to run the roost, a reflection of their own fractured existence. At the end Gotham is saved from total destruction, but once again needs the false lie of a higher man's sacrifice in order to make sense. Bruce Wayne escapes, turns his back on the city, and moves on with his life in a foreign country. . . .
>
> Much like modern America though, Gotham can only make sense for so long before the wheels come undone. What is Nolan really saying then? Is it possible he's challenging our notions of what we actually are conserving? Gotham is reminiscent of modern America, decadent, soulless, and lacking any social capital. Is there a Gotham still worth saving? An America? That's Nolan's real question, and something Batman, like conservatives, omit themselves from ever having to answer.[34]

Hood and Gordon's synopsis of the films explains the appeal to fascists, but it also justifies the esoteric reading of the trilogy with an explicit reference to Leo Strauss.

For these and other white nationalists, the *Dark Knight* trilogy is itself about esotericism, which reflexively invites an esoteric reading. Surface-level appearances, they argue, draw attention to the interplay between exoteric and esoteric structures, essentially thematizing the cultural role of esoteric encoding/decoding. To some extent this is true of any movie centered on an alter ego superhero, but the trilogy takes it a step further. Consider the palatable lie that Batman and Gordon tell the public regarding Harvey Dent/Two-Face; their explicit motive in telling the lie is to protect the public from a truth they believe it cannot handle.

The series also includes numerous instances of surface-level appearances failing to divulge the true story. The Joker tells two mutually exclusive origin stories about how he came by his Glasgow smile—first, that he received it from his abusive father; second, that he inflicted the wounds himself in a grotesque attempt to cheer up his wife. According to Christopher Pankhurst, this narrative contradiction renders the character a cypher and allow his "more mythic qualities" to shine through.[35] When Batman, remarking on the Joker's violent behavior, says, "Criminals aren't complicated," his wise butler, Alfred, disabuses him of that notion: "With respect, Master Wayne, perhaps this is a man you don't fully understand either." Alfred then tells the story of a bandit he fought during his time in Burma, who raided and stole from local caravans, only to later throw away the purloined valuables. The exoteric point of the anecdote is to reveal an existence of an ethical system totally alien to Batman's sense of political justice, one that may require further analysis for Bruce Wayne to comprehend esoterically, and Jason Reza Jorjani argues that the story seems designed to prompt such reflection in the viewer.[36]

When responding to the mainstream conservative interpretations of the films in defense of an esoteric traditionalist reading, Hood and Gordon ask, "But how do we know this? How can we be sure that we aren't like *Big Hollywood,* just reading into the movie our own ideological prejudices? Well, it's pretty easy. Bane *directly* tells us." They argue that Bane tells Batman that the socialist platitudes he spouts are really just him "feeding [Gothamites] hope to poison their souls."[37] The message again is that simple exoteric readings of the film, like those performed by many conservative and liberal critics, are inconsistent with the way the film asks the audience to understand it.

Hood and Gordon present themselves as fans of the trilogy, having conducted in-depth interpretive analyses that show appreciation of the films at virtually every level. They purport to explain the often unstated attraction of white nationalist fans to the films. And they appeal to fans more generally, in what is perhaps a gesture of strategic ambiguity. Hood and Gordon and other contributors essentially ask how a fan, frequently defined by loving attention to detail, could miss all the signs that point to a white nationalist (or traditionalist) reading of the trilogy.

The appeal to, or mimicry of, a fanlike close reading is, however, a hallmark of all esoteric textual interpretation. A call to read something esoterically, "between the lines," presupposes fans as both consumers and producers of fan culture. Of course, that is why there are virtually no esoteric readings of things that do not elicit high levels of subjective adherence, that do not generate fandoms. Esoteric readings are all centered around "great works." And that helps to explain the rhetorical motivation animating white nationalists' esoteric engagement with the *Dark Knight* trilogy; it looks exactly like what true fans would do.

INVITING ESOTERICISM

Being a great work is of course insufficient to attract esoteric readings. *Wuthering Heights* and *1984* aren't accused of containing coded messages. Nolan's Batman films share the characteristics of other pieces of media that receive esoteric readings. This begins with the fact that the films can be seen as offering a justification for esotericism. The films themselves have consistent themes of surface-level appearances hiding what is truly going on. To some extent this is true of any movie centered on a superhero with an alter ego, but the *Dark Knight* trilogy takes it much further. Jorjani compares the palatable lie that Batman and Gordon tell the public about Dent turned Two-Face, because they believe the public cannot handle the truth, to Plato's "noble lie."[38] Another alt-right reviewer refers to this and the other lies necessary to keep Gotham going as "noble lies that would make Leo Strauss blush."[39] Likewise, Richard Spencer, Andy Nowicki, and Colin Liddell discuss the film explicitly in terms of Strauss' concepts of esoteric and exoteric messaging.[40]

Esoteric readings can flourish even when they contradict their creator's publicly stated intent, but the absence of clear authorial direction can serve as fertile ground for esoteric interpretation. In this regard, Nolan's notoriously tight lips about the meaning of his films has likely aided illiberal readings. Nolan has often refused to comment, not just on what his films mean but even on what happens in the story. His film *Inception* (2010) closes with a top spinning on a table; if the top continues to spin, it means the main character is still in a dream state, whereas if the top falls, it means he has returned from dream to reality. The top begins to wobble, but the screen cuts to the credits before a resolution is reached. Nolan would not answer whether the main character was dreaming or not and would skip out of the back of showings to avoid answering this common question.[41] A similar controversy emerges about whether Batman actually lives through the *Dark Knight* series or if the happy ending is simply hallucinated by his butler, which again Nolan refused to weigh in on.

Even after Bane became a meme among the alt-right fan appropriators, Nolan did not denounce them or explain why they were misreading the film, as Matt Furie did when the alt-right co-opted his comic character Pepe the Frog.[42] In the world of (neo)liberal Hollywood, silence on the political implications of the films stands out as an invitation to interpretation; perhaps Nolan is sympathetic to fascist ideology. Throughout the book *Dark Right*, authors will say things like "Who in Hollywood has been reading Rene Guenon and Julius Evola . . . For somebody inside the beast clearly understands that a weaponized traditionalism is the ultimate revolt against the modern world," or that the movies support authoritarianism, "whether or not Nolan will admit it publicly."[43]

Nolan's trilogy clearly rewards careful readings, which lends plausibility to claims that its creator has the desire and capacity to encode hidden messages. There are many cultural objects with critical, cultural, and economic success that do not have an enormous amount of depth. *The Shawshank Redemption* (1994), for example, is much beloved and has numerous moving performances but one does not gain much from closely analyzing the film. The *Dark Knight* trilogy, in contrast, is chock-full of Easter eggs. We meet commissioner Gordon's young daughter, Barbara, who the comics tell us will become Batgirl. A police officer asks Gordon if he saw any giant alligators when searching for Bane in the sewers, a reference to the Batman villain Killer Croc. A police officer with a name patch reading "Allen" references the superhero Spectre, the spirit of murdered cop Crispus Allen, who returns to the mortal realm to fight evil. An executive at Wayne Enterprises who discovers Batman's identity and tries to extort him, goes by the name Coleman Reese but is referred to as Mr. Reese (phonetically identical to *mysteries*). This has been suggested as a reference to the character known as the villain Riddler, whose name is E. Nigma (phonetically identical to *enigma*).[44] The neck tattoos of an unnamed prisoner suggest it is the notorious serial killer Victor Zsasz. There is a vignette in *The Dark Knight* in which a witness testifying against mob boss Sal Maroni pulls a gun and tries to shoot Harvey Dent but his gun

Figure 9. Someone in the crowd holds a sign of an *R* in the distinctive style of Robin's logo. *The Dark Knight Rises* (2012).

misfires. This is a reference to Two-Face's comic book origin story, where Dent receives his extreme facial scarring from a courtroom attack, a traumatic event that results in Dent's psychological transformation into Two-Face.

Hidden details, however, are not only the preserve of comics fans. The mask that the Joker wears to rob a bank in the opening sequences of *The Dark Knight* is strikingly similar to the one Cesar Romero wore in the 1960s Batman TV series. A close-up of the video surveillance of that same robbery shows that it occurred on July 18, 2008, the day the movie was released in theaters. At the football game, one can see a tiny Robin symbol in the stands (figure 9), foreshadowing police officer John Blake's transition to Robin at the end of the series. Bruce Wayne drives a Lamborghini Murcielago, the Spanish word for "bat." And *The Dark Knight* features a *Spider-Man 3* (2007) poster in the background, suggesting that superhero movies exist in Nolan's Batman universe.

The films also make use of foreshadowing that extends to the next film in the series. *Batman Begins* ends with the discovery of a playing card of the Joker. Also in *Batman Begins,* Bruce Wayne needs to clear his mansion of guests, so he insults them all by calling them two-faced, foreshadowing Two-Face's arrival in the sequel. In *The Dark Knight,* Batman complains that his suit did little to protect him from a dog attack. The business manager of Wayne Enterprises, and Batman's tech specialist, Lucius Fox, says about a new gadget that it "should do fine against cats," foreshadowing the arrival of Catwoman in the trilogy's last installment.

The illiberal right does not focus on any of these potentially esoteric elements in their reviews, but that does not make them unimportant. These collected Easter eggs, which come from a variety of the trilogy's paratexts, suggest that the films both invite and reward deep reading. Once one accepts that an auteur has carefully sprinkled clever references throughout a film, references that 99 percent of viewers will not ever realize on their own, it becomes significantly more believable that some other, deeper esoteric message may be buried in the series as well.[45]

That plausibility receives significant rhetorical backing from the trilogy's intertextuality, which appears to invite an esoteric approach. On one level, the *Dark Knight* trilogy *must be* intertextual; it is a reboot of a live-action movie series and both were adapted from a comic book that already had a variety of instantiations, including a live-action TV show, video games, and an animated series. *The Dark Knight* is in conversation with its source material and the variety of other forms that source material has taken, as evidenced by the long list of comics-related Easter eggs. One writer connects the films to Frank Miller's depiction of Batman in the similarly titled comic book *The Dark Knight Returns,* and Zachary O. Ray depicts Miller as a fellow traveler of the illiberal right:

> There is little doubt that Miller, the man who called Occupy Wall Street "nothing but a pack of louts, thieves, and rapists" and author of the unabashedly identitarian *300* and "Islamophobic" *Holy Terror,* was channeling many of the same concerns back in 1986 that the Alt-Right is facing today. While the West is certainly sick, it is a sickness it has brought on itself. Unlike European colonialism of the 19th century, the Global South's colonialism today is strictly the result of self-imposed ethno-masochism of a civilization defeated by centuries of victory (to paraphrase Bane from *The Dark Knight Rises*) and internal warring.[46]

The films' intertextuality, however, extends well beyond their relation to other Batman texts, and there are key intertextual moments that are foundational to an illiberal reading of the series. One intertextual connection deals with the philosophy of Friedrich Nietzsche. Will Windsor, for instance, argues that when Ra's al Ghul trains Bruce Wayne to become Batman he tries to instruct him in Nietzschean philosophy. Ghul blames Wayne's parents for their own murder, saying that Bruce's father failed to act.[47] When Bruce objects that his father had no martial training, Ghul responds, "The training is nothing! The will is everything! The will to act," calling to mind the Nietzschean will to power.[48]

Nietzsche's ideas emerge again in the figure of the Joker. When the Joker robs a mob-run bank at the beginning of *Dark Knight,* a wounded guard calls the Joker a nihilist and demands to know what he "believes in." The Joker responds, "I believe whatever doesn't kill you, simply makes you stranger," a twist on Nietzsche's famous line "What doesn't kill me makes me stronger."[49] The illiberal writers argue that the Joker offers a Nietzschean critique of all the liberal values.

Julius Caesar also plays an important role in the illiberal reading of the films. In *The Dark Knight,* the following exchange occurs between the golden-boy prosecutor Harvey Dent and Batman's love interest, Rachel Dawes:

> Harvey Dent: When their enemies were at the gates, the Romans would suspend democracy and appoint one man to protect the city. It wasn't considered an honor, it was considered a public service.
>
> Rachel Dawes: Harvey, the last man who they appointed to protect the republic was named Caesar, and he never gave up his power.

Exoterically, the film seems to warn against the authoritarianism of Caesar and those who would emulate him. Batman uses an incredibly intrusive surveillance system to track down the Joker but ends the film by destroying the system. Batman thus does what Caser did not: he took hold of ultimate power, used it to deal with an emergency, and then surrendered that power.

Drawing on the work of Nazi jurist Carl Schmitt, Greg Johnson makes the case that the film's invocation of dictatorial powers acts as a powerful critique of liberal democracy.[50] Schmitt's argument is that democracies try to create sets of impersonal rules to govern all behavior, but inevitably there will come a time when someone must make a final decision.[51] This may occur when rules conflict, the rules are vague, something unforeseen happens, or the rules are failing. Schmidt calls the person with the power to decide the "sovereign." The sovereign must work outside the law to fix the system.

The *Dark Knight* series positions Batman as the sovereign and forces a confrontation with the notion that no matter how seemingly liberal a society is, somewhere there exists a dictatorial actor that is necessary for it to function. Johnson makes the case that in America this is the deep state. In recognizing the necessity and inevitability of a sovereign, Johnson proposes a white nationalist deep state, "A League of Shadows, if you like."[52] Jorjani suggests that the films demonstrate that a cessation of a democracy "is not only justified under certain circumstances, but that the suspension of democracy need not be temporary."[53]

The Dark Knight ends with a speech by Gordon praising Batman for taking the blame for Harvey Dent/Two-Face's crimes. Gordon says, "He's not a hero. He's a silent guardian, a watchful protector." This line, combined with the lie Batman tells for the sake of the city, leads Jorjani to the conclusion that "in the closing narration of *The Dark Knight,* with its reference to the 'guardian' and the noble lie, it becomes clear that Nolan is promoting a new interpretation of the idea of Guardianship that we find in Plato's *Republic*—the most antidemocratic political text in the history of philosophy." Jorjani discusses how Plato's characters in his dialogue the *Republic* advocate the use of lies to bring about the ideal city and makes the case that *The Dark Knight* alludes to this and continues Plato's work critiquing democracy. "When Batman decides he must tell a Platonic noble lie, when he realizes that his proper role is as a republican Guardian and not as the hero of a democracy sustained through a social contract . . . To recognize this, in the compelling context of Nolan's films, is to better discern the esoteric Hermetic dimension of the Platonic project."[54] These intertextual allusions to Nietzsche, Caesar, and Plato create points of contact that illiberal fans can use to insert (or from their perspective, excavate) meaning in the text. Fame, discussion of hidden meanings, attention to detail, and intertextuality all rhetorically invite esoteric readings, regardless of the intent of the author.

THE FUTURE IS REACTIONARY ESOTERICISM

Fan studies has long viewed the consumption of texts as an active, creative process rather than mere passive reception. Michel de Certeau compared the act of reading to poaching, a "tactic" by which readers take from a text what they desire and meld it with their own world.[55] Henry Jenkins argues that fans who poach from places of "cultural marginality and social weakness" can create "their own culture built from the semiotic raw materials the media provides."[56] For example, queer fans can write fiction about homosexual couplings between characters who, in the primary source material, are coded as straight. Such textual poaching, in effect, produces texts that critique, expand, or queer the textual "plan" of the source material, developing narratives in ways that may deviate from dominant representations or the intended meanings of the media industry. According to Stuart Hall, societally marginalized fans can assume an oppositional position when decoding a text, interpreting or even altering encoded messages from within a counterhegemonic frame of reference.[57] Although the complexity of textual poaching varies widely, both within and across fan communities, the sophistication of some fan readings is on a par with academic criticism. Some even go so far as to employ a more-or-less worked-out methodology.[58]

White nationalists who appropriate the *Dark Knight* trilogy and read it through an overtly racialized right-wing lens do in fact constitute a distinct subcommunity within the broad, multifarious world of Batman fandom. What's more, relative to other Batman fan groups, their outré political commitments situate them at the margins of both Batman fandom and society at large. Yet their hermeneutical approach to the trilogy cannot be said to fall under the rubric of textual decoding, textual poaching, or indeed any other mainstream critical-cultural practice. In keeping with their "archeofuturist" political predilections, white nationals seem to adhere to a model of interpretation that both predates and goes beyond modernity.

As we have seen, when it comes to Nolan's trilogy, white nationalists prefer to read things esoterically, between the lines. According to Leo Strauss, prior to the nineteenth century, philosophers felt compelled, for reasons of persecution, to write and teach esoterically, to disguise multiple levels of meaning within an exoteric structure of philosophical communication. Using a variety of rhetorical tactics and compositional techniques to encrypt the true meaning of texts—including obscure references, irony or paradox, hyperbole, or even deliberate self-contradictions—these premodern writers deployed esoteric writing to transmit radical, hidden messages to "thoughtful . . . careful readers."[59] Decryption of these messages differs from oppositional reading—even of oppositional texts—because it involves not only the attribution of a perceived oppositional motive on the part of the author, whether

Plato or Maimonides or whomever, but also the encryption, rather than encoding, of what is perceived to be an oppositional message. Thus, common, exoteric readings of a work like Plato's *Republic* function simply as a discursive means of bypassing the censors of a punitive society and safely distributing a truth that is potentially inimical or offensive to common belief and opinion.

To be sure, nothing about the *Dark Knight* trilogy overtly endorses white nationalism; in fact, at the level of exoteric messaging, the movie does not have much at all to say about the politics of racial identity. But white nationalist fan interpretations of the series operate very much between the lines, seeing within the text a secret, intercalated, even risky message designed for their eyes only.

Whether Christopher Nolan esoterically encoded the *Dark Knight* trilogy with white nationalist messages is very close to unknowable, but the same could be said regarding Xenophon or other classical writers whose texts academic Straussians examine like so many animal entrails providing divination. And that is the rhetorical rub of esoteric hermeneutics. Although no esoteric interpretation can be proven, the impossibility of ever becoming certain of one's esoteric reading is one of the conditions that makes esoteric writing possible in the first place; indeed, this interpretive torsion is the source of a paradoxical strength. If it were possible for a reader to prove beyond reasonable doubt that a given author is engaged in esoteric writing, then esoteric writing would simply fail as a strategy of self-protection against a persecutory society. Esoteric writing, in other words, can only work if esoteric reading is always subject to uncertainty. The method presumes what Strauss in a lecture series on Plato refers to as "logographic necessity," that is, it presupposes that a text is constructed like a living organism; each and every part, no matter how apparently accidental their arrangement, functions in coordination with all other parts to create an overall meaning. "Everything is necessary," Strauss says. "Nothing is accidental."[60]

This at once puts the critic of esotericism at a rhetorical disadvantage, since the very question of veracity can be dismissed by an esoteric reader as a red herring (or a MacGuffin). What's more, if a work could be said to invite an esoteric reading, then that reading could take on a life of its own, building discursive communities committed to preserving the hidden meaning of the text. Even so, there is no compelling reason to grant the truth of logographic necessity. And even if the principle were true in general, it would be quite another thing to argue that it applies to any particular text—to Plato's *Gorgias* or to Nolan's Batman.

As progressive values like racial, LGBTQ, and gender equality become increasingly ubiquitous in Western media and popular culture, white nationalists and their fellow travelers on the dissident right are faced with a choice: tune out and turn away from major institutions of communication and culture or adopt interpretive means of repurposing mainstream cultural production (such as it is). The practice of esoteric hermeneutics has ensured that this choice is not merely rhetorical—if it ever was. As we have tried to demonstrate in the case of the *Dark Knight* trilogy, textual esotericism provides an effective mechanism whereby fringe political movements can interstitially decipher their own ideology within and between meaningful structures that are indifferent or even hostile to their worldview.

Regardless of whether mainstream viewers of the trilogy find an esoteric white nationalist reading absurd, that interpretive framework provides a plausible explanation for why the trilogy was enthusiastically embraced by certain segments of right-wing political culture. Given the enthusiasm and obsessional care with which white nationalists took up Nolan's reimagining of the Batman franchise, in combination with a media-cultural environment that is perceived to be overtly left-leaning, it is reasonable to expect the future proliferation of esoteric interpretations of pop cultural artifacts, not only from white nationalists but also from any movement that views itself as the potential object of censure and persecution. In fact, similar esoteric readings frequently emerge among QAnon participants, and Counter-Currents publishes esoterically interpretive analyses of other mainstream American films such as *Dune* (2021) and the 2019 *Dark Crystal: Age of Resistance* television series. It is safe to say that popular texts that reward careful reading, deal with topics controversial enough to provoke actual or perceived persecution, and hint at carefully constructed levels of meaning will continue to invite esoteric readings by those who hold heterodox opinions. In at least the short term, then, the forecast looks like more and more esoteric interpretations from white nationalists and their fellow travelers.

Fan studies research on right-of-center fandoms have tended to treat such groups almost entirely as reactions to what conservatives and rightists perceive as an increasingly progressive pop culture. This is a reasonable approach. After all, "reactionaries" are by their very nature oppositional identities, responding to political or social liberalization or reform. What's more, these works are important if we want to expand our understanding of fandom's intersection with politics, its multifarious vectors of politicization. In the spirit of that project, however, we hope that more fan studies scholars may see fit to scratch beneath the exoteric shell of reactionary or even conservative fandoms and analyze the "hidden" cocreative production of meaning that animates certain right-wing engagements with popular texts. These meanings may center on inegalitarianism, antiprogressivism, and the like, but that should not disguise the fact that they are actively coconstructed. From traditionalists and "normie" conservatives to white nationalists, rightists of all stripes do enjoy popular forms of media and not infrequently find that some of these forms resonate with their worldview and sustain their subjective adherence to it. Right-wing fandoms may not always be as straightforward as left-liberal or progressive ones, though sometimes they are, as in the case of the *Washington Examiner*'s defense of the Galactic Empire of *Star Wars*.[61] But they can just as easily serve as inductors for political subjectivation and action. If fandoms can be politicized—and all signs currently point to increased politicization—then it is important to study this process across the political spectrum and to be alert to its potential to manifest in unorthodox, perhaps even bizarre ways.

5

ALL THAT GLITTERS IS GOLD

Straussians as Rarefied Fandom

> He was like nothing, I told him, but the maniacs who embrace some bedlamitical theory of the cryptic character of Shakespeare.
>
> —Henry James, "The Figure in the Carpet"

Readers may be forgiven for not having heard of, much less read, the independently published book *Bronze Age Mindset.*[1] Part diatribe against egalitarianism in all its forms, part exhortation to achieve a Nietzschean-like state of complete power and self-possession, the book has captured the rapt attention of a certain small but influential slice of the population, among whom it has gained a cult following.[2] Beloved by members of the perpetually online right, disillusioned young conservatives, and apparently Trump's junior staff, the book is to today's youthful, dissident right what Mao's Little Red Book was to the 1960s countercultural left. On conservative college campuses it is not uncommon to see copies of *Bronze Age Mindset* peeking out from among students' academic texts or to find students who can quote it chapter and verse.[3]

Written as a collection of aphorisms under the pseudonym Bronze Age Pervert (commonly referred to among fans as BAP), *Bronze Age Mindset* has much to offer a disaffected, paleoconservative-inflected right.[4] Feminism is an "infection," collectivist policies are the work of "bugmen" (a stand-in for Nietzsche's "last man"), leaders should be martial, and so on. The book spends much of its time discussing aristocratic figures from antiquity, such as Alcibiades and Hippocleides. Still, it manages to shoehorn into this pantheon a paean to Trump as a vector for much-needed political change amid the fallout of progressivism. The book's language seems to be crafted to offend liberal (as well as grammatical) sensibilities, with cancelable words such as *cunt, fag,* and *retard* used throughout.[5] Its message, such as it is, consists of the prescription that young men should drop out of traditional society, lift weights, and live like pirates, preying upon and exploiting the vulnerabilities of a decadent social order—a call to action virtually identical to that of Project Mayhem in Chuck Palahniuk's 1996 novel *Fight Club.* Like Project Mayhem but IRL (in real life), or Ra's al Ghul's League of Shadows, *Bronze Age Mindset* has come to function as a shorthand among devotees for a cultlike male organization centered around a single personality, which trains itself to bring down a civilization it deems corrupt.

The book received a relatively warm review in the *Claremont Review of Books,* one of the premier outlets for Straussian-aligned thought. In it, the political firebrand Michael Anton dismisses much of the book's flamboyant brazenness as a smoke screen, comparing BAP's writing strategy to that of Machiavelli's in *The Prince.* Anton writes, "A great deal of BAP's silly outrageousness seems to be there to provide air cover for the outrageous things he means in deadly earnest. If so, he might be following Niccolò Machiavelli, who once wrote 'that it is a very wise thing to simulate craziness at the right time.'"[6] Anton never uses the word *esoteric* in his review, yet by invoking Machiavelli as an interpretive signpost he is essentially admitting to reading BAP's book esoterically. This interpretive choice would later appear quite prescient for those outside BAP's inner circle.

Bronze Age Mindset was originally published pseudonymously, but thanks to *Politico* the reading public now knows that BAP's real moniker is Costin Alamariu, that he received a PhD in political science from Yale in 2015, and that his adviser, with whom he worked closely, was Steven Smith, an expert on the writings of Leo Strauss.[7] Even more telling is Alamariu's dissertation, "The Problem of Tyranny and Philosophy in the Thought of Plato and Nietzsche," recently revised and self-published as *Selective Breeding and the Birth of Philosophy.* In addition to prefiguring many of the themes found in *Bronze Age Mindset,* the dissertation reads certain of Plato's dialogues esoterically. In treating the *Gorgias,* for instance, Alamariu claims that some of the arguments against nihilistic tyranny that Plato assigns to his supposed philosophical protagonist, Socrates, are in fact an esoteric foil for Plato's preference for just such a system of rule.

The Straussian media and literary critic Paul Cantor wrote persuasively that "a demonstrably esoteric text is a contradiction in terms."[8] And so there may never be a final word on whether Alamariu wrote *Bronze Age Mindset* esoterically, just as there may never be a final word about Taylor Swift's sexual identity or the political intent (if any) behind the *Dark Knight* trilogy. In the final analysis, the esoteric status of any potentially esoteric text (broadly construed and taken on its own) cannot be definitive. Nevertheless, in this instance, the fact that Anton and others presented esoteric readings of a book later revealed to be written by an Ivy League–educated, postgraduate Straussian says something—even if not definitively. As in an *N*-of-1 clinical trial, the data remains inconclusive but the results are promising and deserve further serious attention.

For professional, academic Straussians this means that despite what we have to imagine is a preference for Thucydides and Plato (or even Nietzsche), young, high-achieving right-wingers will for a time associate Strauss and Straussianism not with questions about reason versus revelation or about modern versus ancient liberalism but with an internet personality who ponders questions such as "Chimp in state of nature never jerks off, but in captivity he does, wat [*sic*] does this mean?"[9] The inclusion of BAP in the Straussian fold acts to blur the lines between academic and layperson (as well as sophisticated and vulgar, establishment and insurgent) in a way that opens the whole Straussian project up to reexamination.

Case studies in the previous chapters have detailed some of the ways in which different fandoms and fan-adjacent groups pursue esoteric readings of a range of pop culture textual phenomena. Ranging from the unsound to the plausible, these interpretations deploy the stock-in-trade of Straussian hermeneutics—including intertextual analysis, metaphorical decoding, and close reading—while remaining on high alert for obscure references, irony or paradox, hyperbole, contradiction, and even antagonists who seem a bit too convincing in their arguments. Each of these case studies, from Disney and Taylor Swift to QAnon and Batman, exemplify Henry Jenkins's belief that fan readings can achieve the sophistication and analytical rigor often associated with scholarly discourse, theory, and criticism in particular:

> We tend to think of theory and criticism as specialized practices reserved for an educated elite, for the privileged members of de Certeau's "scriptural economy." Academic criticism and theory builds upon years of training and a complex professional vocabulary that seemingly precludes its duplication on a popular and unschooled level. Yet . . . the intimate knowledge and cultural competency of the popular reader also promotes critical evaluation and interpretation, the exercise of a popular "expertise" that mirrors in interesting ways the knowledge-production that occupies the academy.[10]

This notion of popular mirroring of academic knowledge production is virtually a principle in fan studies scholarship today. One of the contributions of the present study is to highlight the "accidental" spontaneous, though no less real, esoteric dimension of some of that mirroring and the increasingly prominent role it plays in politically charged fan or fan-adjacent readings of popular texts (stars and series included). As we have noted, these esoteric shadings call to mind the pre-/postmodern hermeneutics proposed by Leo Strauss and taken up by his followers. The reasons for this resemblance are multiply complex, having to do with the social psychology of persecution and an emergent mediascape of digitized, networked interactivity. At the same time, popular esoteric readings point to a conspicuous, coherent, and informally coordinative interpretive practice that exploits the media-enabled resources of collective intelligence.

When studying actual, bona fide Straussians, however, the mirroring situation seems to be reversed and we are confronted with a question that has not yet been adequately addressed: If the interpretive analyses of fans, fandoms, and their fellow travelers can be said to exhibit the trappings of academic criticism, could it also be the case that professional academics, in selecting and interpreting their objects of analysis, resemble or even mimic fans? Do fans merely mimic the professionals, or are they mimicked in return? While a series of structural divides (high/low, academic/colloquial, professional/amateur, and others) may obscure any such causal connection, opacity does not constitute evidence of absence. What's more, although the question of influence is particularly thorny—and perhaps, like esotericism itself, ultimately unfalsifiable—in those instances where connections may or even probably exist, their concealment does not erase them but merely hinders their detection (real or imagined).

For instance, it took about seven hundred years (from 1321 to 2020) for someone to make the rather persuasive case that Dante Alighieri's *Divine Comedy,* widely considered a culture-defining literary masterpiece, exhibits many of the tropes associated with the much-maligned genre of fan fiction, including a self-insert protagonist, recycled characters, crossovers, and revenge elements.[11] That is not to say that we unqualifiedly endorse this or any other attribution of influence. Rather, we mention the "Dante's *Divine Comedy* is fanfic" meme to indicate the long-standing cultural tendency to not consider seriously whether professionals poach from the amateurs from time to time—or at the very least covertly mirror their practices in a professional context.[12]

This chapter proposes to push back against that tendency, to act as its Other or counterstatement, if only in some small way. At a fundamental level, many Straussian readings of canonical texts are functionally indistinguishable from the kinds of interpretive analyses we have examined in previous chapters. Here, however, the starting point is different—Straussian rather than popular readings. And that difference makes a difference, to paraphrase Gregory Bateson.[13] Shifting the point of departure reveals that the lack of distinction between popular esoteric readings and professionally Straussian ones is not only a matter of fans and the fan-adjacent accidentally mirroring Straussian hermeneutics but also a matter of academic Straussians behaving like fans in the analysis of philosophical and literary productions.

To this point, our own interpretive analyses have engaged primarily with an informal, nonprofessional mode of esoteric hermeneutics, which we have described as accidentally Straussian. For whatever reason, it is infrequent that academic schools of thought receive cultural studies analysis—perhaps as a courtesy born of a subconscious desire to maintain a self-protective norm. Here, we use the lens of conspiracy and fan culture to assess the Straussian project of esoteric decoding, much as we have in our other case studies. We provide background on the Straussian school and examine a collection of their esoteric readings of the works of William Shakespeare.

WHO ARE THE STRAUSSIANS?

Professional Straussian thought is a particular discourse community within the larger community of academic knowledge production. It thus bears the discursive markings common to that institution: dispassionate argumentation and prose style, theoretical abstraction, careful documentation of evidence, and so on. It is not only esoteric but also hermetic (with a small *h*), giving the impression that it is shaped in a rarefied environment, transcending the prosaic world of human affairs. Appearances notwithstanding, Straussians are academics, and academics are part of what Kenneth Burke felicitously describes as "the Human Barnyard."[14] That is to say that their lives are messier than their words, and that messiness encompasses aspects of their professional lives.

Straussians as a group have been embroiled in a series of long-standing feuds with other academic camps—historicists, social scientists, Marxists, Freudians—but none of these quarrels can hold a candle to their own internecine conflicts, which are driven as much by personality as by doctrine. Outside of these inter- and intra-academic disputes, Straussian controversy even managed to spill into the public sphere in the 2000s, when the by then deceased Leo Strauss and his namesake followers were commonly blamed for helping to launch the Iraq War (2003–2011).[15] None of these controversies, however, can be properly understood apart from the towering figure of Strauss himself.

Leo Strauss was a German Jewish émigré who in 1937 found his way to the United States, where for about three decades he taught political philosophy as a university professor. Hardly an American household name, Strauss lives on today mainly through a legacy built around several famous students. Some of these students, like Allan Bloom and Harvey Mansfield, achieved notoriety inside academia, others in nonacademic fields like journalism (Irving Kristol and his son, Bill) and government (Paul Wolfowitz).

As we have seen, Strauss is perhaps best remembered for his advocacy of close reading. Prior to Strauss, it was fashionable for students in American graduate school programs to read only segments of key works and then supplement that reading with commentary from secondary sources. (Given a highly competitive job market emphasizing metric-based scholarly productivity, this grad school practice remains effectively de rigueur, if not practically necessary, post Strauss.) Strauss endorsed a different approach to postgrad education, instructing students to closely read primary texts in their entirety and then to interpret them on their own, without the aid of secondary material. This opened the door to deeper readings of great (read: canonical) books—and of course to esoteric interpretations.[16]

In keeping with the advocacy of close readings, Strauss also championed a return to certain ancient ways of thinking. For Strauss, the preferred, if not only, way of thinking like an ancient was to deal with perennial and ultimately unresolvable questions—questions such as "What is the purpose of existence?" and "What is *the* good?"[17] Strategically, this mode of thought allowed both superstition and wisdom to coexist in a kind of rhetorical symbiosis or bilevel relationship in which any perceived division between the two would be concealed. According to Strauss, whereas public belief and opinion derive from religious superstition, philosophers achieve true wisdom through abstract reasoning and discursive thought. The challenge—or opportunity—is to convince the public (the many, or hoi polloi) that both they and the philosophers share in *homonoia,* that they are of "one mind together" or share "a union of hearts."[18]

To do that, the intelligentsia would pursue a dual justification in matters affecting life in common, presenting their political judgments—rationally arrived at—in the language of custom and religious superstition familiar to common citizens.[19] This idea, first made famous by Plato in the *Republic,* is often referred to as the noble lie, and it describes a politico-rhetorical method of elite rule—what today we might call hegemony.[20] Strauss positioned classical political thought as both a starting point for judging political action, now as then, and as a means of remedying what he saw as modern liberalism's intrinsic tendency toward scientism, historicism, and extreme relativism and its fruit, nihilism, which could take either a brutalist or a decadent form.[21]

Beyond the broad strokes of calling for a return to classical political philosophy and championing a close reading methodology, Strauss's theoretical profile is notoriously hard to pin down. To begin with, because his method of close reading encouraged an esoteric hermeneutics, one can never be certain of what Strauss believed or the meaning of any of his writings. Knowledgeable readers of Strauss are always confronted with the hermeneutical aporia of always not knowing if they have correctly understood what they have read, even if they think they have—not by accident but by design.[22] This readerly irresolution led Harvey Mansfield to the claim, "There's certainly such a thing as a Straussian, but never such a thing as Straussianism."[23] That notion, which strikes us as bizarre yet oddly reasonable, is probably a bit of an overstatement.

Even in the absence of a formally recognized Straussian*ism,* a kind of doctrinaire approach to Strauss's teachings has emerged. According to J. Scott Johnson, "Leo Strauss was original. His thought was persuasive in part because of its originality. There is much that can be learned from Strauss's work and that of his followers, yet it often seems that the followers are more concerned with being true to Strauss than to their own insights into the works they are commenting upon. This is often true as well of the followers of Freud or Marx."[24] Despite the emphasis on sifting through textual false doors to decode hidden messages, Straussian decryptions tend to coalesce around a rather unitary meaning. As the paleoconservative Paul Gottfried quips:

> Needless to say, the "hidden" views never turn out to be Christian heresies or any belief that would not accord with the prescribed rationalist worldview. A frequently heard joke about this "foreshortening" hermeneutic is that a properly read text for a Straussian would reveal that its author is probably a Jewish intellectual who resides in New York or Chicago. Being a person of moderation, the author, like his interpreter, would have attended synagogue services twice a year, on the High Holy Days—and then probably not in an Orthodox synagogue.[25]

If, as Mikhail Bakhtin argues, heteroglossia is the presence in language of a variety of "points of view, forms for conceptualizing the world in words, specific world views, each characterized by its own objects, meanings, and values," then the operativity of Straussian hermeneutics functions to occlude heteroglossia with "theoretism," the modern tendency to analyze things and events according to a preexisting set of rules to which they conform or the structures they exhibit.[26]

Regardless of whether such homogeneity meets the qualifications of a distinctive *-ism,* Straussians do make up an intellectual movement. And like virtually all intellectual movements, but especially those of a political cast, it is prone to disagreement and division. Hence, despite Strauss's normative view that students ought to avoid mediating influences and engage important texts directly, on a face-to-face or face-to-text basis, that hermeneutic individualism is belied by the tendency of Straussians to become embroiled in doctrinal splits. The most prominent schism falls, somewhat arbitrarily, along the geographic east–west divide popularized by the American East Coast–West Coast hip-hop rivalry from the mid-1990s.[27]

At a granular level, the differences separating East Coast Straussians from their West Coast counterparts may appear incomprehensible, even to insiders. Writing for the conservative news outlet *Washington Examiner,* J.

Bottum maintains, "There are only three people who can sort all this out: The first is dead (Bloom), the second is insane (Jaffa), and the third is Peter Berkowitz (renowned Strauss scholar)."[28] From a broader perspective, some of the reasons for the division are obviously interpersonal: West Coast Straussian Harry Jaffa's inflammatory remarks about gay people were probably less than warmly received by his former coauthor Allan Bloom, the unofficial doyen of the East Coast Straussians.[29] Real ideological differences do exist, to be sure, but their distinctiveness tends to be based on varying degrees of emphasis rather than on hard-and-fast ideological disagreements.

Separate intellectual profiles exist, in other words, but they can be hazy. For instance, West Coast Straussians tend to adopt a more overtly political orientation, advocating direct engagement with public affairs while also embracing America's constitutional history as singularly important.[30] In keeping with those traits, Jaffa, in the 1960s, wrote speeches for the conservative presidential candidate Barry Goldwater, including Goldwater's famous line "Extremism in the defense of liberty is no vice."[31] In a similar vein, though decades later, Michael Anton would pseudonymously write the essay "The Flight 93 Election," characterizing the 2016 presidential election between Donald Trump and Hillary Clinton as an event possessing existential import:

> 2016 is the Flight 93 election: charge the cockpit or you die. You may die anyway. You—or the leader of your party—may make it into the cockpit and not know how to fly or land the plane. There are no guarantees.
>
> Except one: if you don't try, death is certain. To compound the metaphor: a Hillary Clinton presidency is Russian Roulette with a semi-auto. With Trump, at least you can spin the cylinder and take your chances.[32]

While not apolitical, East Coast Straussians, in contrast, prefer what Harvey Mansfield calls a certain "estrangement" between philosophy and politics.[33] By that he means that the East Coast Straussians, of which he is a prominent member, are more stereotypically professorial than the West Coasters, focusing their intellectual efforts on scholarly output, teaching, and the professionalization of PhD students. Even so, that "certain" estrangement is not absolute, and East Coasters have been known, on occasion, to enter the public arena.

Here, Allan Bloom provides what is perhaps the representative anecdote of the porousness of the East–West divide. As we have seen, his *Closing of the*

American Mind helped precipitate the rise in prominence of the American culture war between 1991 and 2001. What's more, some of Bloom's casual political remarks as a public intellectual would be long remembered and widely circulated, taking on the weight of a formal political statement. Such is the case with Bloom's reaction to student protests in the 1960s, recently recollected by Mark Lilla: "Whether it be Nuremberg or Woodstock, the principle is the same."[34] By the same token, but moving in the other direction, West Coast Straussians are also frequently employed as college and university professors, engaging in the same teacherly and erudite endeavors more commonly associated with their East Coast brethren.

Nevertheless, the East–West split runs deep. According to Tim Rice, associate editor of the conservative political journalism website the *Washington Free Beacon,* "Each side had its own conferences, think tanks, and journals, from which they could fight about Aristotle or Spinoza and stoke the embers of decades-old personal grievances."[35] To that point, despite the shortage of PhD-level Straussians, it is a rare (but not impossible) thing to see an East Coast department like Yale hire a West Coaster from, say, Claremont Graduate University, or vice versa.[36] And when such a thing does happen, it tends to generate all manner of interdepartmental political intrigue, such as accusations of tenure denial due to insufficient orthodoxy. The conflict also runs wide, even extending to the realm of popular culture. It was not uncommon, for example, to see instances of a strident West Coaster attack an East Coast publication for promoting "aesthetic relativism" in its positive review of such pop cultural fare as Martin Scorsese's *Gangs of New York* (2002) or Curtis Hanson's *8 Mile* (2002).[37]

STRAUSSIANISM AS ESOTERIC FANDOM

Academic interest in popular culture is obviously not unique to the Straussians. What is peculiar to the Straussian engagement with the popular is that it largely takes place within an ahistorical vacuum (or what Straussians may prefer to call a perennial tradition of philosophical reflection). From the late nineteenth century to today, popular culture has been a persistent topic of conversation among individuals from across the social sciences and humanities, from sociology and critical cultural studies to semiotics, psychoanalysis, and much else besides. Straussians, however, by and large ignore these and any other interpretive approaches to pop cultural objects. As with literary texts, they would appear to prefer "deep," idiosyncratic readings to those bearing the influence of methodological or individual bias. Here, too, Strauss is the model.

While Strauss did not formalize a hermeneutic specific to popular texts or mass media content—indeed, his high culture appraisal of serious writers and "Great Books" would seem to preclude such a project—he greatly enjoyed genre fiction as well as film and television, frequently indulging in informal criticism of the narratives he liked and disliked and sharing these views with his students. Mansfield, for instance, recalls Strauss's love for the comic fiction of P. G. Wodehouse, particularly the characters Bertie Wooster, an amiable but absentminded English gentleman of the "idle rich," and his sagacious valet, Jeeves, whom Strauss saw as representing the respective strengths and weakness of the gentleman and philosopher.[38] Another of Strauss's famous students, Stanley Rosen, relates Strauss's fondness for the Western genre, particularly the television series *Gunsmoke* (1955–1975): "Strauss was a great fan of American television. *Gunsmoke* was his great favorite, and he would hurry home from the seminar, which would end, you know, at 5:30 or so. He'd have a quick dinner so he could be at his seat before the television set when *Gunsmoke* went on."[39] According to Rosen, Strauss claimed to have admired the series for the salutary effect he imagined it had on the American viewing public. For Strauss, *Gunsmoke*, like all good Westerns, demonstrated the conflict between good and evil, and the inevitable triumph of good over evil, in a way that was immediately intelligible to the common viewer (the hoi polloi).

From the perspective of Straussian hermeneutics, these appreciations pertain to a text's exoteric level of meaning. For Strauss the philosopher-cum-television viewer, they coexisted with an enjoyment of texts he regarded as esoterically structured. Alongside *Gunsmoke*, Strauss's other favorite television series was *Perry Mason* (1957–1966). Unlike *Gunsmoke*, the true meaning of *Perry Mason* was not intended for the many but for the few (the *hoi oligoi*), epitomizing the role and function of dual justification. In the character of a criminal defense attorney, "thoughtful . . . careful readers" would infer the message that while in public they should promote the myths necessary to maintain social order, in their private conscience they did not have to believe them.[40] As Stanley Rosen relates, "*Perry Mason* was different from *Gunsmoke:* the extremely cunning man who, *as far as we can see*, is very virtuous and uses his great intelligence and quickness of mind to rescue his clients from dangers but who could be fooling us because he's cleverer than we are. Is he really telling us the truth? Maybe his client is guilty" (emphasis ours).[41]

Per the guidelines of Strauss's hermeneutic argument, "as far as we can see" ought to be interpreted as a democratic euphemism for "the many"—all the less thoughtful and less careful viewers who were not in a graduate seminar on classical political thought immediately prior to watching their favorite television series. While they may enjoy the exoteric dramatic trappings of a series like *Perry Mason*, the true meaning would be lost on them, by design. Strauss's intellectual progeny, in contrast, were inspired to cast their esoteric nets wider and to read not only between the lines but also between the wires, projections, and signal transmissions of the mass media, ferreting out the true philosophical messages of a wide range of pop cultural works, from 1960s sitcoms like *Gilligan's Island* (1964–1967) and 1970s crime drama sagas like *The Godfather* (1972) and *The Godfather Part II* (1974) to the postapocalyptic horror drama series *The Walking Dead* (2010–2022) and the science fiction media franchise *Star Trek* (1966–present).[42]

Mansfield captures the essence of this energized esotericism, when, after relaying the Wodehouse anecdote, he says, "And if you are a Straussian, you go around reading things, and going to movies and trying to find things, sometimes foolishly, or too ambitiously here, or in a silly way, but still [Strauss] teaches that habit in you."[43] In this esoteric free-for-all—free, that is, for the properly educated Straussian critic—the question becomes: Do these critics approach popular works primarily as Straussians or as fans? Or more provocatively: Is there a discernible difference between the two?

We do not raise this question in passing but to signal the possibility of an interpretive phenomenon that stands in an inverse relationship to the poaching of fan culture on display in white nationalist approaches to the *Dark Knight* trilogy. In the latter, political partisans combine the tropes of fandom with an esoteric hermeneutic to inject into popular culture an ideological argument about racial politics and capital-*T* Tradition. In the case of Straussians, we do not observe a simulation of fan culture, exactly, but a dissimulation, a concealment of fan attachment under the guise of an esotericism calibrated to Straussian understandings of classical political philosophy. Instead of smuggling politics in through the allegedly esoteric back door of the popular, like white nationalists, Straussians deploy esotericism to achieve a

Figure 10. Perry Mason interviews a person of interest in another winning case. William D. Russell, dir., "The Case of the Deadly Toy," *Perry Mason*, season 2, episode 27 (1959).

dual purpose: to stake a claim on their preferred popular texts while simultaneously masking the odor of fandom. Both maneuvers are political machinations, but whereas white nationalist readings of Nolan's Batman subserve what they believe to be a world-historical project, Straussian engagements with the popular seem designed for the more "modest" end of expropriating criticism of their fan-favorite works and authors from their academic rivals.

Within the broad field of popular culture, Straussians tend to be drawn to a number of categories: Westerns (both in film and television), particularly the films of John Ford; film noir; and Alfred Hitchcock's oeuvre.[44] However, no pop cultural domain has enjoyed the same depth or persistence of attention as the works of William Shakespeare. Combined, Straussians and their fellow travelers have written close to twenty books exploring the hidden philosophy supposedly animating the Bard's plays.[45] From a professional academic standpoint, the convergence of interest in an English Renaissance writer among scholars trained in ancient classical (and medieval) political thought is perplexing. When considered as an instance of rarefied, high-achieving fandom, the phenomenon gains in intelligibility.

Straussians are fans of Shakespeare, and Straussian criticism of Shakespeare constitutes a niche fan culture. What's more, Shakespeare's plays collectively function as something of an inflection point among Straussians, converting persistent in-group irascibility into mutual appreciation and harmony. It is one of the few areas where East Coast and West Coast Straussians play nicely with one another—an inclusive academic sandbox for the esoterically trained, which boasts multiple collected volumes containing contributions from both groups. (Even Jaffa wrote a chapter for Bloom's *Shakespeare's Politics.*) So ardent is the Straussian love of Shakespeare and Shakespearean analysis that it precipitated a fight between Jaffa and his mentor, Leo Strauss, when Jaffa withdrew an essay on Aristotle from a new edition of Strauss's coedited *History of Political Philosophy,* on the grounds that the work ought to include essays on Shakespeare (as well as Lincoln and Churchill).[46]

Bloom, to his credit, recognizes the unorthodox nature of political philosophers, especially those specializing in classical political thought, writing about drama. Nevertheless, in the introduction to *Shakespeare's Politics,* he follows up this acknowledgment with a stake-depriving claim directed primarily at college English departments: "Shakespeare is not the preserve of any single department in the modern university. He wrote before the university was divided as it is today, and the knowledge he presupposes cuts across these partly accidental lines."[47] Despite the qualifying statement that "we respect the competence of our colleagues in the literature departments and are aware of the contributions of recent scholarship," Bloom in this work initiates what has become the Straussian tendency to largely ignore the vast body of non-Straussian Shakespeare scholarship, professional literary criticism in particular.

For post-Bloom Straussians, more or less all the prevailing schools of literary interpretation and analysis were philosophically or methodologically incapable of discerning the true messages inhering in Shakespeare's plays. New Criticism, for instance, could not achieve appreciative understanding of the plays' ethical dimensions because it focused on texts as self-contained structures of meaning. Marxist and Freudian critics fare no better, but for different and opposite reasons, importing "foreign doctrines" while allegedly "forgetting the plays themselves."[48] Historical analysis may not lose sight of the plays, but according to David Lowenthal, it tends to treat artistic creation as a product of its time, constrained to respond to its historical era. For Straussians like Lowenthal, this historicization means treating so-called Great Thinkers as "historically time-bound and limited, hence never to be looked to for timeless wisdom."[49] Scholarly disagreements are certainly common in academia. They make up part of the professional terrain and often entail some form of public dialogue or debate. Straussians, however, process disagreements differently, which is to say, minimally.

In contrast to other schools of thought, whether Marxists, historicists, structuralists, or others, Straussians have never appeared especially interested in debating Shakespeare critics representing different methodological approaches. They simply state their disagreement with an alternative school (or schools) and move on. At most, there is the occasional negative book review. They have consistently pursued this course of action long enough for it to qualify as an implicit standard operating procedure. The result is not an immunologically secure, stress-tested culture of dispassionate Shakespeare scholars but an exclusive, even hermetically sealed, ecosystem of gatekeepers whose apparent invulnerability presupposes a continual rejection of anything different. This models many pre-/early internet fan communities whose demands for membership went beyond the love of a given shared fan-object and extended to acceptance of a particular set of doctrine interpretations.

STRAUSSIANS AGAINST THE WORLD, AGAINST THEMSELVES

Going against the grain of modern literary criticism, Straussians approach Shakespeare's plays, as they do all other "Great Books," through the lens of logographic necessity.[50] As Bloom writes, "Every rule of objectivity requires that an author first be understood as he understood himself; without that the work is nothing but what we make of it."[51] One might imagine that this interpretive position would require as much historical knowledge of the writer and his or her world as possible, yet as we see in connection with Lowenthal's dismissal of historical analysis, that is not the case. Discussing the writings of the philosopher Spinoza, but in a passage broadly applied by Straussians in their practice of esoteric hermeneutics, Strauss describes an author's historical background as "extraneous" to the task of interpretive analysis. "Such extraneous knowledge," he argues, "can never be permitted to supply the clue to his teaching except after it has been proved beyond any reasonable doubt that it is impossible to make head and tail of his teaching as he presented it."[52]

Bernard Dobski and Dustin Gish echo this axiom and present it as a kind of structuring principle for their edited collection *Shakespeare and the Body Politic.* They write,

> While there is an occasional nod to the context of Elizabethan culture and politics, the chapters herein undertake a more direct approach to understanding what Shakespeare has to teach us about our lives as human beings and citizens. Political context and political actors—whether princes, statesmen, nobles, clergymen, or commoners—come to sight in and inform the arguments developed in these essays. There is, we hope, a freshness and immediacy in an approach that endeavors to draw political wisdom directly from Shakespeare's seemingly bottomless well.[53]

Logographic necessity, in other words, is the key to Straussian objectivity, not social forces, structures of difference, or historical conditions—not even the text, really, as can be seen in Bloom's remark about New Criticism. Esotericism demands that the careful reader see between the lines, that is, *through* the text, to the genius behind it. For Straussians, the great author is the primary and perhaps sole vector of correct interpretive analysis (unless of course extraneous historical factors support an ahistorical thesis, in which case they may be invoked as a form of supererogatory evidence).

Shakespeare—a great author if ever there was one—is certainly no exception, as Jaffa argued vis-à-vis Strauss himself. From that perspective, the only responsible way to approach one of Shakespeare's great works is with a view to unearthing the esoterically hidden messages that constitute their one true meaning, messages that are at once suprahistorical and supratextual. Hence, Straussian analysis of Shakespeare's plays consists almost exclusively of explaining the various ways that Shakespeare signals to all thoughtful readers, across time and space, the presence of an esoteric message: multiple audiences, intertextual references, divergence from source material, and so on. According to Bloom, the first "discovery" to be comprehended by the would-be critic is that "Shakespeare's deepest intention [is] to be the poet-philosopher of the English-speaking peoples, the teacher of its citizens, statesmen, and legislators"[54]

Lowenthal echoes this view, arguing that "Shakespeare devised each play as an artistic whole deriving, in all its parts, from some story he made over or invented as a useful framework for treating an important philosophical issue." Shakespeare, in this view, is not primarily a dramatist, the works not primarily plays; he is a philosopher, and his dramatic works are artistically wrought materials intended to communicate but also disguise their philosophical import. For the Straussians, this is simply axiomatic. Shakespeare is a great premodern philosopher therefore he "generally sought to conceal, rather than reveal, his own systematic thought or philosophy."[55] Or as Timothy Burns claims, borrowing without citing Strauss's iconic phrase, Shakespeare "conveys these truths between the lines."[56]

On that assumption, Straussians manage to find all sorts of secret messages, Easter eggs Shakespeare is believed to have intentionally hidden so that great minds could discover them centuries later. The edited collection *Shakespeare as Political Thinker*, edited by John Alvis and Thomas West, is replete with such esoteric discoveries. Some of the contributors superpose decoded messages onto entire plays and then identify them with the thought of particular philosophers. Jaffa, for example, claims that *The Merchant of Venice* "displays for our approval nearly every vital element of John Locke's political teachings."[57] Dain Trafton similarly argues that *Henry IV* demonstrates Machiavelli's political wisdom.[58] Other critics search tenaciously for positive depictions of philosophers and find them esoterically concealed within dramatis personae such as Prospero (*The Tempest*), Portia and Bassanio (*The Merchant of Venice*), and Duke Vincentio (*Measure for Measure*).[59] Jaffa "uncovers" political history prognostications, arguing that Shakespeare predicts England's "inevitable" transformation into a commercial democratic republic, as well as being a thinker whose defense of the bourgeois nuclear family is conveniently aligned with postwar American conservatism.[60] Barbara Tovey even detects a strategy of elite rule that anticipates Strauss's own theory of dual justification, claiming that *The Merchant of Venice* calls for a hypocritical rapprochement between secular philosophy (reason) and Christianity (revelation): Philosophers will publicly defend Christianity so long as they are free to pursue atheistic inquiry in private.[61]

These instances represent only a sample of the Straussians' engagement with Shakespeare's plays; they are, however, representative. They are not only aloof from established, non-Straussian approaches to Shakespeare criticism but also anachronistic with respect to the prevailing views of the Elizabethan era. This is a feature, not a bug, and stems from Strauss's and the Straussians' antipathy to anything they deem historicist. That aversion obviously includes historicist interpretations of Shakespeare's work, which view his plays and sonnets as reflective of the cultural narratives that prevailed at the time of their composition (and in the case of the dramatic works, their early performances). For Straussians, contextualizing Shakespeare is crudely reductive. Shakespeare was a philosophical-political-artistic genius whose exceptionally keen intellect transcends the historical contingencies and parochial attitudes, interests, and beliefs of Tudor England—or so the thinking goes. Summing up the Straussian opinion of historicist interpretations of Shakespeare, Melzer writes, Shakespeare . . . with all [his] extraordinary gifts and agonized efforts, always end[s] up just confirming the myths of [his] particular 'cave.'"[62]

A similar thinking animates the Straussian rejection of other critical approaches to Shakespeare, such as those based on ideology or psychoanalysis, though here the alleged source of reduction is not historical circumstance but anachronism, possibly combined with "cookie-cutter theory," or inattention to important differences separating Shakespeare from, say, Marx or Freud. One could, of course, question whether the Straussians are not equally guilty of practicing their own brand of anachronism, one that prefers Thomas Hobbes to Marx, John Locke to Freud. However, a properly Straussian esotericism provides a ready-made counterargument: Modern thinkers like Hobbes and Locke belong to the same perennial tradition of rationalist philosophy that stretches back to Plato and includes artistic geniuses such as Shakespeare; sadly, that tradition does not allow for secondary minds suspicious of that tradition (with the possible, very qualified exception of Nietzsche).

With these observations in mind, the wall separating academic Straussian criticism from the interpretive labor of noncredentialed, mostly online fan communities begins to seem more porous than at first glance. The relegation of certain philosophers to a secondary status vis-à-vis the "first-rate minds" of Plato, Machiavelli, Hobbes, and the like, combined with the use of that rank ordering as a mechanism by which to delegitimize swaths of established critical practice, resembles—strategically, structurally—the exclusionary tactics of insular fan communities. One could imagine, for instance, the same series of maneuvers being deployed by insular fans of, say, grunge rock/the Seattle sound. Accordingly, bands such as Nirvana, Soundgarden, and Alice in Chains would be assigned a first-class status by which other musical acts, perhaps Bush, Silverchair, and Stone Temple Pilots, would be invidiously compared. That binarization would then be invoked by exclusionary fans of Nirvana et al. to ignore fans of the latter groups, possibly also to malign them as "posers," in the parlance of the 1990s, and to deny recognition of their claims to expertise in the area of grunge (or pop music in general). These tactics were perhaps more common in a predigital era, but they still crop up on online discussion forums like Reddit and social cataloging services such as Letterboxd and Goodreads.[63]

To be sure, there are significant differences between Straussian criticism and the criticism of fans or fan-adjacent communities. However, the similarities as well as the differences can be explained in terms of what Michel Foucault understands as the rules, systems, and procedures that create, master, and restrain "orders of discourse." For Foucault, these procedures fall into three categories: rules of exclusion; internal rules ("rarefaction"), "where discourse exercises its own control"; and conditions of access to discourse ("application").[64] Both insular fans and Straussians rely on these procedures as strategic resources for exerting control over their respective discursive domains. At the same time, Straussians employ these rules and systems to constitute and police a discourse and discourse community that is exclusive of other discourses and discourse communities, those of fans and non-Straussian critics alike. In other words, they instantiate the procedures differently, according to separate specific criteria, and thereby tactically create their own unique species of discourse.

Despite the pretensions and possible protests of Straussian critics, the differences separating credentialed Straussian esotericism from the esotericism of fans and fan-adjacent groups is first and foremost a matter of discursive operations. (Indeed, having to qualify the former as "credentialed" is already to acknowledge such discursive operability.) The differences may very well be real in their effects, but on Foucault's view, those effects do not result from the innately transcendent qualities of certain ideas, writers, or texts relative to those of a more quotidian variety but from how "the production of discourse is at once controlled, selected, organised, and redistributed by a certain number of procedures."[65]

APOSTATES IN THE ORDER OF DISCOURSE

How then does the proceduralization of Straussian criticism constitute an order of discourse nonidentical to that of the interpretive work of fans? First, it excludes—not by prohibiting fan culture but by "a division and rejection." Specifically, Straussian hermeneutics conjures the class-derived distinction between high and low culture, operationalizing it as a meaningful background difference whose effectiveness takes hold at the level of social perception. Finding elements of Lockean liberalism esoterically concealed in a play by Shakespeare, for instance, invokes an erudite respectability that automatically rejects as unserious, say, a white nationalist decoding of Christopher Nolan's Batman films. Straussianism also excludes by "separating true discourse from false." Properly Straussian interpretations are authentic, good, and "true," according to this order of discourse, because they emanate from a disinterested will to truth and knowledge rather than a desire for valorization or power. Straussian criticism thus superposes the ancient philosophical will to truth onto the more modern "skyscraper" division of culture into a high and low end.

At an even more fundamental level this opposition excludes discourse that is put to work for apparently self-interested ends. While an inappropriate object (such as Batman, Trump, or the sea witch Ursula) may exclude a discourse from the realm of truth, self-serving discourse is always necessarily false because the method is incorrect. Hence, from the standpoint of institutional practice, Gaylors who discover a kindred spirit in their favorite musical artist are participating in an outmoded will to truth that is performative instead of purely semantic, as are QAnon produsers whose decryptions and circulations are experienced as contributing to the triumph of good over evil. Apart from an error in the selection of an object, they also fail to adhere to the methodological delimitations of truth.

Straussian discourse is further closed off from esoteric fandom—or would have itself closed off—because it is limited by internal procedures, disciplinarity in particular. In contrast to even the most exclusive fan communities, Straussian discourse is *academic*, which means it adheres to (or is expected to adhere to) rules of disciplinarity, specifically, the rules governing the discipline of political philosophy or political science more broadly. (Although, to be sure, many Straussians bristle at what they consider the institutional misappropriation of political thought by social science.)

According to Foucault, disciplines are a principle of control of the production of discourse, fixing limits on what can be said or written within the discipline. They are an element of constraint as well as an element of creation and proliferation. Per these guidelines, Straussians are expected to generate new formulations, new propositions within their discipline, but also to publish these new statements in certain venues, typically double-blind peer-reviewed journals or university presses. But disciplines also define the kind of discourse on their objects that will become a part of the discipline, and this is not just any kind of discourse. Such discourses are "defined by groups of objects, methods, their corpus of propositions considered to be true, the interplay of rules and definitions, of techniques and tools: all these constitute a sort of anonymous system, freely available to whoever wishes, or whoever is able to make use of them." Disciplines also lay claim to a theoretical horizon: In order for a proposition to belong to a discipline, in order for it to be true or false, it "must fit into a certain type of theoretical field"; it must be "within the true."[66]

Like other academics in other disciplines, Straussians must in a sense play the game of their discipline and accept its discourses if theirs is to retain a disciplinary status. While the discourse of fan culture may also lay claim to a kind of disciplinarity, that disciplinarity is not subject to the rules of discursive policing particular to academic disciplines (political philosophy included). Fans may generate a great deal of new propositions about their chosen objects or groups of objects; they may even, as we have seen, boast their own methods and collections of statements they consider to be true. These methods may even parrot those practiced by academics. Fan discourse, however, cannot be recognized as belonging to any formal discipline, for the simple reason that it does not belong; it exists beyond the disciplinary pale of academic discourse.

Academic discourse also adheres to and enforces certain conditions of access that fandoms and the fan-adjacent cannot meet. One important condition is the qualification of the speaking subject to enter the order of discourse. This qualification is defined by rituals (such as the completion of comprehensive examinations, a dissertation defense, academic interviews and appointments, or publications and conference presentations, as well as by the signs that must accompany these discourses (postgraduate degrees, academic rank, and so on). The majority of Straussians possess these qualifications; fans qua fans do not (and cannot).

Moreover, as academics, Straussians belong to what Foucault identifies as "fellowships of discourse," societies that preserve discourses and make them circulate within a relatively closed space. Today these societies are relatively open, though not unrestricted. The act of speaking at a conference or writing and publishing in an academic journal is an act of participating in and sustaining a society of discourse in the wider sense. Such fellowships enable conversations among members of the broader academic discourse community, even as the various disciplines set their own constraints. Straussians count themselves as members of this broader community, just as they consider themselves to belong to the discipline of political philosophy and the more specialized fellowship of Straussian discourse.

Fans also enjoy their own societies of discourse, yet here too there is no discursive overlap with their academic counterparts. No matter how intricately esoteric a fan theory may be, it could not qualify as Straussian and would not be admitted into the fold of Straussian fellowship. In terms of the order of discourse, Straussians and fans would seem to belong to mutually exclusive worlds of meaning.

This, then, is the discursive case that one could reasonably make in arguing for a qualitative, unbridgeable difference between Straussian hermeneutics and esoteric fandom. With little modification, the order of discourse heuristic could also be used to shore up the ontic distinction between Dante's *Divine Comedy* and the fanfic found on the open-source repository Archive of Our Own (AO3). Straussians might balk at the use of a thinker as "second-rate" as Foucault and the absence of premodern philosophers, but for the most part they would probably agree with demarcation. At any rate, there is nothing in this Foucauldian account that would warrant a major objection.

However, the case can also be made that Straussians consistently and rather methodically violate the very same discourse norms that guard against the insinuation that Straussian criticism is little more than a glorified, overly credentialed society of fans. This becomes especially clear in the case of the Straussian fixation on rediscovering the esoterically coded, pronoiac messaging said to occur between the lines of Shakespearean drama. There is a non-superficial reason why Straussians' obsession with the Bard of Avon resembles the enthusiastic preoccupations of Gaylors and QAnon produsers. And it is not merely because the latter mimic Strauss's esoteric hermeneutics. It is also because Straussian criticism straddles two different discourse communities: academia and fandom. As it stands, peering behind the order of discourse may just surpass the illuminative power of reading between the lines.

Rules, systems, and procedures for securing academic orders of discourse are no firewall against the lure of conspiratorial pronoia within a group. This temptation affects scholars of all stripes, not only Straussians or political philosophers, but it is more acute among people in the humanities than in the natural or possibly even the social sciences. The reason for this difference in intensity stems from the legacy in the humanities of the author function and commentary principle over and against disciplinarity. In contrast to the disciplines, which are anonymous systems designed to facilitate the production of new statements, the internal procedures of commentary and the author source their meaning in extant canonical works; their point of departure is not the possibility of formulating fresh propositions but "meaning which must be rediscovered, . . . an identity to be reiterated."[67]

Since the Middle Ages, scientific discourses and the humanities have exchanged their faith in the author and commentary principles. Scientific authors are no longer treated as authorities, but in the humanities, the author and commentary are what give the language of literature its unities, nodes of coherence, and insertion in the real. The modern university itself, as a materialized society of discourse, could be said to follow the author function, vis-à-vis Aristotle, in its very division of the various academic disciplines, though here, of course, the author principle is employed in the service of its own (imperfect) obsolescence.[68] To be sure, today there are instances of critical commentary in which writers look to authors and canonical works not for the purpose of rediscovery or reiteration but as means of generating new statements or of finding new applications for established meanings. In these instances, the author and commentary work in the service of disciplinarity. But in general, the specter of these older internal procedures imbues much of humanities discourse with a decidedly fanlike quality.

There are degrees of resemblance, however, and Straussians bear a much closer resemblance to fan culture than their non-Straussian counterparts in the humanities—so much so that the quantitative difference arguably becomes qualitative. Whereas literary criticism from, say, a Marxist or Freudian or poststructuralist perspective may at first glance appear to follow the author and commentary principles, their hermeneutics of suspicion is in fact subversive of these internal procedures of "rarefaction." Instead of assuming Strauss's principle of logographic necessity, these critics (and others) deconstruct that "necessity" as an illusion—of ideology, psychic repression, the infinite play of difference in language, and so on. They superficially play *with* rather than *by* the author-commentary rules in order to expose and ultimately undermine them. As small-*m* critical methods, they have the tendency to calcify and produce redundancies, yet their discursive bias still firmly inclines them toward disciplinarity.

The same cannot be said for all non-Straussian interpretive methods. Some New Critics, for instance, come close to sticking to the author-commentary rules, but even they leverage the clinical language of science to examine works of literature like the Bible or literary movements like French Symbolism as forming vast, apprehensible systems of allusive tendrils and tendencies that often exceed the author as unity and origin of meaning.[69] Straussians, by contrast, are resolutely committed to the author-commentary procedures for the control of discourse. This resolve is present in their commentary on ancient, medieval, and early modern political philosophies but is more obvious in their commentary on canonical literary works, most notably the dramatic works of Shakespeare. What Straussians by and large discover hidden in Shakespeare's texts are the preapproved Straussian political philosophical ideas identified with other great minds of the unofficial, but discursively real, Straussian canon—Locke, Machiavelli, Plato, Xenophon, and the like. Their discoveries are almost always rediscoveries, and their rediscoveries are reaffirmations of their Straussian bona fides.

There is an important, though not obvious, mediological dimension at play in the Straussian critics' rediscovery of meaning and reiteration of identity. The German systems theorist Niklas Luhmann famously describes the dynamics of the media in terms of self-referentiality. For Luhmann, the mass media do not primarily function to make us attentive to the "world as it is"; rather, they constitute a "system which generates a difference of system and environment and which is thereby forced to distinguish internally between self-reference and other-reference and to lend substance to this distinction using its own ever-changing conditions." The system of mass media differs from its environment, first, by carrying out an internal selective coding that separates "information" from "noninformation." This coding is mainly based on a temporal dimension, since information cannot be repeated but becomes noninformation once it has been absorbed within the system. In other words, the self-referential system of the mass media provides itself with information. Once disseminated, that information becomes obsolete, but it paves the way for other information; at the same time, that other, new information will only make sense through internal reference to the first information, which has now become noninformation but serves as background to the appearance of new "facts." For that reason, Luhmann describes the media as circulation systems that constantly renew their material while ensuring the accumulation of knowledge that can serve as a background to the production of constantly renewed figures and what he calls "irritations": "So mass media are not media in the sense of conveying information from those who know to those who do not know. They are media to the extent that they make available background knowledge and carry on writing it as a starting point for communication."[70] Media thus comprise a self-poietic system that makes up a common present. Individuals are situated in relation to it depending on the themes, issues, topics, and so forth presented and discussed.

Like media systems, both fan communities and Straussians operate as self-referential circulation systems. They both perform a certain synchronization that brings people together around certain problems while inviting everyone to situate themselves in relation to these problems. Yet their shared preference for the author function and commentary principles ensures that as circulation systems they are structurally prone to short-circuiting. Their internal selective coding does not separate information from noninformation but rather operationalizes principles of unity and origin of signification as a focus of coherence. Thus, instead of accumulating background knowledge on the appearance of constantly renewed figures and facts, these principles limit chance elements by an identity that takes the form of repetition and sameness.

Not all fandoms operate in this manner. Together, Swifties and Swift form a structural coupling that functions like a media system, articulating the author commentary procedures with an internal dynamic that encodes and circulates information/noninformation. This celebrity–fan assemblage is able function like this because Swift is still producing her "canon." As part of a micromedia system, Swifties remain dependent on their object, an author, and the author's body of work, which in Swift's case is diversely multimodal. Swift generates the information while the Swifties, by producing commentary, absorb that information as background for the appearance of subsequent information.

Straussians, however, along with fandoms working with a finalized body of work, operate differently. In the absence of newly discovered material, they do not generate or receive new information, which could create circumstances enabling the dissemination of subsequent information, but simply produce and circulate among themselves commentary upon commentary. They rediscover Shakespeare again and again, or the original *Star Wars* trilogy, for the purpose of reiterating their identity as interlocutors or fans, respectively. In this regard—as short-circuiting or malfunctioning self-referential systems—Straussian critics and "static" fan cultures more closely resemble anachronistic primary oral cultures than twentieth- or twenty-first-century media systems; they are copious but redundant, conservative (in that their discourse works to preserve itself as well as its object and identity), agonistically toned, empathetic and participatory, and homeostatic.[71] Their activity is not that of generating and interpreting new information tied to a particular moment (or even discipline) but of ceaseless, repetitive commentary on preferred authors and texts.

Beyond the opposition between disciplinarity and the author commentary principles, Straussian literary criticism clearly contravenes the theoretical horizons established by humanities scholarship in general and the discipline of literature in particular. Unlike Marxist or poststructuralist critics, who in many cases could be said to read against the "spirit" of the text or authorial intent, Straussians-cum-literary critics read against the game of the discipline that legitimates their discourse. Their discourse disobeys the rules of discursive policing, which must be reactivated in each of one's discourses if they are to be recognized as such by a discipline. Straussian criticism thus does not fall "within the true" but occupies a space of wild exteriority, a gray zone of indeterminacy that, while not quite literary criticism and not quite philosophy, borders on esoteric fandom. In that zone, Straussians are remarkably distant from the "fellowship" of modern academic discourse, retrieving "the ambiguous interplay of secrecy and disclosure" that characterized premodern monopolies of knowledge, and what Walter Benjamin characterizes as cultlike practices of veneration and devotion directed toward a particular figure or object (not necessarily religious).[72] To be sure, the academic system is a ritualization of speech—a qualification and a fixing of roles for the speaking subject, the constitution of a doctrinal group, and a distribution and appropriation of discourses—but that system is relatively open and gregarious for members.

Straussians, however, are not merely a doctrinal group of qualified speaking subjects among others. They do not simply appropriate and distribute their discourse or police themselves in terms of the orthodoxy–heresy division. They do of course perform all these actions. But they go further, effectively constituting a secret doctrinal society within the broader society of academic discourse—an "entirely different [schema] of exclusivity and disclosure," in the words of Foucault.[73] The literary critic Kenneth Burke famously describes the activity of modern academic discourse communities through the metaphor of a dinner party, which throws into relief the cultish quality of Straussian literary criticism of Shakespeare:

> Imagine that you enter a parlor. You come late. When you arrive, others have long preceded you, and they are engaged in a heated discussion, a discussion too heated for them to pause and tell you exactly what it is about. In fact, the discussion had already begun long before any of them got there, so that no one present is qualified to retrace for you all the steps that had gone before. You listen for a while, until you decide that you have caught the tenor of the argument; then you put in your oar. Someone answers; you answer him; another comes to your defense; another aligns himself against you, to either the embarrassment or gratification of your opponent, depending upon the quality of your ally's assistance. However, the discussion is interminable. The hour grows late, you must depart. And you do depart, with the discussion still vigorously in progress.[74]

In this analogy, the Straussians would be the cliques in the corner who refuse to talk with any out-group attendees, a shadowy presence only obliquely registered by other partygoers, and even then with mild suspicion.

Consider, for example, David Lowenthal's opening remarks in *Shakespeare and the Good Life.* In the preface he makes it clear that he has no interest in engaging the massive body of extant academic work on Shakespeare, writing, "I rarely refer to other things written about these plays."[75] It is a promise on which he delivers. The manuscript cites in total only around twenty sources, including citations of primary literature such as Plato's dialogues, and nowhere does Lowenthal seriously interact with any alternative, exoteric approach to any of Shakespeare's work—not established methods such as ideology, discourse, narrative, representation, psychoanalysis, cognitivism, semiotics, and the like, and certainly not synthetic/multiperspective approaches such as audiences, genre, history and historiography, or stardom and celebrity.[76]

One might assume that a Straussian like Lowenthal would at least be in conversation with other Straussian critics, but even Leo Strauss only merits one citation—and only in justification of Lowenthal's rejection of historicism as a legitimate critical method (!). Crucially, however, there is no citation of any of Strauss's methodological work on esoteric hermeneutics, even though Lowenthal is conducting esoteric readings of the plays. Lowenthal also does not engage with any of the analyses from Alvis and West's landmark *Shakespeare as Political Thinker,* despite referencing, in the notes, Paul Cantor's contributing essay on *The Tempest.*[77]

Those two references to Strauss and to Cantor comprise Lowenthal's only references to other Straussian interpretations of Shakespeare's work, and Lowenthal's citation practice is not an outlier vis-à-vis Straussian literary criticism but a common feature of its innate esotericism, though this quality is perhaps especially pronounced when the object is Shakespeare. It is sufficient to exclude Straussian criticism from the field of contemporary humanities discourse, but it is also suggestive of the extent to which Straussian critics, in constituting a secret discourse society within academic disciplinarity, incline toward idiosyncratic, appropriative societies of one. So perhaps Straussians are not dinner party guests who huddle among themselves so much as attendees who walk into the party, nod to their comrades, and then, like the *Office*'s Dwight Schrute, wander off to give the house a thorough inspection, spending the night alone critiquing the layout and materials.

Straussian publishing habits continue along these lines of Foucault's "secret appropriation and non-interchangeability."[78] In *Straussophobia,* Minowitz alleges that Straussians face persecution from a rogues' gallery of "historians, feminists, behaviorists, Marxists, and postmodernists."[79] However, most Straussian readings are published in Straussian journals (including *Interpretation: A Journal of Political Philosophy, Review of Politics, Perspectives on Political Science, Polis: Ancient Greek Political Thought, American Political Thought*) or in books or collections published by a narrow range of academic presses, such as ISI, Lexington, or Rowman & Littlefield. In other words,

Straussians are not exactly publishing their work in prestigious venues known for entertaining diverse viewpoints. These tendencies, of course, could in part be due to pushback from editors and reviewers who oppose esotericism on methodological rather than ideologically prejudicial grounds, but it is difficult to weigh in on this question with any certainty.

Despite the cloistered nature of esoteric hermeneutics, when Straussians like Minowitz are not grumbling about persecution they tend to gripe about being ignored by their fellow academics. The cognitive dissonance of that dual disposition is evidently lost on Mansfield, who claims that Strauss's own ideas are "arguments held to be not worth stating or refuting." Assuming this assessment is correct, at least some of that neglect would presumably originate from a lack of clarity about which arguments Straussians put forward in their interpretive analyses. Mansfield himself describes how Strauss, in *Thoughts on Machiavelli,* hid his most esoteric interpretations in the notes, and even then did not fully spell out his hermeneutical juijitsu: "And what he did in the footnotes of that book was to set little puzzles for his students to come along and try to discover and some of them were easy and some were hard and I got some of them, but by no means all."[80]

To be clear: Strauss esoterically coded his esoteric interpretations of Machiavelli and esoterically buried them in the notes. If one of Strauss's preeminent students could not fully decipher the master's interpretive arguments, then it is unclear how anyone, especially Mansfield, could reasonably expect non-Straussians (or lesser Straussians) to understand them sufficiently well to respond—or to believe themselves capable of responding. Further complicating matters is the fact that Strauss himself, when writing about Maimonides, raises the question of whether it is even ethical to elucidate the esoteric writings of others, given that the intention of esoteric writing is to keep messages concealed from the many.[81] This quandary is incredibly atypical within academic discourses governed by procedures of disciplinarity. It is relatively common, however, in connection with the discourse rules of exclusive fandoms.

This habit of writing esoterically about esoteric writing has been taken up by Strauss's students, many of whom appear to hide some of their arguments and almost never avail themselves of straightforward discursive argumentation (Barbara Tovey being the exception that proves the rule). While there is certainly no shortage of dense, highly specialized academic prose—see, for instance, the complicated prose style of Judith Butler or Gilles Deleuze and

Félix Guattari—the Straussian practice of concealing one's thesis is diametrically opposed to the discourse norms of the modern academy. Melzer, though, does one better, extending the minoritarian status of this practice beyond the parameters of academic discourse to modernity at large, arguing that "the modern worldview somehow involves a deep aversion to esotericism."[82] Of course, given postmodernism's general disinterest in authorial intent, Melzer could probably get away with expanding the scope of this aversion beyond the limits of modernity.

Nonetheless, Straussians are bound to lose public arguments making use of affective-psychic responses like aversion. One could easily (and persuasively) make the case that individuals who feel compelled to write esoterically to preserve the allegedly hidden meanings of, say, *Macbeth* appear borderline pathological. We can underscore the pathology at play if we imagine someone three hundred years in the future writing in code to discuss the hidden meanings of Quentin Tarantino's oeuvre and how it connects to political ideologies that barely exist in our contemporary moment. Both instances are doubly pathological since they involve both esoteric detection and esoteric writing. And they *are* pathological because they are only intelligible against a background of perceived persecution.

NOT TOO GOOD TO BE HERE

Right or wrong, pathological or nonpathological, Straussians who engage in literary criticism do not behave like other academics; they do not consistently adhere to the rules and systems of discourse that engender and police modern academic humanities scholarship. While not dinner party crashers per se, they certainly do not mingle with others—or sometimes even with one another. They do, however, behave like insular fan communities.[83] This is evident in high expectations of specialized knowledge ("Oh, you like Nirvana? What are your favorite B-sides?"), the use of shibboleths to weed out outsiders ("It's *Aerith* not *Aeris*"), love of Easter eggs unnoticed by broader audiences ("Did you notice that the error message on Swift's website is an anagram for *red herring?*"), and strongly held, inflexible positions ("Ugh, the theatrical release was terrible; release the Snyder cut!"), and so on. Straussians expect their flock to possess a deep understanding of primary ancient texts, to know and preserve the one true canon, to encode their thought in hidden puzzles, and to participate in intergroup conflicts over questions that produce intergenerational rifts, such as the value of modernity or the dichotomy between reason and revelation.

The other chapters in this book illustrate the academic level of analysis that many fan cultures bring to their esoteric interpretations of cherished pop cultural objects. One could easily imagine a different world, where Gaylors fill university press anthologies with in-depth examinations of Swift's lyrics and aesthetic choices while Straussians populate Reddit and TikTok with posts about the hidden meanings operating within Shakespeare's plays. Even though Straussians may have paved the hermeneutic way—by rehabilitating the "lost art" of esoteric reading and highlighting the analytic tools useful for esoteric decryption—it is difficult to imagine members of a fan/conspiracy culture like QAnon reading their work or taking it seriously. The implication of this "Elseworld," we argue, is that the "Straussian method" evolved independently—and many times—like the carcinization phenomenon in evolutionary biology.[84]

And just as esoteric decodings foster bonds and connections among fandoms/pronoiac conspiracy theorists (as it does with the Gaylors and with QAnon adherents), it is difficult not to view the same effect in play vis-à-vis Straussian analyses of Shakespeare. The East and West Coast rivalry has all the rancor of a forum throw-down over whether *Star Trek: Deep Space Nine* (1993–1999) is better than *Star Trek: The Next Generation* (1987–1994). One can hear the nostalgia and pride in Mansfield's voice when he retells stories about decoding Machiavelli's mysteries with his mentor, Strauss. Esoteric knowledge (understood in both the specialized and the common parlance) creates and nurtures significant connections through the use of shared meaning-making structures, regardless of object.

CONCLUSION

This Conclusion Is Not Esoteric

> If one seeks with sufficient ingenuity in any sample, one can create cryptographic rationale for any output text—therefore in any investigation the key problem is not how to begin, but where to stop.
>
> —Nick Harkaway, *Gnomon*

As you read this book, you may have caught an odd turn of phrase, a nonreferential clause, or a defunct endnote and paused to wonder whether the text contained hidden esoteric content. Before we proceed, let us assure you that this is not the case. This conclusion was not designed to have any deeper meaning for "thoughtful, careful readers."[1] The "unintentional errors and shortcomings" that may express esotericism in "great masterpieces and works of rare genius" are here just pedestrian mistakes of a middling work. Melzer begins his history of philosophical esotericism by stating that "my goal here is not to get people to like esotericism (I am no great lover of it myself), or to engage in it themselves (as I do not)."[2] One imagines he felt the need to offer an explicit denial of engaging in esoteric shenanigans, given that anyone who writes a book-length study on the workings of literary secret codes becomes, by default, suspect. We join him in that explicit denial and apologize for not placing it earlier in the work. Unfortunately for Melzer (and us!), authors do not have the final say over how their texts are interpreted.

Although Straussians and their fellow travelers have long acknowledged esotericism as a rhetorical endeavor, they have yet to do much to explore that rhetoricity, and indeed they have made little effort to examine it in the context of the modern field of media and cultural studies analysis. Rhetoric, for them, operates in the classical and humanistic modes, where "rhetoric" refers to conscious choices on the part of a rhetor to influence and persuade an audience. However, on the question of textual authority over meaning, contemporary rhetorical studies firmly sides with the poststructuralist tradition of literary theory, which, since Roland Barthes's 1967 essay "The Death of the Author," has assumed that the author should not be seen as the ultimate authority over the meaning of the text, arguing instead that the focus should be on the text itself and its interaction with readers.[3]

In light of that hermeneutic principle, we have argued that if a text is popular, makes intertextual references, rewards close reading, and offers a lens for interpretation, then it is rhetorically esoteric, regardless of whether the author intended to hide messages between the lines. The obverse, of course, is that authors may have painstakingly coded their texts with esoteric designs, only for audiences to interpret them solely on the exoteric, surface level. And even if an audience reads a coded text esoterically, that does not guarantee that their decodings will match the intended encryptions. For instance, it is close to undeniable that Taylor Swift hides messages in her songs, but that probability does not mean that Gaylors are correct in their interpretations. There may exist texts with intentionally hidden messages that have never been decoded or, indeed, texts with esoteric messages read into them that were not there but are simply figments of a fan's individual or fandom's collective imagination.

Is the distinction between esoteric reading and esoteric intent not best understood as a hermeneutic question? Certainly this is a much easier position to defend methodologically. A person unwilling or unable to read between the lines might interpret, say, Bulgakov's *Heart of a Dog* as a whimsical tale of a dog transforming into a human rather than as an indictment of the New Soviet man. Conversely, a disturbed individual might see secret codes embedded in the menu items of their local Chinese restaurant.

While treating esotericism as a reading practice is an incredibly fruitful avenue for research—certainly more so than unknowable philosophical esotericism—considering a text as rhetorically esoteric allows one to assess its qualities independently of atomized readings. That a text may possess rhetorically esoteric features unintentionally or without notice is irrelevant; rhetoric does not always produce its intended effects. A person might listen to a great orator and remain unmoved and unaware of the anaphora, allegory, or allusions at play. Likewise, rhetorical devices need not be intentional—an oblivious orator may unconsciously structure a speech with anaphora, allegory, or allusions. Viewing esotericism solely as an individual hermeneutic is limiting; it offers no predictive power regarding which texts will cultivate mass followings of esoteric readers, nor does it provide a blueprint for shaping a text to invite esoteric interpretations. That said, our inclusion of popularity as a rhetorical feature means esotericism cannot be entirely divorced from reception.[4]

While this book has focused on some of the hermeneutic practices of pronoiac fans and the fan-adjacent—examining rhetorically esoteric elements of pop cultural phenomena and how audiences interact with them—it also offers something in the way of a practical guide. Academic Straussians like Melzer may not wish to encourage others to engage in esoteric writing. Still, by cataloging esoteric tropes and maneuvers, Melzer provides a manual as much as a history. The present work functions similarly. By framing our study of esoteric fandom in terms of cultural studies and rhetoric, we offer, in effect, a template for produsing esoterically invitational surfaces. At its core, after all, rhetoric is a practical and productive tradition, regardless of its mode (for classical, humanistic, poststructural, or other). Just as we argue that it is not an accident but the work of esoteric tropes that have caused certain fan-objects to attract deep readings, one could likewise use our case studies as a model either to create encrypted meaningful surfaces (or aesthetic phenomena more broadly) or to signal the presence of encrypted encodings—regardless of whether such encryptions are really encoded or merely simulated. In other words, they could imitate the subjects of our case studies to invite esoteric engagement. A singer-songwriter, for example, could follow in Swift's footsteps and rhetorically invite fans to read hidden messages in their multimodal output (results may vary). Showrunners of prestige television series like *Rick and Morty* (2013–present), *From* (2022–present), and *Lost* (2004–2010) understand this and have adopted many esoteric tropes to encourage wild fan speculation and create buzz. The first season of *True Detective* (2014) is a paradigmatic example of an audiovisual text that presents as rhetorically esoteric while delivering no more profound meaning.[5]

Our book also expands on the explanation for *why* a singer-songwriter might choose to engage in esoteric messaging. Past studies of esotericism focus almost entirely on the transmission of philosophical truths designed to remake society or the individual—what Meltzer calls political and pedagogical esotericism. This approach, however, takes esoteric decoders (or their fan communities) at their word and thus inevitably portrays them in the most favorable light. Straussians and QAnon followers alike see their work of interpreting their "fan-objects" as revealing noble truths that have been hidden from the hoi polloi.

Our case studies demonstrate other effects of esoteric reading, such as creating shared bonds among practitioners and providing the foundation for identity, the second of which explains how the genre of esoteric decoding sustains itself in the face of various forms of resistance to esotericism. Such determination in the face of opposition is evident in the case of QAnon produsers who stick to their pronoiac, Trumpian, Q guns despite all evidence to the contrary; it is also apparent in the Straussian commitment to decoding centuries-old texts regardless of limited job prospects or the derision of their peers. But that is not the whole story. QAnoners and Gaylors form relationships with individuals around the world with their shared worldview. Straussians have their own academic clique, complete with their own conferences, journals, and tight mentor–mentee bonds. Perhaps then the real esoteric gain is the friends made along the way, or the strengthened sense of self—a price worth the pushback from mainstream society. Such psychosocial effects of pronoiac fandom help explain its longevity. Changing your interpretation of Swift's lyrics or Shakespeare's plays may be relatively easy, but how difficult would it be to stop being a Gaylor—or a Straussian critic of Shakespeare?

It is no accident that our pronoiac case studies revolve around works of popular culture. As our analyses demonstrate, various discourse communities can quite capably blend the inventive resources of conspiracy and fan culture in mutually reinforcing ways. That porousness assumes a structurally persuasive force when the supposed conspiratorial agent is ascribed a benevolent motive. In those instances, fan-objects—whether Trump, Swift, or Shakespeare—are primed to function, psychically, as watchdogs or champions for those who occupy or believe themselves to occupy a marginal position within society. Moreover, as we have seen, in a media sphere characterized by digitized forms of networked interactivity, such pronoiac fandoms work to blur the boundaries between the work of fans and professional (specifically, academic) criticism. In that ecosystem, it becomes increasingly common to observe scholars who approach texts with a fanlike appreciation and fans who engage texts with scholarly tools and an analytic attitude (allowing that the engagement itself tends to be that of a nonspecialist).

These border crossings, however, are an emergent feature of conspiracy theory in the pronoiac mode. In many ways, conspiracy theories and the study of conspiracy theories continue to operate in the shadow of Hofstadter's paranoid style. Most academic analyses of conspiracy thinking and conspiracy theories focus on speculations about secret, malign forces, whether shape-shifting reptilian overlords, government-sponsored political assassinations, or false flag operations carried out by rogue elements of the national security apparatus. This tends to be the case even among scholars whose methodologies do not demand that their objects of study posit malevolent agents of change or control.

Popular media representations also tend to focus primarily on conspiracies related to harmful hidden forces grounded in a paranoid worldview—from postwar American paranoia novels by William S. Burroughs, Thomas Pynchon, and Don DeLillo to conspiracy theory movies and television shows like *JFK* (1991), *Conspiracy Theory* (1997), and *The X-Files* (1993–2002).[6] Perhaps this tendency is unsurprising given that the word *paranoia* goes back at least to the tragic dramas of classical antiquity whereas *pronoia* is a late-twentieth-century American coinage. One of the things we have tried to accomplish with the present work is to make a convincing case that conspiracy theories may—and with increasing frequency do—operate in pronoiac fashion, especially when such theorization is of a piece with a real or imagined fear of persecution—that is, with paranoia.

CONSPIRACY AND CYBERCULTURE

There is a media-technical angle to this "contradictory" situation in which the pronoiac suspends the IRL agency of the individual and rational subject while simultaneously enjoying the hermeneutical hyperactivity of collaborative decryption. We gestured toward this viewpoint in the chapters on QAnon and Strauss, but it has been chiefly a background consideration informing all our analyses. In his magnum opus, *Underworld,* Don DeLillo reaffirmed Thomas Pynchon's definition of paranoia from twenty-five years earlier. Whereas the narrator of Pynchon's *Gravity's Rainbow* called paranoia "the leading edge of the discovery that *everything is connected,*" DeLillo saw this tendency to see connections as having become concretized in the structure of the internet and literalized in the lived experience of everyday American life.[7] In an increasingly networked world, one of *Underworld*'s characters observes, "Everything is connected. All human knowledge gathered and linked, hyperlinked."[8]

The internet's precise role in twenty-first-century conspiracy theory is a matter of ongoing debate. (Does it *cause* more conspiracy speculation or simply make it more visible? Is there even a significant difference between the two in a digital media environment of omnipresent, always-connected, hyperfast mobile touch screens where visibility is reality and productive of reality effects?)[9] Even so, DeLillo's concretization of the paranoia thesis with regard to the internet, while not wrong, overlooks an equally powerful technical affordance of digitized, networked interactivity: the restoration via virtual means of what media ecologists like Marshall McLuhan and Walter Ong refer to as secondary orality, where psychosocial traces of orality, or "oral residue," reemerge with changes of technology.[10] While the internet's hyperconnectivity may exacerbate the paranoia of co-isolated, hyperindividualistic, neoliberal subjects, it is also positioned to nourish the pronoiac togetherness and cocreativity characteristic of primary oral cultures, cultures that believed not only in malefic forces roaming the world but also in a host of benevolent ones as well, local gods and angels inspiring cultic devotion, whose coded messages are decipherable for those communities of interpretation possessing the collective intelligence to read between the lines.

Despite the profit-making structure of Web 2.0 and its myriad interactive platforms, social media has helped usher in and superposed onto liberal modernity a throwback world of esoteric, group-based pronoia, a fiber-optic world of benevolent "conspiracy" theorizing in which neo-scribal fan practices of decryption tend to substitute for a world of paranoia- and panic-induced action. Of course, this world existed for the Straussians before the advent of networked social interaction, making them in a sense the "original gangstas" of esoteric fan culture, capable of persisting as a community, seemingly despite changes in media technology.

THE FINAL WORD

Esoteric authenticity has a "use by" date. Although the Straussian view of the esoteric aligns with popular conceptions, that meaning is, if not moribund, increasingly eclipsed by a new esoteric mode of thought shaped by the current media and political environment.[11] Absent violent censorship in today's liberal democracies, esoteric encoders can afford to make their cyphers more beginner-friendly—or at least offer explanations about why esoteric codes can be cracked by the terminally online as opposed to just the terminally credentialed or those with terminal degrees. The internet, in other words, has expanded the inner circle of esoteric reading from exclusive, face-to-face groups as small as two (one encoder, one decoder) to those including millions of participants connected via digitally networked channels. Gaylors, QAnon sleuths, and culturally literate white nationalists, for example, do not require secret initiatory rites for admission; they are, in fact, happy to teach any aspiring novitiate their methods of decipherment.

The severed connection between esoteric reading/writing and philosophical truth also contributes to the changing nature of esotericism. In the *Gorgias,* Plato defines art (or *techne*) as a rational enterprise, the procedure of which can be explained as contributing to an end, contrasting it with the mere knack for "producing a certain gratification and pleasure."[12] According to that division, the gratification queer folk derive from seeing queerness celebrated in animated feature films produced or distributed by Disney would probably point to an esoteric knack for creating pleasure, not an art. Although these films may be satisfying to a queer or queer-friendly audience, animated encomia to queerness do not address perennial questions of epistemology, metaphysics, or the "good life."

This and other examples of esoteric fandom are a far cry from Plato's understanding of art and from what the classically biased Straussians view as the proper ambit of esotericism *as an art.* For Straussians, esotericism is not only a means of avoiding persecution but also a means of conveying and decoding deep philosophical truths. Although white nationalists like Greg Johnson may counter that Nolan's *Dark Knight* trilogy does just that (esoterically traffics in profound ideas about tradition, the proper sociopolitical order, and so on), and Straussians such as Paul Cantor see value in practicing esoteric criticism of pop culture films and television shows, this strikes us—and would presumably strike many classically trained Straussians—as a (mostly) unacknowledged sacrifice of the premodern esoteric tradition on the altar of cultural relevance.

But is this truly a bastardization of philosophical esotericism, a downgrade from art to knack, or does the changing, mediological face of esotericism constitute a modern evolution and expansion of the art, such that pop cultural esoterica that were always present are now legible—and thanks to networked digital information technology, increasingly legible—to pronoiacally savvy fans? Or could we flip the formula and ask whether Straussians are the keepers of an almost lost art or simply diehard participants in a convoluted form of self-gratification? Perhaps the biggest lingering question about esoteric fandom—which we stated in the introduction would remain unanswered—is whether and to what extent any of the allegedly hidden messages identified by Gaylors, white nationalists, and the like were *really* real, actually encrypted messages—"real" in the sense of the sender-receiver model of communication, "real" in the sense of intentionally disguised and clandestinely disseminated truth—and not the product of an overactive collective imagination.

Abstracted from a rhetorical context, each instance of esoteric decoding merits a binary yes/no regarding its validity. How these yeses and noes break down offers some interesting possibilities. Perhaps Plato's dialogues are not esoteric (and what you see is what you get), while Taylor Swift is in reality a master of the encrypted message. Likewise, maybe Shakespeare's tragedies and historical works are purely exoteric in their messaging but Nolan's *Dark Knight* trilogy is Delphic in its esotericism. For, in a strictly philosophical sense, a TikTok video by river_witch7, grouponmom, or heyitsmoog may be truer—more in keeping with an author's intended yet hidden meaning—than any given formal esoteric analysis of a so-called great work.

NOTES

INTRODUCTION

1. Quoted in *Kanye Quest 3030*.

2. Strauss would go on to restate this general argument throughout many subsequent writings, most notably in *City and Man* (1964).

3. Strauss, *Persecution and the Art of Writing*, 25.

4. Melzer, *Philosophy Between the Lines*, 2.

5. The quote is widely attributed to Jorge Luis Borges, though it is difficult to find a primary source on this issue. See International Federation of Library Associations and Institutions, "Quotes on Intellectual Freedom and Censorship."

6. Melzer, *Philosophy Between the Lines*, 4, 91–92, 105, 118, 158, 128–35, 243–44, 227–30, 278, 280–83, 302.

7. The Straussians would have us believe that esoteric messaging extends back a couple thousand years, even being the dominant mode of communication for philosophers prior to modernity, used by everyone from Plato to Shakespeare.

8. Cantor, "Leo Strauss and Contemporary Hermeneutics," 277.

9. Mellor, "90s Art Collective."

10. Reslen, "10 Clues."

11. Melley, *Empire of Conspiracy*, 22.

12. According to Van Prooijen and Van Vugt, this adaptive feature evolved "(a) to alert ancestral humans to the possibility that others were forming dangerous coalitions against them and (b) to stimulate appropriate actions to fend off such threats." Van Prooijen and Van Vugt, "Conspiracy Theories," 771.

13. Roisman, *Rhetoric of Conspiracy;* Pagán, *Conspiracy Narratives in Roman History;* Pagán, "Toward a Model of Conspiracy Theory," 27–49; Pagán, *Conspiracy Theory in Latin Literature.*

14. For rumors about Nero's alleged role in the Great Fire, see Brotherton, *Suspicious Minds*, 21–24; for other speculations regarding the cause of the fire, see Pagán, *Conspiracy Theory in Latin Literature*, 119–22. The Great Fire episode is particularly illustrative of the potency of conspiracy theory in Roman political discourse. Based on a passage in Tacitus's *Annals*, some scholars argue that Nero countered the public insinuation that he opportunistically started the fire with his own counter conspiracy: The Nazoreans/Christians did it. See Jones, "Historicity of the Neronian Persecution," 146–52; and Pollini, "Burning Rome," 212–36. Richard Carrier claims that Tacitus's reference to Christians and their scapegoating at the hands of Nero was anachronistically added to the original manuscript by a late antique Christian copyist. Carrier, "Prospect

of a Christian Interpolation," 264–83. Brent Shaw, in contrast, argues that the passage is Tacitean but that Tacitus was wrong about Nero's persecution of early Christians. In this account, Nero did not persecute Christians; the link between the fire and Christians was a later development by Roman officials to respond to and exploit local communities upset by Christian activity and to offset growing negative populist mythology about Nero. Shaw, "Myth of the Neronian Persecution."

15. See Barber, "Lepers, Jews and Moslems"; Ginzburg, *Ecstasies.* For an alternative interpretation of the persecution of social minorities in fourteenth-century France, see Nirenberg, *Communities of Violence.*

16. Barber, *Trial of the Templars,* 70–74.

17. Thalmann, *Stigmatizing of Conspiracy Theory.* Until Thalmann, the commonsense view was that the Kennedy assassination constituted the most important caesura in the history of American conspiracy theory, as encapsulated in Peter Knight's statement that "following the assassination . . . , conspiracy theories have become a regular feature of everyday political and cultural life." Knight, *Conspiracy Culture,* 2. Michal Butter argues that the opposite is true. He writes, "The Kennedy assassination was the first event in American history that triggered large-scale conspiracy theories that were problematised immediately and on a completely new level." Butter, "Conspiracy Theories," 654.

18. Bratich, *Conspiracy Panics.*

19. See Thalmann, *Stigmatizing of Conspiracy Theory,* 25–69; Butter, *Plots, Designs, and Schemes;* and Butter, *Nature of Conspiracy Theory.*

20. Thalmann, *Stigmatizing of Conspiracy Theory,* 30.

21. Fenster, *Conspiracy Theories,* 3–21.

22. Hofstadter, *Paranoid Style,* 4–5, 17, 31–32, 36.

23. Fenster, *Conspiracy Theories,* 13.

24. Hofstadter, *Paranoid Style,* 9.

25. See McKenzie-McHarg, "Conspiracy Theory," 62–81.

26. Thalmann, *Stigmatizing of Conspiracy Theory,* 30.

27. Fenster, *Conspiracy Theories,* xvi.

28. Knight, *Conspiracy Culture,* 11.

29. As Michael Butter has recently argued, the current clash between domains where conspiracy theories are accepted once again as legitimate knowledge and those where they are rejected as illegitimate signal that "we are entering a third phase in the history of conspiracism. After the long period of widespread acceptance and the short one of complete stigmatization, we in the West are now living in a world where conspiracy theories are simultaneously legitimate and illegitimate knowledge." Butter, *Nature of Conspiracy Theory,* 7–8.

30. Robins and Post, *Political Paranoia;* Barkun, *Culture of Conspiracy.*

31. Hofstadter, *Paranoid Style,* 7.

32. Barkun, *Culture of Conspiracy,* 15–38.

33. Hofstadter's influence has also enjoyed an extended impact on the literary criticism of conspiracy theory as it appears in American literature. Critics such as Tony Tanner (1971), Patrick O'Donnell (2000), and Samuel Chase Coale (2005), for example, investigate the pervasive theme of cultural paranoia in contemporary American literature and culture, exploring how this paranoia is intertwined with national identity, historical consciousness, and narrative form.

34. Matheson, "'What Does Obama Want of Me?'"

35. Beckman, *Paranoid Chronotope*, 2, 11–27.

36. See in particular, Dean, *Aliens in America;* Fenster, *Conspiracy Theories;* Knight, *Conspiracy Culture;* Melley, *Empire of Conspiracy;* Birchall, *Knowledge Goes Pop;* and Bratich, *Conspiracy Panics.*

37. Butter and Knight, "Conspiracy Theory in Historical, Cultural and Literary Studies," 31.

38. Dean, "Theorizing Conspiracy Theory." For the works examined by Dean, see Fenster, *Conspiracy Theories;* and Melley, *Empire of Conspiracy.*

39. Marcus, "Introduction," 2.

40. Melley, *Empire of Conspiracy*, 8, 14.

41. Knight, *Conspiracy Culture*, 8. On the concept of conspiracism (a worldview in which conspiracies are seen as central to the unfolding of history), see Mintz, *Liberty Lobby.*

42. Several cultural studies scholars go as far as to detail many well-documented examples of official conspiracies (Olmsted, *Real Enemies*); the creation in the U.S. state apparatus of an official, bureaucratized culture of secrecy and conspiring (Melley, *Covert Sphere*); and the long history of abusive treatment of African Americans by mainstream American medical institutions and practices (Washington, *Medical Apartheid;* Turner, *I Heard It;* Fiske, "Blackstream Knowledge"; Knight, *Conspiracy Culture*).

43. Jameson, "Cognitive Mapping," 356.

44. Dean, *Publicity's Secret*, 47–78.

45. Dean, *Aliens in America*, 8. See also Dean, "Theorizing Conspiracy Theory."

46. Rice, *Awful Archives*, 15.

47. Matheson, "Stasis in the Net of Affect," 71–77.

48. Kelly, "COVID-19 Conspiracy Rhetoric," 132–53; Matheson, "'What Does Obama Want of Me?,'" 133–49.

49. Hallsby, *Sovereign, Settler, Leaker, Lie*, 12, 51. For Hallsby, conspiracy theories are tropological formations that operate largely independently of the specific claims being asserted about any given plot or hidden scheme: "No matter how new the information," he argues, we gain the sense that "we have been in this place before; that despite our not-knowing, we can still locate ourselves within the bounds of a familiar plot" (51).

50. Gunn, *Modern Occult Rhetoric.*

51. Douglas and Sutton, "What Are Conspiracy Theories?," 283.

52. See, for instance, Cubitt, "Conspiracy Myths"; and Barkun, *Culture of Conspiracy*, 3–4.

53. Under the second Trump administration, QAnon has evolved, with factions denouncing Trump for failing to release what they see as key evidence, notably documents tied to the pedophile and sex trafficker Jeffrey Epstein.

54. See, for instance, Enders et al., "Who Supports QAnon?"

55. Strauss, *Persecution and the Art of Writing*, 25.

56. According to Liddell and Scott's *Greek-English Lexicon*, *paranoia* (παράνοια) is defined as "madness, derangement" and is derived from *para-* ("beside," "beyond") and *nous* ("mind"). It was used in both medical contexts, by the likes of Hippocrates, and in philosophical contexts, by, for instance, Plato and Aristotle

57. Goldner, "Pronoia."

58. Flusser, *Post-History.*

59. See Ricoeur, *Freud and Philosophy,* 33, 35.

60. Sedgwick, "Paranoid Reading," esp. 127.

61. Best and Marcus, "Surface Reading," 9–13.

62. Jenkins, "Fan Studies."

63. See Hellekson and Busse, "Introduction"; and Booth and Williams, "Introduction."

64. Hinck, *Politics for the Love of Fandom.*

65. See Stanfill, *Fandom Is Ugly.*

66. Click, *Anti-Fandom.*

67. The #FreeBritney movement is a grassroots campaign that began in 2009 and gained significant traction around 2019. It advocated for the end of the conservatorship placed on pop star Britney Spears in 2008, which granted her father, Jamie Spears, and other legal guardians control over her finances, personal life, and career decisions.

68. Smith and Southerton, "FreeBritney."

69. Reinhard et al., "Fans of Q."

70. See Jenkins, *Textual Poachers,* 23–24, 33–34; de Certeau, *Practice of Everyday Life,* 171–76.

71. Jenkins, *Textual Poachers,* 26–27.

72. Hall, "Encoding/Decoding," 128–38. Hall's encoding/decoding formulation is similar but not identical to the notion of textual poaching. Jenkins lays out the important differences between the two in *Textual Poachers,* 34–35.

73. Melzer, *Philosophy Between the Lines,* 112.

74. Jenkins, *Convergence Culture.*

75. At the same, however, fan cultures are known to appropriate critical-cultural vernacular, viewing their own behavior through the lens of previously cloistered academic terms. For example, if one fan disagrees with another fan's commentary on a shared fan-object, the former may accuse the latter of lacking "media literacy." See "Media Literacy," *Know Your Meme,* https://knowyourmeme.com/memes/media-literacy. One such instance occurred when one Taylor Swift fan on TikTok criticized critics of fans who read Taylor Swift esoterically: "We all went to liberal universities, OK? And we have been analyzing written work and poetry for a very, very long time. In fact, most of the lesbians that anybody knew until, like, twenty years ago were writers, like Gertrude Stein and Emily Dickinson. So what you are seeing right now is the world's biggest poetry class, and this is like game time." theonlykmac, "#PSA on How," 2022. A reflexivity is at play here, such that cultural and media studies exist simultaneously as analytic tools and objects.

76. *Archeofuturist* is a neologism that combines the words *archaic* and *futuristic.* Typically this is understood as a society in which archaic or medieval values are paired with futuristic technologies.

1. I CAN SHOW YOU [A] WORLD

1. Kendrick Lamar, "Not Like Us." American rapper Lamar has built a career around embedding coded messages in his music and visuals, crafting intricate narratives that invite deep analysis from his audience. See, for instance, fan-generated analyses of the song "Not Like Us" and of his performance at the Super Bowl LIX halftime show on February 9, 2025. New Rockstars,

"NOT LIKE US Music Video Breakdown!," YouTube video, July 10, 2024, https://youtu.be/TITLwfqtUzw; Tisa Tells, "Every Hidden Easter Egg in Kendrick Lamar's Super Bowl Performance," YouTube video, February 10, 2025, https://youtu.be/oYoffn7eo8k.

2. The two hosts are not credited or identified but are likely some combination of Ryan Williams, James Poulos, and Spencer Klavan. "Leo Strauss and Queer Theory."

3. Jaffa, "Aristotle and the Higher Good."

4. Robinson, "Conservative Hero's Dark Side." It is worth noting that Bloom himself was gay and succumbed to AIDS four years later, and Jaffa's critique primarily focused on the absence of a condemnation of homosexuality in Bloom's popular work.

5. Minowitz, *Straussophobia,* 8.

6. According to the jurist Richard Posner, *Public Intellectuals,* Bloom's *Closing of the American Mind* and Camille Paglia's *Sexual Personae* are examples of "difficult academic works that mysteriously strike a chord with a broad public" (103). The same can be said of Jaffa's work *Crisis of the House Divided,* about the Lincoln–Douglas debates, which appeared decades earlier.

7. Snyder, "America Will Never Move Beyond the Culture Wars."

8. Sedgwick, *Epistemology of the Closet,* 55–58.

9. Smith, "Bronze Age Pervert's Dissertation."

10. Baker, *Fabulosa!*

11. Reilly and Saethre, "Hankie Code Revisited."

12. Mohan, "Secret Language of Lesbian Love."

13. Doty, *Making Things Perfectly Queer,* 26.

14. Child, "Why Has Hollywood Put Ben-Hur Back in the Closet?"

15. Video of this moment was posted on TikTok by user sarahinfilm, "Poker Face (Vegas Edition)." It's worth mentioning that Lady Gaga had previously revealed the bisexual meaning and origin of the song's lyrics during a private gig in London, in 2013, but they again became a viral sensation across social media in 2023, thirteen years after its debut, when some of the song's lesser-known lyrics came to light. Ramsden, "Real Meaning."

16. "Leo Strauss and Queer Theory."

17. Whitten, "Disney Accounted."

18. Hallman, "Every Company Disney Owns."

19. Alexander, "Every Entertainment Company."

20. Scarcella, "Disney Must Face Consumer Antitrust Claims"; Heinz, "It's Time to Break Up Disney."

21. Gomery and Pafort-Overduin, *Movie History,* 1–2, 137–62, 167–93.

22. Pallant, *Demystifying Disney,* 89–110. Attesting to this revival is the fact that the ten highest-grossing films of the 1990s were produced by Disney. Brayton and Singer, "Top 10 Animated Movies."

23. Riquier, "Disney Reanimated."

24. Straight-to-video sequels of these films include *The Little Mermaid II: Return to the Sea* (2000), *The Return of Jafar* (1994), and *Aladdin and the King of Thieves* (1996).

25. The trend seems to have begun in 2004 with Pixar's *The Incredibles,* two years before Disney would purchase Pixar Animation. Spelling, "No More G-Rated Films?"

26. Jennifer Lee wrote and codirected *Frozen,* but the songs were written and composed by

the husband-and-wife songwriting team of Robert Lopez and Kristen Anderson-Lopez. "Frozen Director Now Apologizes."

27. It should be noted that the basis for the film *Aladdin*, "Aladdin and the Wonderful Lamp," from the Arabic folktale compilation *One Thousand and One Nights* (often known in English as *Arabian Nights*), was not part of the original Arabic versions of the collection but was added by its French translator, Antoine Galland, after appropriating the story from the Syrian writer Hannah Diyab during Diyab's visit to Paris. Even so, the origin would still be Middle Eastern. See Horta, *Marvelous Thieves*, 8, 11.

28. Kaczynski, "Mike Pence Argued."

29. Griffin, *Tinker Belles and Evil Queens*, 48–49, 54–56, 60–62, 64–66, 69–70; Benshoff and Griffin, *Queer Images*, 74ff.

30. The first openly gay character to feature in a Disney animated film is Officer Specter in Pixar's *Onward* (2020).

31. Of the two films, *Priest* was the more controversial. It was condemned by the Catholic Church, and in the United States, Catholic organizations, including the Catholic League and the American Life League, staged a national boycott, demanded that the film be withdrawn, and called for Disney president Michael Eisner to be fired. Evans, "'Priest' Foes."

32. Decades prior to Disney's purchase of ABC in 1996, ABC released *That Certain Summer* (1972), a made-for-television drama film focusing on a father who comes out to his fourteen-year-old son.

33. Griffin, *Tinker Belles and Evil Queens*, xii.

34. Cloud, "How Gay Days Made a Home."

35. Andreas Deja is credited as the supervising animator for King Triton in *The Little Mermaid*, Gaston in *Beauty and the Beast*, Jafar in *Aladdin*, Scar in *The Lion King*, and the title character in *Hercules* (1997).

36. Thomas Schumacher is currently president of Disney Theatrical Group, the theatrical production division of the Walt Disney Company. In the *Advocate* article, Schumacher noted that his partner, Matt White, accompanied him to an annual company beach party and to long company retreats. He remarked that while some executives were uncomfortable with Schumacher bringing his partner, higher executives did not seem bothered, and in any case, they did not give him or White any trouble.

37. Provenzaon, "Lion in Summer," 64–71.

38. Griffin, *Tinker Belles and Evil Queens*, 108.

39. Project on Disney, *Inside the Mouse*, 153.

40. At the time of his hiring, Ashman was best known for his work on the theatrical musicals *Little Shop of Horrors* (1982) and *Smile* (1986).

41. Sunderland, "Beauty and the Plague."

42. Determan, "Many Merry Eras"; Hahn, *Howard*, 46:00. Films from the so-called dark ages of Disney Animation include *The Fox and the Hound* (1981), *The Black Cauldron* (1985), *The Great Mouse Detective* (1986), and *Oliver & Company* (1988).

43. Hahn, *Howard*, 61:00.

44. *The Little Mermaid* made $84,355,863 at the domestic U.S. box office, *Beauty and the Beast* earned $145,863,363 domestically and $102,939,158 internationally, and *Aladdin* made

$217,350,219 domestically and $129,126,077 internationally. These are significant sums in today's dollars, but even more so when adjusted for inflation. In comparison, *The Fox and the Hound* (1981) made only $39.9 million domestically, while *The Black Cauldron* (1985) earned $21,288,692. The success of *The Little Mermaid, Beauty and the Beast,* and *Aladdin* continued into the twenty-first-century era of streaming, each receiving a live-action adaptation on the Disney+ platform.

45. Hahn, *Howard,* 1:23:37, 1:25:11.

46. Bell et al., "Walt's in the Movies."

47. Andresen, "I Track Murder Cases"; Von Delden, "Sex, Gender, Sexuality, and Victimology," 452–56; Michalski and Nunez, "When Is 'Gay Panic' Accepted?"

48. Lawler, "Beauty and the Beast's 'Gay Moment.'"

49. Wiseman, "Disney/Pixar's 'Onward' Banned."

50. Li and Goh, "China's Censors Drop Gay Scenes"; Ellis-Petersen, "China Bans Depictions"; Sala, "'No Ghosts.'"

51. Rather, "AIDS Metaphor."

52. Erb, "Another World."

53. Griffin, *Tinker Belles and Evil Queens,* 137.

54. Cmandra, "LGBTQ Disney Princess"; Nikolas, "It's Not Just *Frozen.*"

55. Stroude, "How One Gay Man's Battle with Aids Shaped Disney's 'Beauty and the Beast.'"

56. Brew, "Don Hahn Interview."

57. Spencer, "Performing Transgender Identity."

58. Welsh, "How the Little Mermaid Found a Place."

59. JennyJaneWrites, "Alternative Lens | Disney Animation," YouTube video, November 26, 2017, https://youtu.be/uBlorZDjgRY.

60. Brown, "How Ursula and 'The Little Mermaid' Changed Disney History."

61. Landis, "'Little Mermaid' Has Been Subverting Expectations"; Nikolas, "It's Not Just *Frozen*"; Myers, "Queer Subtext in *The Little Mermaid.*"

62. Melzer, *Philosophy Between the Lines,* 302–3.

63. Strauss, *Persecution and the Art of Writing,* 36.

64. Howard Ashman apparently referred to the appearance of the film's burly villain, Gaston, as "rough trade," "a slang term for masculine-looking and straight-identifying men who engage in a bit of man-on-man action on the downlow." Stroude, "Disney's Gaston."

65. Jessica Kellgren-Fozard, "The Little Mermaid Is Queerer Than You Think," YouTube video, June 15, 2023, https://youtu.be/4PT2kjwE_aY.

66 Landis, "'Little Mermaid' Has Been Subverting Expectations."

67. Geisinger, "Little Mermaid."

68. La'Ron Readus, "*How Queer Is* The Little Mermaid?," YouTube video, May 10, 2023, https://youtu.be/7aSYzK6VaxY.

69. Martinez, "Fabulously Fiendish."

70. Brown, "How Ursula and 'The Little Mermaid' Changed Disney History."

71. Myers, "Queer Subtext in *The Little Mermaid.*"

72. Booth, *Just As Well I'm Leaving,* 226; Ageeva, "Unrequited Gay Love."

73. Geisinger, "Little Mermaid."

74. Calfa, "Dear Straight Women."

75. Readus, "How Queer Is *The Little Mermaid?*"

76. See Dowling. "Why There's So Little Left."

77. Slash fiction is a genre of fanfiction in which characters are placed in romantic (typically gay male male) pairings. Jenkins, *Textual Poachers*, 159.

78. Lynskey, "Why *Frozen*'s Let It Go Is More Than a Disney Hit."

79. St. James, "Why Elsa from *Frozen* Is a Queer Icon."

80. Tsjeng, "'Mulan' Was the Most Bisexual Cartoon Ever."

2. YOU CAN WANT WHO YOU WANT

1. Jesse Watters took over the prime-time slot left vacant at Fox News after Tucker Carlson's sudden departure in April 2023, which roughly coincided with the network's nearly $787.5 million settlement to Dominion Voting Systems. Almost any Swift-related conspiracy hook would be arbitrary. For years, Swift has been the focus of many paranoid/pronoiac speculations about the book/film *Argylle*, her relationship to Travis Kelce, and so on. Arkin, "Tucker Carlson and Fox News Part Ways."

2. Luciano, "Jesse Watters Runs Fake Story."

3. Deville, "Taylor Swift Not a Pentagon PsyOp."

4. Novak, "Why Conspiracy Theorists Think Taylor Swift Is a Pentagon 'Psy-Op.'"

5. Luciano, "Jesse Watters Runs Fake Story."

6. Laclau, *Emancipation(s)*.

7. Hallsby, "Imagine There's No President," 354–78.

8. For a recent partisan synthesis of the different faces and permutations of contemporary left-liberalism, see Slack, *War on the American Republic*.

9. Boot Staff, "14 Years Ago."

10. Pietroluongo, "Taylor Swift Debuts 10 'Speak Now' Songs."

11. The platinum certification was introduced in 1976 for the sale of 1 million units for albums and 2 million for singles, with the gold certification redefined to mean sales of five hundred thousand units for albums and 1 million for singles.

12. Smith, "World's Most Admired 2021."

13. "Apple Changes Tune on Royalties."

14. Smith, "Taylor Swift Signs a Huge New Record Deal."

15. In the first of the rerecordings, she released her 2008 album *Fearless* as *Fearless (Taylor's Version)* in 2021.

16. Rosenbaum and Michael, "Taylor Swift's Instagram."

17. Braver, "Taylor Swift Fans, and Congress, Take on Ticketmaster."

18. Doornbos, "Senators Drop Cringe-Worthy Taylor Swift Puns."

19. Winters and Jensen, "Egg Prices Increased 70%"; Balao, "Taylor Swift Fan Stunned."

20. Garfinkle-Crowell, "Taylor Swift Has Rocked My Psychiatric Practice."

21. Rutledge, "Why So Many Care."

22. Morris, "Drew a Map," 14.

23. Swifties Land, "Taylor Swift Reveals Her Easter Eggs About TS7," YouTube video, May 9, 2019, https://youtu.be/o3YGh73XQU8.

24. Yahr, "How the Search for Clues."

25. Way, "Taylor Swift's Very First Cheating Ex Bragged."

26. Brunker, "Taylor Swift Just Confirmed a Major Easter Egg."

27. Shen, "Taylor Swift's Biggest Music Easter Eggs."

28. Cohen, "Taylor Swift's *Fearless* Announcement."

29. Not all of Swift's Easter eggs are so easily decoded. At least one of her cyphers required fans to conduct amateur numerological sleuthing. Taking to Twitter, one fan, samisntokay, noted the obscure significance of the number twelve vis-à-vis Swift's age and the release of *Midnights:* "Taylor is going to be 12,000 days old when Midnights is released on Friday. 12,000 exactly. Like how a clock has 12 numbers." Describing the music video for *Reputation*'s (2017) lead single "Look What You Made Me Do," Swift claims, "Literally the whole video is just an Easter egg. It's like thousands of Easter eggs. There are some that people still haven't found. It will be decades before people find them all." Swifties Land, "Taylor Swift Reveals," 2:50.

30. Capatides, "Match These Taylor Swift Songs"; kkayden, "Jimmy Fallon Breaks Down Several Midnights Easter Eggs and Clues During the Monologue on His Show," Reddit, https://www.reddit.com/r/TaylorSwift/comments/xiyega/jimmy_fallon_breaks_down_several_midnights_easter/; Merinuk, "How Taylor Swift Turned Fandom Into a Scavenger Hunt."

31. Dyer, *Stars,* 60; Dyer, *Heavenly Bodies,* 2.

32. Schüll, *Addiction by Design.*

33. Swifties Land, "Taylor Swift Reveals Her Easter Eggs About TS7," YouTube video, May 9, 2019, https://youtu.be/o3YGh73XQU8.

34. Suskind, "New Reputation."

35. Fleras and Elliott, *Mass Media Communication,* 379; Katz and Liebes, "No More Peace!"

36. Yahr, "How the Search for Clues."

37. O'Sullivan and Carr, "Masspersonal Communication," 1161–80.

38. Martin, "World's Celebrity Billionaires"; Parker, "Taylor Swift Makes One Million Dollars, Every Day."

39. Yvonne Eadon argues that the Gaylor phenomenon represents a unique form of conspiracy theory categorized as a "closeting conspiracy theory," which she says typically involves the examination of a public figure's sexuality, the collection of relevant evidence, and the informal sharing of insights among fans on social media platforms. Eadon, "'You Could Hear a Hair Pin Drop.'"

40. Cruz, "Enduring Fervor of Gaylor Fan Theory"

41. Duberman, *Stonewall;* Carter, *Stonewall;* Daw, "Everything You Need to Know"; U.S. Congress, House, *Equality Act,* HR 5, 117th Cong., 1st sess., introduced in House March 1, 2021.

42. Holmes, "No Shade."

43. Kornhaber, "Queasy Double Message."

44. McDermott, "Taylor Swift Has Angered Many People."

45. Greenburg, "Nine of the 10."

46. Marks, "Look What We Made Taylor Swift Do."

47. The stitching and duetting features on TikTok are similar, but there are key differences between them. The most basic difference is that duets play side by side (or picture-in-picture), at the same time, while stitches are shown in sequence—first the original clip, then one's own recording, which responds to the former. Because of these and other variances, either switching or duetting may be better for a specific use case.

48. The ancient Greeks believed that in the afterlife, souls (σκιά or shades) were forced to drink from the river of Lethe, which caused them to lose all memories of their earthly lives. See also pessimism rearticulated. Packer and Stoneman, *A Feeling of Wrongness*, 171–74.

49. Keith Hdez., "Miss Americana—Creation of ME! (Clip)," YouTube video, February 6, 2020, https://youtu.be/TjLVEs9LHpw.

50. Melzer, *Philosophy Between the Lines*, 309.

51. De la Cretaz, "Postcard from Camp Gaylore."

52. Dajches and Aubrey, "Queer *Folklore*," 255–67.

53. Dajches, "We're Here."

3. WHERE WE PRODUCE ONE, WE PRODUCE ALL

1. This chapter examines QAnon from 2017 to 2021. Over that span, the conspiracy evolved, and early signs of disillusionment emerged, with some adherents faulting President Trump for not releasing files purportedly related to Jeffrey Epstein.

2. Hofstadter, *Paranoid Style*.

3. Neville-Shepard, "Paranoid Style and Subtextual Form"; Stempel et al., "Media Use"; Goodnight and Poulakos, "Conspiracy Rhetoric."

4. Jameson, "Cognitive Mapping," 356.

5. Strauss, "On a Forgotten Kind of Writing."

6. Strauss, *Persecution and the Art of Writing*, 25.

7. Bruns, *Blogs, Wikipedia, Second Life, and Beyond*.

8. We have seen similar conspiracy produsage in contexts like Sandy Hook denial, but QAnon operates on a previously unprecedented scale. We believe its fusion of conspiracy with esotericism partly explains the expanded produsage ecosystem.

9. Created as an unofficial counterpart to the Japanese imageboard 2chan, 4chan is an anonymous, English-language, image-based bulletin board website. Launched by Christopher "moot" Poole in October 2003, 4chan hosts boards dedicated to a wide range of topics, from anime and manga to video games, music, literature, television and film, technology, sports, and weapons, among others. It is a hub of Internet subculture as well as of political and hacktivist movements. 4chan has also often been the subject of media attention as a source of controversy, particularly in connection with Gamergate, an online harassment campaign primarily conducted through the use of the hashtag #gamergate, which served as a backlash to growing feminism and diversity in video games.

10. For archived messages, see https://archive.4plebs.org/pol/thread/146981635/#147012719, October 28, 2017. All in-text citations to Q posts refer to them by their original post number.

11. Barkun, *Culture of Conspiracy*.

12. M, "Plan to Save the World," 4.

13. Victor, *Satanic Panic.*

14. Zadrozny and Collins, "How Three Conspiracy Theorists Took 'Q' and Sparked Qanon."

15. "QAnon Book."

16. Cohen, "Head of NYPD Union Gives Fox News Interview"; Sen and Zadrozny, "QAnon Groups."

17. Roose, "Think QAnon Is on the Fringe?"

18. "Report: Americans Pessimistic."

19. Baudrillard, *Fatal Strategies,* 219.

20. Matheson, "Stasis in the Net of Affect," 74–75.

21. See Baudrillard, *Fatal Strategies.*

22. Coleman, *Hacker, Hoaxer, Whistleblower, Spy,* 201.

23. Shannon and Weaver, *Mathematical Theory.*

24. Pamphlet and Radix, "Changing the Narrative," 100.

25. Sandvoss, *Fans;* Duffett, *Understanding Fandom.*

26. Stanfill, *Fandom Is Ugly,* 6–8.

27. Bruns, *Blogs, Wikipedia, Second Life, and Beyond,* 215.

28. McLuhan, *Understanding Media,* 7.

29. Kuhn, *Structure of Scientific Revolutions,* 10.

30. Colley, "The Day I Knew," 32.

31. Cowley, *QAnon;* Hayes, *Calm Before the Storm;* Paine, *QAnon Phenomenon;* Knight and Geddes, *QAnon and the Great Awakening;* RedpillTheWorld, *QAnon and 1000 Years of Peace,* 2019; WWG1WGA, *QAnon;* Quincy, *Questions Answered.*

32. Grassi, *Rhetoric as Philosophy,* 20.

33. Cixous, "Fiction and Its Phantoms."

34. Rice, *Awful Archives,* 17.

35. Strauss, *Persecution and the Art of Writing,* 25.

36. Wilson, "Reddit Crackdown."

37. Landler, "What Did President Trump Mean."

38. Strauss, *Persecution and the Art of Writing,* 25.

39. Flynn, "Describing the Digital Army," 14.

40. "Speech: Donald Trump Holds a Political Rally."

41. Colley, "The Day I Knew," 31.

42. Pizzagate is the conspiracy theory that Democratic Party was running a pedophilia ring out of the basement of the restaurant Comet pizza. Colley, "The Day I Knew," 31–32, 38–39.

43. SerialBrain2, "Decoding and Deciphering Q," 76–81.

44. Colley, "The Day I Knew," 33.

45. Pamphlet and Radix, "Changing the Narrative," 102.

46. Melzer, *Philosophy Between the Lines,* 301.

47. Lacan, "Instance of the Letter in the Unconscious," 146–78.

48. Lundberg, *Lacan in Public,* 28, 52, 56, 62, 131–32.

49. Pramuk, "Trump: I Don't Give Specific ISIS Plan."

50. Tan, "Timeline of Trump's Clearly Made-Up 'Secret Plan.'"

51. Hendrix, "Trump and His Strategy of Ambiguity."

52. Rogers, "Trump on Releasing His Tax Returns." Despite Trump's refusal (or in his words, inability) to release his tax returns, in 2020 the *New York Times* obtained Trump's tax information extending over more than two decades. These documents revealed struggling properties, vast write-offs, an audit battle, and hundreds of millions in debt coming due. Buettner et al., "President's Taxes."

53. On the three fundamental levels of media analysis—individual, organizational, and institutional—see McQuail, *McQuail's Mass Communication Theory*, 278–80.

54. "Donald Trump: 'What You're Seeing and What You're Reading Is Not What's Happening.'" *BBC*, video, July 25, 2018, https://www.bbc.com/news/av/world-us-canada-44959340.

55. Baudrillard, *Simulacra and Simulation*, 6.

56. Burke, *A Rhetoric of Motives*, 21.

57. Kaplan, "Trump Has Repeatedly Amplified QAnon Twitter Accounts."

58. SpaceShot76 and RedPill78, "When Will it Become Mathematically Impossible?," 26.

59. Associated Press, "Trump Dodges QAnon Conspiracy Theory Question," YouTube video, August 14, 2020, https://youtu.be/oesJCQdkblQ.

60. NBC News, "'They Like Me Very Much': Trump Discusses the QAnon Conspiracy Theory Movement," YouTube video, August 19, 2020, https://youtu.be/GNI553Np__k.

61. Melzer, *Philosophy Between the Lines*, 251, 296, 306, 309, 311, 320–22.

62. Yack, "*Philosophy Between the Lines.*"

63. Fritze and Collins, "Trump Calls Himself 'Extremely Stable Genius'"; Healy, *Cult of the Presidency*, 3.

64. Fritze and Collins, "Trump Calls Himself 'Extremely Stable Genius.'"

65. Britzky, "Everything Trump Says He Knows 'More About Than Anybody.'"

66. Wolf, "Donald Trump Is Not Sorry"; McGann, "Let's Stop Pretending"; Swan, "Why Trump's White House Never Says Sorry"; "I'm Sorry, by Donald Trump"; Hanania, "Donald Trump Never Apologizes."

67. Garber, "The First Lie."

68. Cummings, "Trump Posts Vague, Midnight Tweet"; Estepa, "Covfefe."

69. LaFrance, "Six Hours."

70. Colley "The Day I Knew," 39.

71. Bataille, "Solar Anus."

72. Roose, "Shocked by Trump's Loss."

73. Greenspan, "QAnon Conspiracy Theory."

74. Palmer, "Why QAnon Followers Think Donald Trump Will Be Sworn Back In."

75. QAnon returned briefly after the Supreme Court's Dobb's decision but has not been nearly as active. Fletcher, "After Two Years."

76. Bridle, *New Dark Age*, 211.

4. THE ESOTERIC HERO THE DISSIDENT RIGHT NEEDS

1. Spencer et al., "Batman—Anarcho-Fascist?," 46:00. *Dissident right* is a term of unknown origin that began circulating in right-wing or far-right internet circles (blogs, tweets, podcasts, and the like) following 2017's Unite the Right rally in Charlottesville, Virginia, and the ensuing

rhetorical fallout of the terms *alt-right* or *alternative right.* Like *alt-right, dissident right* functions as a descriptive genus for any radical right-wing group that does not fit into the American conservative movement or mainstream right-wing categories. Such radical groups include civic nationalists, ethno- or white nationalists, national socialists, fascists, neoreactionaries, and others. For this discussion, which focuses on white nationalists' fan readings of the *Dark Knight* trilogy, the term *dissident right* refers to the white nationalist core of the radical right. We maintain that this metonymy of *dissident right* for *white nationalism* is justified insofar as each group of the dissident right is implicitly white nationalist (in effect, if not in principle), though to be sure, certain radical right-wing groups, like the Proud Boys, reject the white nationalist label. We avoid using the terms such as *neo-Nazi* or *white supremacist* to refer to white nationalists on the grounds that the self-identified white nationalists we deal with typically reject the supremacist label, and more importantly, do not invoke overtly supremacist arguments in their interpretations of the Batman films.

2. Hinck, *Politics for the Love of Fandom,* 6.

3. Mueller, *Politics of Fandom.*

4. Stanfill, "Introduction," 124.

5. See Johnson, "Playing with Lynching," 169–83; Serazio and Thorson, "Weaponized Patriotism," 151–68; and Blodgett, "Media in the Post #GamerGate Era," 184–200.

6. See Lewis, "'This Is What the News Won't Show You,'" 201–17; Miro, "Who Are the People?," 59–74; and Miller, "*Wolfenstein II* and MAGA as Fandom."

7. Johnson, "Walter White(ness)," 14–28; Salter, "#RelationshipGoals?," 135–50.

8. Whitbrook, "As the Punisher Skull Re-Emerges."

9. See Devarenne, "'A Language Heroically Commensurate,'" 48–54; Gavaler, "Rise and Fall of Fascist Superheroes"; Holder, "Vigilantism and Violent Forms"; and Pellitteri, "Alan Moore."

10. Southern Poverty Law Center, "Greg Johnson."

11. Jenkins, "Fan Studies."

12. Ebert, "Batman Begins."

13. For an insightful cultural history of Batman in film and on television, see Weldon, *Caped Crusade.*

14. Lieberman, "Rush Limbaugh."

15. Zuckerman, "Watching 'The Dark Knight Rises.'"

16. Klavan, "What Bush and Batman Have in Common."

17. Shapiro, "**Spoiler Alert**."

18. Nolte, "'Dark Knight Rises' Review."

19. See Bedard, "Romney's New Foe."

20. Gaba, "Bain/Bane Memes Begin!"

21. O'Hehir, "'Dark Knight Rises.'"

22. Taibbi, "Batman Shrugged," 24.

23. From the perspective of auteurship, Christopher Nolan's rendering of Batman marks a significant departure from Tim Burton's, which, beginning with *Batman* (1989) and continuing with *Batman Returns* (1992), functioned as the Hollywood gold standard for successfully adapting the superhero to film. Burton's films revel in a gothic aesthetic, framing the hero's identity through an operatic, mythic lens, with visual excess and a playfully grotesque vision of Gotham

that encodes his thematic preoccupations in stylistic extravagance. Burton's Batman does not read as a political figure per se but as an expression of a personalized artistic mythology, one indebted equally to German expressionism and outsider sensibilities. In that view, Batman's schizophrenic duality could be seen as a projection of America's fractured selfhood, just as German expressionist films like *The Cabinet of Dr. Caligari* (1920) explored the idea of the "divided self" and the double. See Terrill, "Put on a Happy Face," 319–35; and Terrill, "Spectacular Repression."

Nolan's *Dark Knight* trilogy, in contrast, operates within a mode of "realist" interpretation and could be said to invite political engagement and to be open to allegorical overdetermination. Critical readings of Nolan's Batman thus tend to emerge from political hermeneutics: He is variously construed as a neoconservative enforcer of state power (McGowan, "Exceptional Darkness of *The Dark Knight*"), a post-9/11 traumatized figure mediating America's war on terror (Feblowitz, "Hero We Create"), or a locus of ideological instability in a neoliberal crisis (Fradley, "What Do You Believe In?").

We depart from these readings by situating Batman not within auteur readings (ideological or stylistic) but within the rhetorical-esoteric frameworks of pronoia and conspiracism. The book, for instance, does not seek to relitigate whether Nolan's Batman is Bush, Bane is Marx, or Gotham is Iraq. Instead, it examines how Batman functions as an esoteric icon for the dissident right—how he is "white knighted" by communities that locate in his image a secret, encoded confirmation of their worldview. Rather than treating Batman as an ideological barometer, *Cypher Culture* tracks the reception history of Batman as an esoteric text, appropriated and read conspiratorially by contemporary media subcultures. This reading positions Batman not merely as an object of ideological contestation but also as a figure within the broader historical phenomenon of rhetorical esotericism—the coded messaging that fans and ideologues alike perceive as hidden within mass culture.

24. Hood, "Order in Action," 47.

25. Burke, *Permanence and Change*, 7.

26. Hood and Gordon, "Conservatism's League of Stupidity," 65.

27. Lynch, "*The Dark Knight Rises,*" 38; Hood and Gordon, "Conservatism's League of Stupidity," 51.

28. Broderick, "Trump Supporters and Neo-Nazis Are Using Secret Chatrooms."

29. See Michel, "Bane of the Alt-Right."

30. McLuhan, *Understanding Media.*

31. Bluestone, "Donald Trump Plagiarized Bane."

32. Hood and Gordon, "Conservatism's League of Stupidity," 65.

33. Ibid., 64.

34. Ibid., 64–65

35. Pankhurst, "Caesar Without Gods," 99.

36. Jorjani, "Gotham Guardian."

37. Hood and Gordon, "Conservatism's League of Stupidity," 60.

38. Jorjani, "Gotham Guardian," 76.

39. Hood and Gordon, "Conservatism's League of Stupidity," 64.

40. Spencer et al., "Batman—Anarcho-Fascist?," 46:56.

41. Child, "Christopher Nolan Explains Inception's Ending."

42. Hunt, "Pepe the Frog Creator Kills Off Internet Meme."

43. Lynch, "*Batman Begins,*" 14; Jorjani, "Gotham Guardian," 74. For representative texts of the authors mentioned in Spencer et al., "Batman—Anarcho-Fascist?," see Guénon, *Crisis of the Modern World;* and Evola, *Revolt Against the Modern World.*

44. Thrash, "15 Shocking Things."

45. Some fans have even pointed to connections between Nolan's earlier low-budget films and the *Dark Knight* trilogy. For example, Batman logos are visible in both *Following* (1998) and *Memento* (2000). While it is unlikely that Nolan, still a largely unknown director, had the prescience to determine that he would direct a major comic book movie, there is a connection that seems deliberate. Thomas Lennon, best known for his comedic roles in *Reno 911* and *I Love You, Man,* had a small, serious role as a doctor in Nolan's film *Memento.* Lennon says that Nolan asked for him specifically to fill another small doctor role in *The Dark Knight Rises,* leading him to believe that both doctors are the same character. Rosen, "'Dark Knight Rises.'"

46. Ray, "The Alt Knight," 152.

47. Windsor, "Dark Knight Without a King," 111.

48. "The will to power" is a central concept in the philosophy of Friedrich Nietzsche. It describes what Nietzsche, following Arthur Schopenhauer, may have believed to be an irrational force (and main driving force), found in all individuals, that can be channeled toward different ends. Despite its importance to Nietzsche's philosophy, Nietzsche never systematically defined the concept, categorizing it at various points as a psychological, biological, or metaphysical principle. For this reason, the will to power is one of Nietzsche's most misunderstood ideas. The psychological interpretation, which is probably the one invoked by Ra's al Ghul, traces to Nietzsche's middle work, *Thus Spoke Zarathustra,* and can be summarized broadly as self-determination or heroic self-surpassing, that is, as actualizing one's will onto one's self or surroundings. See Nietzsche, *Thus Spoke Zarathustra,* 42–44, 88–90, 109–12.

49. Nietzsche, *Twilight of the Idols,* 157. See also Lynch, "*Batman Begins,*" 14.

50. Johnson, "Superheroes, Sovereignty, and the Deep State."

51. Schmitt, *Political Theology,* 5–15.

52. Johnson, "Superheroes, Sovereignty, and the Deep State," 94.

53. Jorjani, "Gotham Guardian," 74.

54. Jorjani, "Gotham Guardian," 74, 76–77, 81–82.

55. De Certeau, *Practice of Everyday Life,* 31ff.

56. Jenkins, *Textual Poachers* 26, 46.

57. Hall, "Encoding/Decoding."

58. Jenkins, *Textual Poachers,* 86. See also Sharratt, "Politics of the Popular?"

59. Strauss, *Persecution and the Art of Writing* 25.

60. Strauss, "Plato's *Gorgias,*" 19.

61. Last, "Case for Empire."

5. ALL THAT GLITTERS IS GOLD

1. Bronze Age Pervert, *Bronze Age Mindset.*

2. Raspail, "What Their Chosen Reading Says."

3. Zerofsky, "How the Claremont Institute Became a Nerve Center."

4. Paleoconservatives have traditional social values but also reject globalism, integration into international markets, and foreign intervention.

5. Schreckinger, "Alt-Right Manifesto."

6. Anton, "Are the Kids Al(t) Right?" Michael Anton was deputy assistant to the president for strategic communications on the National Security Council under Trump. Culturally, however, Anton is probably best known as the author of the influential essay "The Flight 93 Election." Published pseudonymously in the *Claremont Review of Books*, the essay compared the prospect of conservative voters allowing Hillary Clinton to win the election with passengers not charging the cockpit of the United Airlines aircraft hijacked by Al-Qaeda terrorists during the 9/11 attacks. It was one of the first endorsements of Trump during the 2016 presidential campaign. See Publius Decius Mus, "Flight 93 Election."

7. Gray, "How Bronze Age Pervert Built an Online Following."

8. Cantor, "Leo Strauss and Contemporary Hermeneutics," 277.

9. Bronze Age Pervert, *Bronze Age Mindset*, 32.

10. Jenkins, *Textual Poachers*, 86. See also de Certeau, *Practice of Everyday Life*, 171–75; and Sharratt, "Politics of the Popular?"

11. Martin, "Dante's Masterpiece." In 2020, Martin's interpretive claim became a meme (though here, too, it is virtually impossible to know whether her essay "caused" the meme) and became a point of contention on social media and among online fan fiction communities. Interestingly enough, the two most common arguments against the fanfic interpretation are not substantive but circumstantial: The term *fanfic*, or even the concept, did not exist prior to the twentieth century, and copyright laws did not exist in the fourteenth century. See, for instance, PluralCohomology's Reddit post, "Dante's Divine Comedy is fanfiction."

12. Although the present study is not sociological, we find it probable that the tendency to ignore or even dismiss the possible mirroring of amateurs by professionals is a function of what Pierre Bourdieu calls "distinction": the ways in which individuals and social groups use cultural preferences and consumption patterns to distinguish themselves from others and assert their social status. Bourdieu argues that people's tastes and preferences are not merely personal choices but are deeply influenced by their social position, education, and upbringing.

13. Bateson, *Mind and Nature*, 99.

14. Burke, *Rhetoric of Motives*, 23.

15. See Atlas, "The Nation: Leo-Cons"; Hersh, "Selective Intelligence"; Curtis, *Power of Nightmares;* and Horton, "Leo Strauss and the Iraq War."

16. Strauss, "Exoteric Teaching," 275. See also Henrie, "Straussianism."

17. Despite Strauss's claim that this mode of thought was characteristic of ancient philosophy, including if not especially ancient Greek philosophy. Aristotle argues in *Categories* that universals (like justice, existence, and the good) are incorporeal and universal, existing only where they are instantiated, that is, only in particular things. See Klima, "Medieval Problem of Universals."

18. De Mauriac, "Alexander the Great" 106; Knoche, "Of One Mind."

19. See Paley and Staub, "Jewish Philosophy," 215.

20. Plato, *Republic*, 414b–515d. See also Hersh, "Selective Intelligence."

21. See Strauss, *City and Man*, 10–11.

22. This quandary of interpretation is different from Roland Barthes's "death of the author" argument, according to which the meaning of a text is determined not by an author's intention but rather by the reader's. In the case of Strauss and of esoteric hermeneutics in general, a text's polysemy or ambiguity is a function of the author's intentional design. Part of that intent is that a text's "true readers," and only its true readers, will be able to parse the text's multiple layers of meaning to discover its true meaning hidden between the lines. That is, of course, not to say that Barthes's argument does not apply, only that readers of Strauss are confronted with an additional hermeneutic difficulty. See Barthes, "Death of the Author," 142–48.

23. "Harvey Mansfield IV."

24. Johnson, "Review of *Shakespeare and the Good Life*," 933.

25. Gottfried, *Strauss and the Conservative Movement*, 99.

26. Bakhtin, "Discourse and the Novel," 291. On "theoretism," see Morson and Emerson, *Mikhail Bakhtin*, 49–50.

27. Straussians in the know will reference a third intellectual division, the Midwest Straussians. These Straussians are more open to embracing modernity than either their East Coast or West Coast counterparts. See Zuckert and Zuckert, *Truth About Leo Strauss*, 22.

28. Bottum, "Warren Report."

29. Bloom and Jaffa, *Shakespeare's Politics*.

30. See O'Neill, "Straussian Constitutional History," 459–78.

31. Perlstein, *Before the Storm*, 390–91.

32. Publius Decius Mus, "Flight 93 Election."

33. "Harvey Mansfield IV."

34. Lilla, *Shipwrecked Mind*, 60.

35. Rice, "Saving Strauss."

36. Unlike the world of 1990s hip-hop, the east–west division among Straussians is not (or is no longer) strictly geographic. For instance, the Department of Political Science at the University of Notre Dame is probably East Coast in its orientation, while the Van Andel Graduate School of Statesmanship at Hillsdale College leans to the West. Both programs, however, are in the Midwest, in Indiana and Michigan, respectively, and about two hours' driving distance away from each other.

37. See Warren, "Conservative Generation Gap."

38. "Harvey Mansfield IV."

39. Adam Curtis Documentaries, *The Power of Nightmares*, part 1, "Baby It's Cold Outside," YouTube video, April 7, 2024, 8:58–9:11, https://youtu.be/jxBbw13Y3Gc.

40. Strauss, *Persecution and the Art of Writing*, 25.

41. Adam Curtis Documentaries, *Power of Nightmares*, 10:05–10:24.

42. See, for instance, Cantor, *Gilligan Unbound;* and Cantor, *Pop Culture and the Dark Side of the American Dream*.

43. "Harvey Mansfield IV."

44. See, for instance, Pearson, *Print the Legend;* Pippin, *Hollywood Westerns and American Myth;* McMaken, *Commie Cowboys;* Pippin, *Fatalism in American Film Noir;* and Pippin, *Philosophical Hitchcock*. This sample is by no means comprehensive and does not consider the

many one-off book chapters, essays, and reviews that could qualify as Straussian approaches to the study of film and television.

45. See, for instance, Bloom and Jaffa, *Shakespeare's Politics;* White, *Copp'd Hills Towards Heaven;* Platt, *Rome and Romans According to Shakespeare;* Cantor, *Shakespeare: Hamlet;* Aluius and Sullivan, *Shakespeare's Political Pageant;* Lowenthal, *Shakespeare and the Good Life;* Alvis and West, *Shakespeare as Political Thinker;* Craig, *Of Philosophers and Kings;* McGrail, *Tyranny in Shakespeare;* Spiekerman, *Shakespeare's Political Realism;* Smith and Curtright, *Shakespeare's Last Plays;* Dobski and Gish, *Souls with Longing;* Burns, *Shakespeare's Political Wisdom;* Dobski and Gish, *Shakespeare and the Body Politic;* Altschuler and Genovese, *Shakespeare and Politics;* Craig, *Philosopher's English King;* Cantor, *Shakespeare's Roman Trilogy;* and Habib and Herbert, *Soul of Statesmanship.*

46. Strauss and Cropsey, *History of Political Philosophy.* See also Masugi, "Straussian Civil Wars."

47. Bloom and Jaffa, *Shakespeare's Politics,* 4. In applying historical circumstance as evidence (namely, Shakespeare wrote before the invention of the modern research university; therefore, Shakespearean analysis is not the exclusive preserve of English departments), Bloom is inverting the Reddit posters' argument that Dante's *Divine Comedy* could not be considered fanfic because copyright laws and the concept of fan fiction are modern inventions. German media theory, however, provides the basis for a compelling counterargument to Bloom: "Cultural techniques—such as writing, reading, painting, counting, making music—are always older than the concepts that are generated from them." Winthrop-Young, "Cultural Techniques," 11. To be sure, the skills and technique of literary analysis existed before the complex actor network that makes up today's university. And while that practice may have changed in many important ways since the university's formation, its existence does not do away with the media-cultural fact that the practice, tools, and development of literary analysis in part helped give rise to modern English departments. This would mean that from an academic standpoint—the credentials Bloom is most certainly invoking—scholars trained in literary theory and criticism, generally speaking, would be the types of scholars best suited to the task of literary analysis.

48. Bloom and Jaffa, *Shakespeare's Politics,* 2, 4.

49. Lowenthal, *Shakespeare and the Good Life,* viii–ix.

50. Strauss, "Plato's *Gorgias,*" 19.

51. In Bloom and Jaffa, *Shakespeare's Politics,* 10.

52. Strauss, *Persecution and the Art of Writing,* 159. An exception that proves the rule is Minowitz, *Straussophobia;* see, for instance, 224.

53. Dobski and Gish, *Shakespeare and the Body Politic,* x.

54. In Bloom and Jaffa, *Shakespeare's Politics,* 43.

55. Lowenthal, *Shakespeare and the Good Life,* vii, x.

56. Burns, *Shakespeare's Political Wisdom,* 217.

57. Jaffa, "Chastity as a Political Principle," 42.

58. Trafton, "Shakespeare's *Henry IV,*" 104–6.

59. See de Alvarez, "Nature and the City," 181; Cantor, "Prospero's Republic," 235, 242.

60. Jaffa, "Chastity as a Political Principle," 57, 54.

61. Tovey, "Golden Casket," 85. One could easily imagine these kinds of modern ideas (or

premodern, if you believe the Straussians) running afoul of the ruling social forces of Shakespeare's time, whether the monarchy or the Anglican Church. John Locke's teachings were in tension with the power of the monarchy, and as in many European states, Christianity provided a backbone for British society. The threat of violence from the hegemonic forces and the socially disruptive nature of these esoteric readings, both largely unexplored by the Straussians, would justify Shakespeare writing in code.

62. Melzer, *Philosophy Between the Lines,* xiv.

63. A host of scholarship exists on how fan communities police their members, limit membership, and create hierarchies by creating rigid definitions of what it means to be a "good" fan. See, for instance, Hadas, "Web Planet"; Bennet, "Discourses of Order and Rationality," 214–27; and Geraghty, "It's Not All About the Music." A significant body of work also focuses on how fan communities police membership based on identity and one's feelings about making media more diverse. For example, see Busse, "Geek Hierarchies," 73–91; Condis, "No Homosexuals in *Star Wars?*," 198–212; Yodovich, "'Little Costumed Girl at a Sci-Fi Convention'"; and Rouse et al., "Making Fandom Great Again."

64. Foucault, "Orders of Discourse," 12.

65. Ibid., 8.

66. Ibid., 16, quoting Georges Canguilhem.

67. Ibid., 8–10, 15–16, 18.

68. See Broedel, "Rise of Universities."

69. See, for instance, Frye, *Great Code;* and Wilson, *Axel's Castle.*

70. Luhmann, *Reality of the Mass Media,* 13–14, 19–20, 66.

71. On the distinction between literary and primary oral cultures, see Ong, *Orality and Literacy,* 36–76.

72. Benjamin, "Work of Art," 106.

73. Foucault, "Orders of Discourse," 18.

74. Burke, *Philosophy of Literary Form,* 110–11.

75. Lowenthal, *Shakespeare and the Good Life,* xi.

76. The case could be made that Straussians do inflect their esoteric criticism of Shakespeare with an intertextual (but not paratextual) quality. It is very important to them, for instance, if Hamlet slightly paraphrases chapter 5 of Epictetus's *Enchiridion* when he declaims, "There is nothing either good or bad, but thinking makes it so" (Shakespeare, *Hamlet,* act 2, scene 2)—even though Epictetus is not included in the unofficial Straussian canon of first-rate minds. Nevertheless, it would be difficult to classify any instance of Straussian criticism as intertextual when the Straussian "fellowship of discourse" does not acknowledge intertextuality itself as a discourse, that is, as a dynamic set of ideas that is constantly challenged internally and externally; and when Straussian "intertextuality" does not generate new statements about the object but merely rediscovers in Shakespeare, and reiterates his association with, the Straussian-approved canon.

77. Lowenthal, *Shakespeare and the Good Life,* 68, note 1. See also Cantor, "Prospero's Republic."

78. Foucault, "Orders of Discourse," 18.

79. Minowitz, *Straussophobia,* 164.

80. "Harvey Mansfield IV."

81. Strauss, *Persecution and the Art of Writing*, 55.

82. Melzer, *Philosophy Between the Lines*, 7.

83. This chapter will leave unexplored the very real question of how much other academic disciplines have in common with less insular fan communities.

84. Elseworlds serves as the publication imprint for American comic books created by DC Comics, featuring narratives that occur outside the established canon of the DC Universe. The stories under the Elseworlds label are situated in alternate realities that diverge from the continuity of DC's standard comics. The trademark for the name Elseworlds was registered in 1989, coinciding with the release of the inaugural Elseworlds publication.

CONCLUSION

1. To be fair, conclusions are not the place you want to hide your esoteric messages. Cicero counsels rhetoricians to put the message they want to highlight at the beginning and the end of their speech; however, if they seek a level of obscurity, he advises it is best to hide their message in the middle. See Melzer, *Philosophy Between the Lines*, 321–22.

2. Ibid., xii; also 311.

3. See Barthes, "Death of the Author," 142–48. Two years later, in 1969, Michel Foucault delivered a lecture responding to and elaborating upon Barthes's already influential essay, thereby cementing and broadening the scope of the latter's "death of the author" thesis. See Foucault, "What Is an Author?" 205–22.

4. Richard Weaver's notion of rhetoric as a carrier of tendency reinforces this perspective. According to Weaver, language is identical to rhetoric, and rhetoric is sermonic—always promoting values and reflecting choices among competing goods. Rhetoric, in this sense, is never neutral but is inherently purposeful, exerting a form of compulsion that steers interpretation in particular directions. In the case of esoteric readings, the sermonic quality of rhetoric suggests that texts implicitly guide interpretation, even when authors disavow intent. Every utterance, every expression "proceeds from the will to alter something." This point is also reinforced by the philosophical concept of the hermeneutic circle—the idea that meaning does not reside solely in a "text" or "reader" but emerges through an iterative process of interaction, whereby apprehension is continuously shaped by the interpreter's prior knowledge and expectations, which forms a feedback loop that refines and reconfigures meaning with each engagement. With respect to esotericism, this dynamic process ensures that esoteric readings are not passively uncovered but are actively constructed as part of a broader hermeneutic engagement. Weaver, "Language Is Sermonic," 222. On the concept of the hermeneutic circle, see Gadamer, *Truth and Method*, 265–307.

5. For cultural studies approaches to *True Detective* season 1 (and *Rick and Morty*), readers could do a lot worse than consulting our previous book: Packer and Stoneman, *Feeling of Wrongness*.

6. See Melley, "Conspiracy in American Narrative." Despite *The X-Files*'s unofficial status as the ur-conspiracy theory television series, Michael Butter argues that "in the twenty-first century, conspiracy theories have figured more prominently than ever in television shows." By his count, there are dozens of such shows, including *Stranger Things* (2016–2025), *Designated Survivor* (2016–2019), and *Bodyguard* (2018). Butter, "Conspiracy Theory," 466.

7. Pynchon, *Gravity's Rainbow,* 703.

8. DeLillo, *Underworld,* 827.

9. See Butter, *Nature of Conspiracy Theory;* Stano, "Internet and the Spread of Conspiracy Content," 483–96; and Birchall and Knight, *Time of COVID-19.*

10. McLuhan, *Understanding Media;* Ong, *Orality and Literacy.*

11. The *Oxford English Dictionary,* for instance, defines *esoteric* as "Of philosophical doctrines, treatises, modes of speech, etc.: Designed for, or appropriate to, an inner circle of advanced or privileged disciples; communicated to, or intelligible by, the initiated exclusively."

12. Plato, *Gorgias,* 465a, 462c.

BIBLIOGRAPHY

Alamariu, Costin. *Selective Breeding and the Birth of Philosophy.* Self-published, 2023.

Alexander, Cristina. "Every Entertainment Company Disney Owns in 2023." *IGN,* September 25, 2023.

Allen, Karma. "Hallmark Channel Apologizes for Pulling Gay-Themed Wedding Ad." *ABC News,* December 15, 2019.

Altschuler, Bruce E., and Michael A. Genovese, eds. *Shakespeare and Politics: What a Sixteenth-Century Playwright Can Tell Us About Twenty-First-Century Politics.* Paradigm, 2014.

Aluius, Joseph, and Vickie Sullivan, eds. *Shakespeare's Political Pageant.* Rowman & Littlefield, 1996.

Alvis, John E., and Thomas G. West, eds. *Shakespeare as Political Thinker.* 2nd ed. ISI Books, 2000.

Andersen, Hans Christian. "The Little Mermaid." In *Fairy Tales,* translated by Tiina Nunnally. Penguin, 2006.

Andresen, W. Carsten. "I Track Murder Cases That Use the 'Gay Panic Defense,' a Controversial Practice Banned in 9 States." *The Conversation,* January 29, 2020.

Anton, Michael. "Are the Kids Al(t) Right?" *Claremont Review of Books,* Summer 2019.

"Apple Changes Tune on Royalties After Taylor Swift Complains." Associated Press, June 22, 2015.

Aristotle. "Categories." In *The Complete Works of Aristotle,* translated by J. L. Ackrill. 2 vols. Princeton University Press, 2014.

Arkin, Daniel. "Tucker Carlson and Fox News Part Ways." *NBC News* [online], April 25, 2023.

Ashford, J. Wesson, and Sue Binkley Tatem. "Michelangelo's Presentations in the Sistine Chapel: Brain Evolution and the Relationship of the Brain to Specific Cognitive Functions." *Neuroscientist* 30, no. 5 (2024): 520–24.

Atlas, James. "The Nation: Leo-Cons; A Classicist's Legacy: New Empire Builders." *New York Times,* May 4, 2003.

Baker, Paul. *Fabulosa! The Story of Polari, Britain's Secret Gay Language.* Reaktion Books, 2019.

Bakhtin, Mikhail. "Discourse and the Novel." In *The Dialogic Imagination: Four Essays,* edited by Michael Holquist, translated by Caryl Emerson and Michael Holquist. University of Texas Press, 1981.

Balao, Neia. "Taylor Swift Fans Stunned to Learn Swifties May Have Lowered Price of Eggs in the U.S." *Yahoo! Life,* February 17, 2023.

Banias, M. J. "QAnon and UFO Conspiracies Are Merging." *Vice,* October 29, 2019.

Barber, Malcolm. "Lepers, Jews and Moslems: The Plot to Overthrow Christendom in 1321." *History* 66, no. 216 (1981): 1–17.

———. *The Trial of the Templars.* 2nd ed. Cambridge University Press, 2006.

Barker, Tyson. "Germany Is Losing the Fight Against QAnon." *Foreign Policy,* September 2, 2020.

Barkun, Michael. *A Culture of Conspiracy: Apocalyptic Visions in Contemporary America.* University of California Press, 2003.

Barsam, Richard, and Dave Monahan. *Looking at Movies.* 6th ed. W. W. Norton, 2018.

Barthes, Roland. "The Death of the Author." In *Image-Music-Text,* translated by Stephen Heath. Hill and Wang, 1977.

Bartlett, Jamie, and Carl Miller. *The Power of Unreason.* Demos, 2010.

Bataille, Georges. *The Accursed Share.* Vol. 1: *Consumption.* Translated by Robert Hurley. Zone Books, 1988.

———. "Solar Anus." In *Visions of Excess: Selected Writings, 1927–1939,* edited by Allan Stoekl. University of Minnesota Press.

Bateson, Gregory. *Mind and Nature: A Necessary Unity.* E. P. Dutton, 1979.

Baudrillard, Jean. *Fatal Strategies.* Translated by Philip Beitchman and W. G. J. Niesluchowski. Semiotext(e), 2008.

———. *Simulacra and Simulations.* Translated by Sheila Faria Glaser. University of Michigan Press, 1994.

Beckman, Frida. *The Paranoid Chronotope: Power, Truth, Identity.* Stanford University Press, 2022.

Bedard, Paul. "Romney's New Foe: Batman's 'Bane.'" *Washington Examiner,* July 16, 2012.

Bell, Elizabeth, Lynda Haas, and Laura Sells, eds. "Walt's in the Movies." In *From Mouse to Mermaid: The Politics of Film, Gender, and Culture.* Indiana University Press, 1995.

Benjamin, Walter. 2006. "The Work of Art in the Age of Its Technological Reproducibility: Second Version." In *Walter Benjamin: Selected Writings,* vol. 3, *1935–1938,* edited by Howard Eiland and Michael W Jennings, translated by Edmund Jephcott et al. Belknap Press of Harvard University Press.

Bennet, Lucy. "Discourses of Order and Rationality: Drooling R.E.M. Fans as 'Matter out of Place.'" *Continuum* 27, no. 2 (2013): 214–27.

Bennett, Dashiell. "Newtown Conspiracy Theories, Debunked." *Atlantic,* December 18, 2013.

Benshoff, Harry M., and Sean Griffin. *Queer Images: A History of Gay and Lesbian Film in America.* Rowman & Littlefield, 2006.

Berger, J. M. *Extremism.* MIT Press, 2018.

Best, Stephen, and Sharon Marcus. "Surface Reading: An Introduction." *Representations* 108, no. 1 (2009): 1–21.

Bierwiaczonek, Kinga, Sam Fluit, Tilmann von Soest, Matthew J. Hornsey, and Jonas R. Kunst. "Loneliness Trajectories Over Three Decades Are Associated with Conspiracist Worldviews in Midlife. *Nature Communications* 15, no. 3629 (2024).

Birchall, Clare. *Knowledge Goes Pop: From Conspiracy Theory to Gossip.* Berg, 2006.

Birchall, Clare, and Peter Knight. *Conspiracy Theories in the Time of COVID-19.* Routledge, 2023.

Blodgett, Bridget M. "Media in the Post #GamerGate Era: Coverage of Reactionary Fan Anger and the Terrorism of the Privileged." *Television & New Media* 21, no. 2 (2020): 184–200.

Bloom, Allan. *The Closing of the American Mind: How Higher Education Has Failed Democracy and Impoverished the Souls of Today's Students.* 25th anniversary ed. Simon and Schuster, 2012.

———. "*Richard II.*" In Alvis and West, *Shakespeare as Political Thinker.*

Bloom, Alan, and Harry V. Jaffa. *Shakespeare's Politics.* University of Chicago Press, 1964.

Bluestone, Gabrielle. "Donald Trump Plagiarized Bane in His Inaugural Speech." *Jezebel,* January 20, 2017.

Bollinger, Alex. "Delta Censors Gay Scenes from In-Flight Movies." *LGBTQ Nation,* October 31, 2019.

Boone, John. "'Joker' Tops 'The Dark Knight' as the Most Oscar-Nominated Superhero Film of All Time." *ET,* January 13, 2020.

Boot Staff. "14 Years Ago: Taylor Swift Sets a Record with Grammy's Album of the Year Win." *The Boot,* January 31, 2024, https://theboot.com/taylor-swift-youngest-winner-grammy-awards-album-of-the-year/

Booth, Michael. *Just as Well I'm Leaving: To the Orient with Hans Christian Andersen.* Vintage, 2005.

Booth, Paul, and Rebecca Williams, eds. "Introduction." In *A Fan Studies Primer: Method, Research, Ethics.* University of Iowa Press, 2021.

Bottum, Joseph. "The Warren Report." *Washington Examiner,* January 21, 2003.

Bourdieu, Pierre. *Distinction: A Social Critique of the Judgement of Taste.* Translated by Richard Nice. Harvard University Press, 1984.

Bratich, Jack Z. *Conspiracy Panics: Political Rationality and Popular Culture.* State University of New York Press, 2008.

Braver, Rita. "Taylor Swift Fans, and Congress, Take On Ticketmaster." *CBS News* [online], February 5, 2023.

Brayton, Emily, and Jesse Singer. "Top 10 Animated Movies of Each Year (1990–1999)." *WatchMojo,* December 22, 2023.

Brew, Simon. "Don Hahn Interview: Beauty and the Beast, Howard Ashman, The Lion King, South Park and Frankenweenie." *Den of Geek,* November 3, 2010.

Bridle, James. *New Dark Age: Technology and the End of the Future.* Verso, 2018.

Britzky, Haley. "Everything Trump Says He Knows 'More About Than Anybody.'" *Axios,* January 5, 2019.

Broderick, Ryan. "Trump Supporters and Neo-Nazis Are Using Secret Chatrooms to Harass Shia LaBeouf." *BuzzFeed News,* January 25, 2017.

Broedel, Hans Peter. "The Rise of Universities and the Discovery of Aristotle." In *History of Applied Science and Technology,* edited by Danielle Skjelver, David Arnold, Hans Peter Broedel, Sharon Bailey Glasco, Bonnie Kim, and Sheryl Dahm Broedel. Digital Press at the University of North Dakota, 2021.

Bronze Age Pervert [pseud.]. *Bronze Age Mindset.* Self-published, 2018.

Brotherton, Rob. *Suspicious Minds: Why We Believe Conspiracy Theories.* Bloomsbury Sigma, 2015.

Brown, Tracy. "How Ursula and 'The Little Mermaid' Changed Disney History—in More Ways Than One." *Los Angeles Times* [online], August 2, 2022.

Bruner, Raisa. "Here's Why Taylor Swift Is Re-Releasing Her Old Albums." *Time* [online], March 25, 2021.

Brunker, Alicia. "Taylor Swift Just Confirmed a Major Easter Egg in 'Folklore.'" *InStyle,* August 9, 2020.

Bruns, Axel. *Blogs, Wikipedia, Second Life, and Beyond: From Production to Produsage.* Peter Lang, 2008.

Buettner, Russ, Susanne Craig, and Mike McIntire. "The President's Taxes: Long-Concealed Records Show Trump's Chronic Losses and Years of Tax Avoidance." *New York Times* [online], September 27, 2020.

Burke, Kenneth. *Permanence and Change: An Anatomy of Purpose.* 3rd ed. University of California Press, 1984.

———. *The Philosophy of Literary Form.* University of California Press, 1974.

———. *A Rhetoric of Motives.* University of California Press, 1969.

Burns, Timothy W. *Shakespeare's Political Wisdom.* Palgrave Macmillan, 2013.

Busse, Kristina. "Geek Hierarchies, Boundary Policing, and the Gendering of the Good Fan." *Participations* 10, no. 1 (2013): 73–91.

Butter, Michael. "Conspiracy Theories in American History." In Butter and Knight, *Routledge Handbook of Conspiracy Theories.*

———. "Conspiracy Theory in Films and Television Shows." In Butter and Knight, *Routledge Handbook of Conspiracy Theories.*

———. *The Nature of Conspiracy Theory.* Translated by Sharon Howe. Polity Press, 2020.

———. *Plots, Designs, and Schemes: American Conspiracy Theories from the Puritans to the Present.* de Gruyter, 2014.
Butter, Michael, and Peter Knight. "Conspiracy Theory in Historical, Cultural and Literary Studies." In Butter and Knight, *Routledge Handbook of Conspiracy Theories.*
———, eds. *Routledge Handbook of Conspiracy Theories.* Routledge, 2020.
Calfa, Chris. "Dear Straight Women: The Little Mermaid Is Not About You, or *The Little Mermaid* and the Queer Experience." *Medium,* May 10, 2023.
Cantor, Paul A. *Gilligan Unbound: Pop Culture in the Age of Globalization.* Rowman & Littlefield, 2001.
———. "Leo Strauss and Contemporary Hermeneutics." In *Leo Strauss's Thought: Toward a Critical Engagement,* edited by Alan Udoff. Lynne Rienner, 1991.
———. *Pop Culture and the Dark Side of the American Dream: Con Men, Gangsters, Drug Lords, and Zombies.* University Press of Kentucky, 2019.
———. "Prospero's Republic: The Politics of Shakespeare's *The Tempest.*" In Alvis and West, *Shakespeare as Political Thinker.*
———. *Shakespeare: Hamlet.* Cambridge University Press, 1989.
———. *Shakespeare's Roman Trilogy: The Twilight of the Ancient World.* University of Chicago Press, 2017.
Capatides, Christina. "Match These Taylor Swift Songs to Her Ex-Boyfriends." *CBS News* [online], September 7, 2016.
Carrier, Richard. "The Prospect of a Christian Interpolation in Tacitus, *Annals* 15.44." *Vigiliae Christianne* 68, no. 3 (2014): 264–83.
Carter, David. *Stonewall: The Riots That Sparked the Gay Revolution.* St. Martin's Griffin, 2009.
Chatman, Seymour. *Story and Discourse: Narrative Structure in Fiction and Film.* Cornell University Press, 1978.
Child, Ben. "Christopher Nolan Explains Inception's Ending: 'I Want You to Chase Your Reality.'" *Guardian* [online], June 5, 2015.
———. "Why Has Hollywood Put Ben-Hur Back in the Closet?" *Guardian* [online], August 17, 2016.
Chitwood, Adam. "Worldwide Box Office Records: *The Dark Knight Rises* Passes $1 Billion While *The Avengers* Hits $1.5 Billion." *Collider,* September 2, 2012.
Cixous, Hélène. "Fiction and Its Phantoms: A Reading of Freud's *Das Unheimliche* (The 'Uncanny')." *New Literary History* 7, no. 3 (1976): 525–48.
Click, Melissa A. *Anti-Fandom: Dislike and Hate in the Digital Age.* New York University Press, 2019.
Cloud, John. "How Gay Days Made a Home at Disney World." *Time* [online], June 21, 2010.
Cmandra. "Is the World Ready for an LGBTQ Disney Princess (or Prince)?" *Artifice,* December 25, 2015.

Coady, David. "Conspiracy Theory as Heresy." *Educational Philosophy and Theory* 55, no. 7 (2021): 756–59.

Coale, Samuel Chase. *Paradigms of Paranoia: The Culture of Conspiracy in Contemporary American Fiction.* University of Alabama Press, 2005.

Cohen, Jess. "Taylor Swift's *Fearless* Announcement Included a Major Easter Egg." *E! News,* February 12, 2021.

Cohen, Marshall. "Head of NYPD Union Gives Fox News Interview with QAnon Mug in Background." *CNN* [online], July 17, 2020.

Coleman, Gabriella. *Hacker, Hoaxer, Whistleblower, Spy: The Many Faces of Anonymous.* Verso, 2014.

Colley, Lori. "The Day I Knew Q Wasn't a Hoax." In WWG1WGA, *QAnon.*

Condis, Megan. "No Homosexuals in *Star Wars?* BioWare, 'Gamer' Identity, and the Politics of Privilege in a Convergence Culture." *Convergence: The International Journal of Research into New Media Technologies* 21, no. 2 (2015): 198–212.

Conger, Cristen. "Unladies Room: The Little Feminist Mermaid." *Unladylike,* July 1, 2023.Podcast.

Couch, Robbie. "Amid Backlash, Target Still Launched Its Annual LGBTQ Pride Line. Hell Yeah." *Upworthy,* May 11, 2017.

Cowley, Frank R. *QAnon: An Understanding of Conspiracy Theories and the Great Awakening. The Battle for Our Souls and the Earth.* Self-published, 2020.

Cowsill, Alan, Alex Irvine, Steve Korte, Matt Manning, Win Wiacek, and Sven Wilson. *The DC Comics Encyclopedia: The Definitive Guide to the Characters of the DC Universe.* DK Publishing, 2016.

Craig, Leon Harold. *Of Philosophers and Kings: Political Philosophy in Shakespeare's Macbeth and King Lear.* University of Toronto Press, 2001.

———. *The Philosopher's English King: Shakespeare's "Henriad" as Political Philosophy.* University of Rochester Press, 2015.

Cruz, Caitlin. "The Enduring Fervor of Gaylor Fan Theory." *Jezebel,* March 25, 2022.

Cubitt, Geoffrey. "Conspiracy Myths and Conspiracy Theories." *Journal of the Anthropological Society of Oxford* 20, no. 1 (1989): 12–26.

Cummings, William. "Trump Posts Vague, Midnight Tweet About 'Negative Press Covfefe.'" *USA Today* [online], May 31, 2017.

Curtis, Adam, dir. *The Power of Nightmares: The Rise of the Politics of Fear.* 3 parts. BBC, 2004.

Dajches, Leah. "We're Here, We're Queer, and We're Stressed: Using the Minority Stress Model to Explore the Impact of Queer Readings on Mental Health Outcomes Among Sexual Minority Youth." PhD diss., University of Arizona, 2022.

Dajches, Leah, and Jennifer Stevens Aubrey. "Queer *Folklore:* Examining the Influence of Fandom on Sexual Identity Development and Fluidity Acceptance among Taylor Swift Fans." *Psychology of Popular Media* 12, no. 3 (2023): 255–67.

Darcy, Oliver. "Taylor Swift's Associates Dismayed by *New York Times* Piece Speculating on Her Sexuality: 'Invasive, Untrue and Inappropriate.'" *CNN* [online], January 6, 2024.

Daw, Stephen. "Everything You Need to Know About the Equality Act and Taylor Swift's Petition to Pass It." *Billboard,* June 17, 2019.

De Alvarez, Leo Paul S. "Nature and the City: *Timon of Athens.*" In Alvis and West, *Shakespeare as Political Thinker.*

de Certeau, Michel. *The Practice of Everyday Life.* Translated by Steven Rendall. University of California Press, 1984.

de la Cretaz, Frankie. "Postcard from Camp Gaylore." *Cosmopolitan,* August 31, 2023.

de Mauriac, Henry M. "Alexander the Great and the Politics of 'Homonoia.'" *Journal of the History of Ideas* 10, no. 1 (1949): 104–14.

Dean, Jodi. *Aliens in America: Conspiracy Cultures from Outerspace to Cyberspace.* Cornell University Press, 1998.

———. *Publicity's Secret: How Technoculture Capitalizes on Democracy.* Cornell University Press, 2002.

———. "Theorizing Conspiracy Theory. *Theory & Event* 4, no. 3 (2000).

DeLillo, Don. *Underworld.* Viking, 1997.

Determan, Sophie. "The Many Merry Eras of Disney." *BFI,* February 18, 2021.

Devarenne, Nicole. "'A Language Heroically Commensurate with Her Body': Nationalism, Fascism, and the Language of the Superhero Comic." *International Journal of Comic Art* 10, no. 1 (2008): 48–54.

Deville, Chris. "Taylor Swift Not a Pentagon PsyOp, Says US Department of Defense." *Stereogum,* January 10, 2024.

Dobski, Bernard J., and Dustin A. Gish, eds. *Shakespeare and the Body Politic.* Lexington Books, 2013.

———, eds. *Souls with Longing: Representations of Honor and Love in the Plays and Poetry of William Shakespeare.* Lexington Press, 2011.

Doornbos, Caitlin. "Senators Drop Cringe-Worthy Taylor Swift Puns at Ticketmaster Hearing." *New York Post,* January 24, 2023.

Doty, Alexander. *Making Things Perfectly Queer: Interpreting Mass Culture.* University of Minnesota Press, 1993.

Dougherty, Michael Brendan. "The Sad Cult of Esoteric Trumpism." *National Review,* July 30, 2020.

Douglas, Karen M., and Robbie M. Sutton. "What Are Conspiracy Theories? A Definitional Approach to Their Correlates, Consequences, and Communication." *Annual Review of Psychology* 74 (2023): 271–98.

Dowling, Stephen. 2019. "Why There's So Little Left of the Early Internet." BBC [online], April 2, 2019.

Downard, James Shelby, and Michael A. Hoffman II. "King/Kill-33: Masonic Symbolism in the Assassination of John F. Kennedy." In *Apocalypse Culture*, edited by Adam Parfrey. Amok Press, 1988.

Duberman, Martin. *Stonewall: The Definitive Story of the LGBTQ Rights Uprising That Changed America*. Plume, 2019.

Duffett, Mark. *Understanding Fandom*. Bloomsbury Academic, 2013.

Dyer, Richard. *Heavenly Bodies: Film Stars and Society*. Routledge, 2004.

———. *Stars*. BFI Publishing, 1998.

Eadon, Yvonne M. "'You Could Hear a Hair Pin Drop': Queer Utopianism and Informal Knowledge Production in the Gaylor Closeting Conspiracy Theory." *Social Media + Society* 10, no. 2 (2024).

Ebert, Roger. "Batman Begins." *RogerEbert.com*, June 13, 2005.

Ellis-Petersen, Hannah. "China Bans Depictions of Gay People on Television." *Guardian* [online], March 4, 2016.

Enders, Adam M., et al. "Who Supports QAnon? A Case Study in Political Extremism." *Journal of Politics* 84, no. 3 (2022): 1844–49.

Erb, Cynthia. "Another World or the World of an Other? The Space of Romance in Recent Versions of Beauty and the Beast." *Cinema Journal* 34, no. 4 (1995): 50–70.

Estepa, Jessica. "Covfefe, One Year Later: How a Late-Night Trump Tweet Turned into a Phenomenon." *USA Today* [online], May 31, 2018.

Evans, Greg. "'Priest' Foes Pass Over Miramax, Boycott Disney." *Variety* [online], April 3, 1995.

Evola, Julius. *Revolt Against the Modern World*. Translated by Guido Stucco. Inner Traditions International, 1995

Farivar, Masood. "How the QAnon Conspiracy Theory Went Global." *Voice of America*, August 15, 2020.

Feblowitz, Joshua C. "The Hero We Create: 9/11 & the Reinvention of Batman." *Inquiries Journal* 1, no. 12 (2009).

Fenster, Mark. *Conspiracy Theories: Secrecy and Power in American Culture*. University of Minnesota Press, 2000.

Fiske, John, ed. "Blackstream Knowledge: Genocide." In *Media Matters: Everyday Culture and Political Change*. University of Minnesota Press, 1994.

Fleras, Augie, and Jean Leonard Elliott. *Mass Media Communication in Canada*. 4th ed. Harcourt Brace Canada, 2003.

Fletcher, Harry. "After Two Years, QAnon's Creator Q Returns in the Wake of Roe v Wade Decision." *Indy100*, June 25, 2022.

Florez, StormMiguel, dir. *The Whistle*. What Do We Want Films, 2019.

Flusser, Vilém. *Post-History*. Translated by Rodrigo Maltez Novaes. Univocal, 2013.

Flynn, Michael. "Describing the Digital Army." In WWG1WGA, *QAnon*.

Foucault, Michel. "Orders of Discourse: Inaugural Lecture Delivered at the Collège de France." Translated by Rupert Swyer. *Social Science Information* 10, no. 2 (1971): 7–30.

———. "What Is an Author?" Translated by Robert Hurley et al. In *Essential Works of Foucault, 1954–1984*, vol. 2, *Aesthetics, Method, and Epistemology*, edited by James D. Faubion. The New Press, 1998.

Fradley, Martin. "What Do You Believe In? Film Scholarship and the Cultural Politics of the *Dark Knight* Franchise." *Film Quarterly* 66, no. 3 (2013): 15–27.

Frankfurter, David. *Evil Incarnate: Rumors of Demonic Conspiracy and Satanic Abuse in History*. Princeton University Press, 2008.

Fritze, John, and Michael Collins. "Trump Calls Himself 'Extremely Stable Genius' While Responding to Pelosi Criticism." *USA Today*, May 23, 2019.

"*Frozen* Director Now Apologizes to Parents for 'Let It Go.'" *Time*, December 15, 2014.

Frye, Northrop. *The Great Code: The Bible and Literature*. Mariner Books, 2002.

Gaba, Charles. "Let the Bain/Bane Memes Begin!" *Daily Kos*, January 13, 2012.

Gadamer, Hans-Georg. *Truth and Method*. Translated by Joel Weinsheimer and Donald G. Marshall. Bloomsbury Academic, 2004.

Garber, Megan. "The First Lie of the Trump Presidency." *Atlantic*, January 13, 2019.

Garfinkle-Crowell, Suzanne. "Taylor Swift Has Rocked My Psychiatric Practice." *New York Times* [online], June 7, 2023.

Gavaler, Chris. "The Rise and Fall of Fascist Superheroes." *Journal of Graphic Novels and Comics* 7, no. 1 (2016): 70–87.

Geisinger, Gabriella. "The Little Mermaid: How Disney Made a Classic More Queer." *Gay Times Magazine*, May 25, 2023.

Geraghty, Lincoln. "It's Not All About the Music: Online Fan Communities and Collecting Hard Rock Café Pins." *Transformative Works and Cultures* 16 (2014).

Ginzburg, Carlo. *Ecstasies: Deciphering the Witches' Sabbath*. University of Chicago Press, 2004.

Goldner, Fred. H. "Pronoia." *Social Problems* 3, no. 1 (1982): 82–91.

Gomery, Douglas, and Clara Pafort-Overduin. *Movie History: A Survey*. 2nd ed. Routledge, 2011.

Goodnight, G. Thomas, and John Poulakos. "Conspiracy Rhetoric: From Pragmatism to Fantasy in Public Discourse." *Western Journal of Speech Communication* 45, no. 4 (1981): 299–316.

Gottfried, Paul Edward. *Leo Strauss and the Conservative Movement in America: A Critical Appraisal*. Cambridge University Press, 2012.

Graeupner, Damaris, and Alin Coman. "The Dark-Side of Meaning-Making: How Social Exclusion Leads to Superstitious Thinking." *Journal of Experimental Social Psychology* 69 (March 2017): 218–22.

Grassi, Ernesto. *Rhetoric as Philosophy: The Humanist Tradition.* Translated by John Michael Krois and Azizeh Azodi. Southern Illinois University Press, 2001.

Gray, Richard. "Did Disney Shape How You See the World?" BBC [online], July 31, 2019.

Gray, Rosie. "How Bronze Age Pervert Built an Online Following and Injected Anti-Democracy, Pro-Men Ideas into the GOP." *Politico,* July 16, 2023.

Greenburg, Zack O'Malley. "Nine of the 10 Highest-Paid Musicians of 2021 Were Men." *Rolling Stone,* January 14, 2022.

Greenspan, Rachel E. "The QAnon Conspiracy Theory and a Stew of Misinformation Fueled by the Insurrection at the Capital." *Insider,* January 7, 2021.

Griffin, Sean P. *Tinker Belles and Evil Queens: The Walt Disney Company from the Inside Out.* New York University Press, 2000.

Grubb, Brian. "Death to the Gritty Reboot." *Uproxx,* August 13, 2020.

Guénon, René. *The Crisis of the Modern World.* Translated by Marco Pallis, Arthur Osborne, and Richard C. Nicholson. Sophia Perennis, 2004.

Gunn, Joshua. *Modern Occult Rhetoric: Mass Media and the Drama of Secrecy in the Twentieth Century.* University of Alabama Press, 2005.

Habib, Khalil, and L. Joseph Herbert Jr., eds. *The Soul of Statesmanship: Shakespeare on Nature, Virtue, and Political Wisdom.* Lexington Press, 2018.

Hadas, Leora. "The Web Planet: How the Changing Internet Divided 'Doctor Who' Fan Fiction Writers." *Transformative Works and Cultures* 3 (2009).

Hahn, Don, dir. *Howard.* Stone Circle Pictures, 2018.

Hall, Stuart. "Encoding/Decoding." In *Culture, Media, Language,* edited by Stuart Hall, Dorothy Hobson, Andrew Lowe, and Paul Willis. Hutchinson, 1980.

Hallman, Carly. "Every Company Disney Owns: A Map of Disney's Worldwide Assets." TitleMax, December 20, 2023.

Hallsby, Attila. "Imagine There's No President: The Rhetorical Secret and the Exposure of Valerie Plame." *Quarterly Journal of Speech* 101, no. 2 (2015): 354–78.

———. *Sovereign, Settler, Leaker, Lie.* The Ohio State University Press, forthcoming.

Hanania, Richard. "Donald Trump Never Apologizes for His Controversial Remarks. Here's Why He Shouldn't." *Washington Post* [online], October 21, 2015.

"Harvey Mansfield IV." *Conversations with Bill Kristol,* episode 27, chapter 4, "Great Contemporaries (1:10:32–1:36:38)," May 11, 2015. Podcast transcript.

Hayes, Dave. *Calm Before the Storm (Q Chronicles).* Dhayes Media, 2020.

Healy, Gene. *The Cult of the Presidency: America's Dangerous Devotion to Executive Power.* Cato Institute, 2008.

Heinz, Brett. "It's Time to Break Up Disney." *American Prospect,* October 1, 2019.

Hellekson, Karen, and Kristina Busse, eds. "Introduction: Why a Fan Fiction Studies Reader Now?" In *The Fan Fiction Studies Reader.* University of Iowa Press, 2014.

Hendrix, Jerry. "Trump and His Strategy of Ambiguity." *National Review,* January 8, 2018.

Henrie, Mark C. "Straussianism." *First Principles: ISI Web Journal,* May 5, 2011, http://www.firstprinciplesjournal.com/articles.aspx?article=871. Archived December 21, 2018, at the WayBack Machine.

Hersh, Seymour M. "Selective Intelligence." *New Yorker,* May 4, 2003.

Hinck, Ashley. *Politics for the Love of Fandom: Fan-Based Citizenship in a Digital World.* Louisiana State University Press, 2019.

Hinck, Ashley, and Amber Davisson, eds. "Fandom and Politics." Special issue, *Transformative Works and Cultures,* no. 32 (2020).

Hofstadter, Richard. *The Paranoid Style in American Politics and Other Essays.* Harvard University Press, 1996.

Holder, Matthew. "Vigilantism and Violent Forms in Frank Miller's *The Dark Knight Returns.*" *ImageTexT* 13, no. 2 (2022).

Holmes, Dave. "No Shade, but There's a Wrong Way to Make a Gay Anthem." *Esquire,* June 15, 2019.

Hood, Gregory. "The Order in Action: *The Dark Knight Rises.*" In Johnson and Hood, *Dark Right.*

Hood, Gregory, and Luke Gordon. "Conservatism's League of Stupidity: Christopher Nolan as Fascist Filmmaker?" In Johnson and Hood, *Dark Right.*

Horta, Paulo Lemos. *Marvelous Thieves: Secret Authors of the Arabian Nights.* Harvard University Press, 2019.

Horton, Scott. "Leo Strauss and the Iraq War." *Harper's Magazine,* June 3, 2009.

Hunt, Elle. "Pepe the Frog Creator Kills Off Internet Meme Co-Opted by White Supremacists." *Guardian* [online], May 7, 2017.

Hunt, Stacey Wilson. "'Frozen' Director Apologizes to Parents for 'Let It Go.'" *Hollywood Reporter,* December 12, 2014.

"I'm Sorry, by Donald Trump." *Los Angeles Times* [online], August 18, 2019.

International Federation of Library Associations and Institutions. "Quotes on Intellectual Freedom and Censorship." https://repository.ifla.org/rest/api/core/bitstreams/43acfb95-b592-4ea2-89b3-dcd650c75370/content.

Irwin, Neil. "Presidents Have Less Power Over the Economy Than You Might Think." *New York Times* [online], January 17, 2017.

Jaffa, Harry V. "Aristotle and the Higher Good." *New York Times* [online], July 1, 2011.

———. "Chastity as a Political Principle: An Interpretation of Shakespeare's *Measure for Measure.*" In Alvis and West, *Shakespeare as Political Thinker.*

———. *Crisis of the House Divided: An Interpretation of the Issues in the Lincoln-Douglas Debates.* 50th anniversary ed. University of Chicago Press, 2009.

———. "The Unity of Tragedy, Comedy, and History: An Interpretation of the Shakespearean Universe." In Alvis and West, *Shakespeare as Political Thinker.*

Jagernauth, Kevin. "Michael Caine Says, Yes, Alfred Really Did See Bruce Wayne and Selina Kyle at The End of 'The Dark Knight Rises.'" *IndieWire,* December 5, 2012.

Jameson, Fredric. "Cognitive Mapping." In *Marxism and the Interpretation of Culture,* edited by Cary Nelson and Lawrence Grossberg. Macmillan, 1988.

Jardina, Ashely, and Michael Traugott. "The Genesis of the Birther Rumor: Partisanship, Racial Attitudes, and Political Knowledge." *Journal of Race, Ethnicity, and Politics* 4, no. 1 (2019): 60–80.

Jenkins, Henry. *Convergence Culture: Where Old Media and New Media Collide.* New York University Press, 2006.

———. "Fan Studies." *Oxford Bibliographies,* last modified August 29, 2012.

———. *Textual Poachers: Television Fans and Participatory Culture.* Routledge, 1992.

Johnson, Greg. "Superheroes, Sovereignty, and the Deep State." In Johnson and Hood, *Dark Right.*

Johnson, Greg, and Gregory Hood, eds. *Dark Right: Batman Viewed from the Right.* Counter-Currents, 2018.

Johnson, J. Scott. "Review of *Shakespeare and the Good Life: Ethics and Politics in Dramatic Form* by David Lowenthal." *American Political Science Review* 92, no. 4 (1998): 933–34.

Johnson, Paul Elliott. "Walter White(ness) Lashes Out: *Breaking Bad* and Male Victimage." *Critical Studies in Media Communication* 34, no. 1 (2017): 14–28.

Johnson, Poe. "Playing with Lynching: Fandom Violence and the Black Athletic Body." In Stanfill, "Reactionary Fandom."

Johnston, Casey. "Chat Logs Show How 4chan Users Created #GamerGate Controversy." *Ars Technica,* September 9, 2014.

Jones, Christopher, "The Historicity of the Neronian Persecution: A Response to Brent Shaw." *New Testament Studies* 63, no. 1 (2017): 146–52.

Jorjani, Jason Reza. "Gotham Guardian: Will the Real Batman Please Stand Up?" In Johnson and Hood, *Dark Right.*

Kaczynski, Andrew. "Mike Pence Argued in an Op-Ed That Disney's 'Mulan' Was Liberal Propaganda." *Buzzfeed News,* July 17, 2016.

"*Kanye Quest 3030:* The Video Game (Supposedly) Tied to a Cult." *Your Everyday Games,* https://youreverydaygames.com/kanye-quest-3030.

Kaplan, Alex. "Trump Has Repeatedly Amplified QAnon Twitter Accounts. The FBI Has Linked the Conspiracy Theory to Domestic Terror." *Media Matters for America,* August 1, 2019.

Katz, Elihu, and Tamar Liebes. "'No More Peace!' How Disaster, Terror and War Have Upstaged Media Events." In *Media Events in a Global Age,* edited by Nick Couldry, Andreas Hepp, and Friedrich Krotz. Routledge, 2010.

Kelly, Casey Ryan. "COVID-19 Conspiracy Rhetoric and Other Primal Fantasies." *Quarterly Journal of Speech* 109, no. 2 (2023): 132–53.

Klavan, Andrew. "What Bush and Batman Have in Common." *Wall Street Journal,* July 25, 2008.

Klima, Gyula. "The Medieval Problem of Universals." In *The Stanford Encyclopedia of Philosophy,* Spring 2022, edited by Edward N. Zalta.

Knight, Michael, and Martin Geddes. *QAnon and the Great Awakening.* North Star, 2019.

Knight, Peter. *Conspiracy Culture: From the Kennedy Assassination to The X-Files.* Routledge, 2000.

Knoche, Grace F. "Of One Mind, of One Heart." *Sunrise,* October 1974.

Kornhaber, Spencer. "The Queasy Double Message of Taylor Swift's 'You Need to Calm Down.'" *The Atlantic* [online], July 17, 2019.

Kuhn, Thomas S. *The Structure of Scientific Revolutions.* 50th anniversary ed. University of Chicago Press, 2012.

Lacan, Jacques. "The Instance of the Letter in the Unconscious, or Reason Since Freud." In *Écrits: A Selection,* translated by Alan Sheridan. W. W. Norton, 1977.

Laclau, Ernesto. *Emancipation(s).* Verso, 2007.

Labbe, Chine, Virginia Padovese, Marie Richter, and Anna-Sophie Harling. "QAnon's Deep State Conspiracies Spread to Europe." *NewsGuard,* July 21, 2020.

LaFrance, Adrienne. "Six Hours and Three Minutes of Internet Chaos." *Atlantic* [online], January 13, 2019.

Landis, Michael. "'The Little Mermaid' Has Been Subverting Expectations for Decades." *Smithsonian Magazine* [online], April 11, 2023.

Landler, Mark. "What Did President Trump Mean by 'Calm Before the Storm'?" *New York Times* [online], October 6, 2017.

Last, Jonathan V. "The Case for Empire." *Washington Examiner,* May 16, 2002.

Lawler, Kelly. "Beauty and the Beast's 'Gay Moment' May Have Been Much Ado About Nothing." *USA Today* [online], March 21, 2017.

Lee, Benjamin. "Radicalisation and Conspiracy Theories." In Butter and Knight, *Routledge Handbook of Conspiracy Theories.*

Leguichard, Stephanie. "Why 'Gaylor' Believers Like Me Think Taylor Swift Is Bisexual." *An Injustice!,* February 24, 2021.

"Leo Strauss and Queer Theory." *The Roundtable,* episode 35, segment3, September 17, 2020. *The American Mind* podcast.

Lewis, Rebecca. "'This Is What the News Won't Show You': YouTube Creators and the Reactionary Politics of Micro-celebrity." In Stanfill, "Reactionary Fandom."

Li, Pei, and Brenda Goh. "China's Censors Drop Gay Scenes from 'Bohemian Rhapsody' Film." Reuters [online], March 27, 2019.

Lieberman, David. "Rush Limbaugh: Batman Villain Was Named 'Bane' to Hurt Mitt Romney." *Deadline,* July 17, 2012.

Lilla, Mark. *The Shipwrecked Mind: On Political Reaction.* New York Review Books, 2016.

Lilti, Antoine. *The Invention of Celebrity.* Polity Press, 2017.

Ling, Justin. "QAnon's Madness Is Turning Canadians into Potential Assassins." *Foreign Policy* [online], July 13, 2020.

Lowenthal, David. "The New Shakespeareans: A Review of *Shakespeare as Political Thinker*, edited by John Alvis and Thomas G. West." *Claremont Review of Books*, July 10, 2014.

———. *Shakespeare and the Good Life*. Rowman & Littlefield, 1997.

Luciano, Michael. "Jesse Watters Runs Fake Story About the Pentagon Wanting to Turn Taylor Swift into a PsyOp: 'That's Real.'" *Mediaite*, January 9, 2024.

Luey, Beth. *Expanding the American Mind: Books and the Popularization of Knowledge*. University of Massachusetts Press, 2010.

Luhmann, Niklas. *The Reality of the Mass Media*. Translated by Kathleen Cross. Polity Press, 2000.

Lundberg, Christian. *Lacan in Public: Psychoanalysis and the Science of Rhetoric*. University of Alabama Press, 2013.

Lynch, Trevor. "*Batman Begins.*" In Johnson and Hood, *Dark Right*.

———. "*The Dark Knight Rises.*" In Johnson and Hood, *Dark Right*.

Lynskey, Dorian. "Why *Frozen*'s Let It Go Is More than a Disney Hit—It's an Adolescent Aperitif." *Guardian* [online], April 10, 2014.

M, Joel [pseud.]. "The Plan to Save the World." In WWG1WGA, *QAnon*.

Macho, Thomas. "Zeit und Zahl. Kalender-und Zeitrechnung als Kulturtechniken." In *Bild, Schrift, Zahl*, edited by Sybille Krämer and Horst Bredekamp. Wilhelm Fink, 2003.

Marcus, George E, ed. "Introduction to the Volume: The Paranoid Style Now." In *Paranoia Within Reason*.

———, ed. *Paranoia Within Reason: A Casebook on Conspiracy as Explanation*. University of Chicago Press, 1999.

Marks, Anna. "Look What We Made Taylor Swift Do." *New York Times* [online], January 4, 2024.

Martin, Devin Sean. "The World's Celebrity Billionaires 2024." *Forbes*, April 2, 2024.

Martin, Kalea. "Dante's Masterpiece 'La Divina Commedia' Is Actually Fanfiction." *Medium*, September 17, 2020.

Martinez, Ren. "Fabulously Fiendish: Disney Villains and Queer-Coding." *Quail Bell Magazine*, December 15, 2015.

Masugi, Ken. "Straussian Civil Wars." *Law and Liberty*, August 25, 2013.

Matheson, Calum. "Stasis in the Net of Affect." *Philosophy & Rhetoric* 52, no. 1 (2019): 71–77.

———. "'What Does Obama Want of Me?' Anxiety and Jade Helm 15." *Quarterly Journal of Speech* 102, no. 2 (2016): 133–49.

McCluskey, Megan. "Let Michael Caine Finally Explain the Ending of *Inception* Once and for All." *Time*, August 15, 2018.

McDermott, Maeve. "Taylor Swift Has Angered Many People with Her 'You Need to Calm Down' Release. Here's Why." *USA Today* [online], June 21, 2019.

McGann, Laura. "Let's Stop Pretending Trump Is Just Pretending." *Vox*, October 30, 2018.

McGowan, Todd. "The Exceptional Darkness of *The Dark Knight*." *Jump Cut*, no. 51 (Spring 2009).

McGrail, Mary Ann. *Tyranny in Shakespeare*. Lexington Books, 2001.

McKenzie-McHarg, Andrew. "Conceptual History and Conspiracy Theory." In Butter and Knight, *Routledge Handbook of Conspiracy Theories*.

———. "Conspiracy Theory: The Nineteenth-Century Prehistory of a Twentieth-Century Concept." In *Conspiracy Theories and the People Who Believe Them*, edited by Joseph E. Uscinski. Oxford University Press, 2019.

McLuhan, Marshall. *Understanding Media: The Extensions of Man*. MIT Press, 1964.

McMaken, Ryan W. *Commie Cowboys: The Bourgeoisie and the Nation-State in the Western Genre*. 2nd ed., rev. Self-published, 2012.

McQuail, Denis. *McQuail's Mass Communication Theory*. 6th ed. Sage, 2010.

Melley, Timothy. "Conspiracy in American Narrative." In Butter and Knight, *Routledge Handbook of Conspiracy Theories*.

———. *The Covert Sphere: Secrecy, Fiction, and the National Security State*. Cornell University Press, 2000.

———. *Empire of Conspiracy: The Culture of Paranoia in Postwar America*. Cornell University Press, 2000.

Mellor, Louisa. "The 90s Art Collective That Infiltrated Melrose Place." *Den of Geek*, March 17, 2016.

Melzer, Arthur M. *Philosophy Between the Lines: The Lost History of Esoteric Writing*. University of Chicago Press, 2014.

Merinuk, Madeline. "How Taylor Swift Turned Fandom Into a Scavenger Hunt of Clues." *Today* [online], October 21, 2022.

Michalski, Nicholas D., and Narina Nunez. "When Is 'Gay Panic' Accepted? Exploring Juror Characteristics and Case Type as Predictors of a Successful Gay Panic Defense." *Journal of Interpersonal Violence* 37, no. 1–2 (2022): 782–803.

Michel, Casey. "The Bane of the Alt-Right." *Medium*, June 12, 2016.

Miller, Frank, with Klaus Janson and Lynn Varley. *Batman: The Dark Knight Returns*. DC Comics, 2002.

Miller, Lucy. 2020. "*Wolfenstein II* and MAGA as Fandom." *Transformative Works and Cultures*, no. 32 (2020).

Minowitz, Peter. *Straussophobia: Defending Leo Strauss and Straussians Against Shadia Drury and Other Accusers*. Lexington Books, 2009.

Mintz, Frank P. *The Liberty Lobby and the American Right: Race, Conspiracy, and Culture*. Greenwood Press, 1985.

Miro, Clara Juarez. "Who Are the People? Using Fandom Research to Study Populist Supporters." *Annals of the International Communication Association* 45, no. 1 (2021): 59–74.

Mohan, Megha. "The Secret Language of Lesbian Love: The Wives, Mothers and Friends Who Hide Their Sexuality." BBC [online], February 2019.

Morris, Amelia. "Drew a Map on Your Bedroom Ceiling: Fandoms, Nostalgic Girlhood and Digital Bedroom Cultures in the Swiftie-Sphere." *Celebrity Studies* 16, no. 1 (2024): 77–95.

Morson, Gary Saul, and Caryl Emerson. *Mikhail Bakhtin: Creation of a Prosaics.* Stanford University Press, 1990.

Mueller, Hannah. *The Politics of Fandom: Conflicts That Divide Communities.* McFarland and Company, 2022.

Myers, Maddy. "Queer Subtext in *The Little Mermaid,* from Hans Christian Andersen's Original to Disney's Adaptation." *The Mary Sue,* May 10, 2016.

Neon Revolt [pseud.]. *Revolution Q: The Story of QAnon and the 2nd American Revolution.* Salterrae, 2019.

Neville-Shepard, Ryan. "Paranoid Style and Subtextual Form in Modern Conspiracy Rhetoric." *Southern Communication Journal* 83, no. 2 (2018): 119–32.

Nguyen, Tina. "Trump Isn't Secretly Winking at QAnon. He's Retweeting Its Followers." *Politico,* July 12, 2020.

Nietzsche, Friedrich. *Thus Spoke Zarathustra: A Book for All and None.* Edited by Adrian Del Caro and Robert Pippin. Translated by Adrian Del Caro. Cambridge University Press, 2006.

———. *Twilight of the Idols,* translated by Judith Norman. In *The Anti-Christ, Ecce Homo, Twilight of the Idols,* edited by Aaron Ridley and Judith Norman. Cambridge University Press, 2005.

Nikolas, Akash. "It's Not Just *Frozen:* Most Disney Movies Are Pro-Gay." *Atlantic* [online], April 23, 2014.

Nirenberg, David. *Communities of Violence: Persecution of Minorities in the Middle Ages.* Updated ed. Princeton University Press, 2015.

Nolte, John. "'Dark Knight Rises' Review: Nolan Slaps Obama with a Masterpiece." *Breitbart,* July 21, 2012.

Norton, Rictor, ed. *My Dear Boy: Gay Love Letters Through the Centuries.* Leyland Publications, 1998.

Novak, Matt. "Why Conspiracy Theorists Think Taylor Swift Is a Pentagon 'Psy-Op.'" *Forbes* [online], January 10, 2024.

O'Donnell, Patrick. *Latent Destinies: Cultural Paranoia and Contemporary U.S. Narrative.* Duke University Press, 2000.

O'Hehir, Andrew. "'The Dark Knight Rises': Christopher Nolan's Evil Masterpiece." *Salon,* July 19, 2012.

Olmsted, Kathryn S. *Real Enemies: Conspiracy Theories and American Democracy, World War I to 9/11.* Oxford University Press, 2009.

O'Neill, Jonathan. 2009. "Straussian Constitutional History and the Straussian Political Project." *Journal of Theory and Practice* 13, no. 4: 459–78.

Ong, Walter J. *Orality and Literacy: The Technologizing of the Word.* 30th anniversary ed. Routledge, 2012.

O'Sullivan, Patrick B., and Caleb T. Carr. "Masspersonal Communication: A Model Bridging the Mass-Interpersonal Divide." *New Media & Society,* 20, no. 3 (2018): 1161–80.

Packer, Joseph, and Ethan Stoneman. *A Feeling of Wrongness: Pessimistic Rhetoric on the Fringes of Popular Culture.* Pennsylvania State University Press, 2018.

Pagán, Victoria Emma. *Conspiracy Narratives in Roman History.* University of Texas Press, 2004.

———. *Conspiracy Theory in Latin Literature.* University of Texas Press, 2012.

———. "Toward a Model of Conspiracy Theory for Ancient Rome." *New German Critique,* no. 103 (2008): 27–49.

Paglia, Camille. *Sexual Personae: Art and Decadence from Nefertiti to Emily Dickinson.* Yale University Press, 1990.

Paine, T. J. *QAnon Phenomenon: A Detailed Report on the "Storm" That Is About to Destroy the Deep State That Conspires Against the United States and on the "Great Awakening" That Will Make America Great Again!* LP Business and Management Limited, 2020.

Paley, Michael, and Jacob J. Staub. "Jewish Philosophy: Medieval and Modern." In *The Schocken Guide to Jewish Books,* edited by Barry W. Holtz. Schocken Books, 1992.

Pallant, Chris. *Demystifying Disney: A History of Disney Feature Animation.* Bloomsbury Academic, 2013.

Palmer, Ewan. "Why QAnon Followers Think Donald Trump Will Be Sworn Back In as President on March 4." *Newsweek,* February 8, 2021.

Pamphlet and Radix [pseud.]. "Changing the Narrative: Trump and the Media." In WWG1WGA, *QAnon.*

Pankhurst, Christopher. "Caesar Without Gods." In Johnson and Hood, *Dark Right.*

Parker, Mike. "Taylor Swift Makes One Million Dollars, Every Day." *Express,* October 19, 2015.

Pearson, Sidney A. Jr., ed. *Print the Legend: Politics, Culture, and Civic Virtue in the Films of John Ford.* Lexington Books, 2009.

Pellitteri, Marco. "Alan Moore, *Watchmen* and Some Notes on the Ideology of Superhero Comics." *Studies in Comics* 2, no. 1 (2011): 81–91.

Perlstein, Rick. *Before the Storm: Barry Goldwater and the Unmaking of American Consensus.* Nation Books, 2009.

Pietroluongo, Silvio. "Taylor Swift Debuts 10 'Speak Now' Songs on Hot 100." *Billboard* [online], November 4, 2010.

Pippin, Robert B. *Fatalism in American Film Noir: Some Cinematic Philosophy.* University of Virginia Press, 2012.

———. *Hollywood Westerns and American Myth: The Importance of Howard Hawks and John Ford for Political Philosophy.* Yale University Press, 2010.

———. *The Philosophical Hitchcock: Vertigo and Anxieties of Unknowingness.* University of Chicago Press, 2017.

Plato. *Gorgias.* Translated by Donald J. Zeyl. Hackett, 1987.

———. *Republic.* 2nd ed. Translated by G. M. A. Grube. Revised by C. D. C. Reeve. Hackett, 1992.

Platt, Michael. *Rome and Romans According to Shakespeare.* University Press of America, 1983.

Pollini, John. "Burning Rome, Burning Christians." In *The Cambridge Companion to the Age of Nero,* edited by Shadi Bartsch, Kirk Freudenburg, and Cedric Littlewood. Cambridge University Press, 2017.

Popper, Karl. *The Open Society and Its Enemies.* 2nd ed. Princeton University Press, 1956.

Posner, Richard A. *Public Intellectuals: A Study of Decline.* Harvard University Press, 2001.

Pramuk, Jacob. "Trump: I Don't Give Specific ISIS Plan Because I Don't Want Enemies to Know It." CNBC, September 7, 2016.

The Project on Disney. *Inside the Mouse: Work and Play at Disney World.* Duke University Press, 1995.

Provenzaon, Tom. "The Lion in Summer." *Advocate,* June 28, 1994.

Publius Decius Mus [Michael Anton]. "The Flight 93 Election." *Claremont Review of Books,* September 5, 2016.

Pynchon, Thomas. *Bleeding Edge.* Penguin, 2013.

———. *Gravity's Rainbow.* Viking, 1973.

"QAnon Book Is Now Among the Top 15 Titles Sold on Amazon." *Daily Beast,* March 5, 2019.

Quincy, Pat. 2018. *Questions Answered: An Introduction to QAnon and the Great Awakening.* Self-published, 2018.

Ramsden, Sam. "The Real Meaning Behind Poker Face by Lady Gaga." *The List,* May 4, 2022.

Raspail, Jean. "What Their Chosen Reading Says About America's Far-Right." *Economist,* February 20, 2021.

Rather, Dan. "The AIDS Metaphor in 'Beauty and the Beast.'" *Los Angeles Times* [online], March 22, 1992.

Ray, Zachary O. "The Alt Knight: A Retrospect of Frank Miller's *Dark Knight Returns* for the Current Year. In Johnson and Hood, *Dark Right.*

RedpillTheWorld [pseud.]. *QAnon and 1000 Years of Peace: Destroying the New World Order and Taking the Kingdom of Christ by Force.* Self-published, 2019.

Reilly, Andrew, and Saethre, Eirik J. "The Hankie Code Revisited: From Function to Fashion." *Critical Studies in Men's Fashion* 1, no. 1 (2013): 69–78.

Reinhard, CarrieLynn, David Stanley, and Linda Howell. "Fans of Q: The Stakes of QAnon's Functioning as Political Fandom." *American Behavioral Scientist* 66, no. 8 (2022): 1152–72.

Relman, Eliza. "Taylor Swift Slams Tennessee Sen. Marsha Blackburn as 'Trump in a Wig' and Says She's 'Sad' She Didn't Come Out Against Trump in 2016." *Business Insider,* January 31, 2020.

"Report: Americans Pessimistic on Time Frame for Coronavirus Recovery." *Civiqs,* September 2, 2020.

Reslen, Eileen. "10 Clues Britney Spears Posted that Fans Thought Were a Cry for Help." *Page Six,* June 25, 2021.

Rice, Jenny. *Awful Archives: Conspiracy Theory, Rhetoric, and Acts of Evidence.* The Ohio State University Press, 2020.

Ricoeur, Paul. *Freud and Philosophy: An Essay on Interpretation.* Translated by Denis Savage. Yale University Press, 1970.

Riquier, Andrea. "Disney Reanimated: How Eisner Brought the Magic Back." *Investor's Business Daily,* April 15, 2014.

Robins, Robert S., and Jerrold Post. *Political Paranoia: The Psychopolitics of Hatred.* Yale University Press, 1997.

Robinson, Nathan. "Conservative Hero's Dark Side: How an 'Intellectual' Icon's Real Legacy Got Sanitized." *Salon,* January 20, 2015.

Rogers, Katie. "Trump on Releasing His Tax Returns: From 'Absolutely' to 'Political Persecution.'" *New York Times,* July 9, 2020.

Roisman, Joseph. *The Rhetoric of Conspiracy in Ancient Athens.* University of California Press, 2006.

Roose, Kevin. "Shocked by Trump's Loss, QAnon Struggles to Keep the Faith." *New York Times,* November 10, 2020.

———. "Think QAnon Is on the Fringe? So Was the Tea Party." *New York Times,* August 13, 2020.

Rosen, Christopher. "'Dark Knight Rises': Thomas Lennon Explains How His Appearance Connects to 'Memento.'" *HuffPost,* July 23, 2012.

Rosenbaum, Claudia, and Michael Blackmon. "Taylor Swift's Instagram Post Has Caused a Massive Spike in Voter Registration." *BuzzFeed News,* October 9, 2018.

Rosenberg, Matthew, Astead W. Herndon, and Nick Corasaniti. "Marjorie Taylor Greene, a QAnon Supporter, Wins House Primary in Georgia." *New York Times,* August 11, 2020.

Rosenfield, Kat. "Why Taylor Swift Can't Deny Being Gay." *UnHerd,* January 12, 2024.

Rouse, Lauren, Megan Condis, and Mel Stanfill. "Making Fandom Great Again: Si-

lencing Discussions of Racism in Reactionary and Transformative Fandoms." *Popular Communication* 22, no. 2 (2024): 67–79.
Ruiz, Michelle. "Seeking: Bestie Who Loves Brunch, Netflix Binges, and Going Down on Each Other." *Cosmopolitan* [online], April 26, 2015.
Rutledge, Pamela B. "Why So Many Care Who Taylor Swift Dates." *Psychology Today,* October 2, 2023.
Ryan, Joel. "Biggest Movie Franchises: Marvel, *Star Wars,* Harry Potter and More Ranked by Box Office." *CBS News* [online], January 24, 2020.
Sala, Ilaria Maria. "'No Ghosts. No Gay Love Stories. No Nudity': Tales of Film-Making in China." *Guardian* [online], September 22, 2016.
Salter, Anastasia. "#RelationshipGoals? Suicide Squad and Fandom's Love of 'Problematic' Men." In Stanfill, "Reactionary Fandom."
Sandvoss, Cornel. *Fans: The Mirror of Consumption.* Polity Press, 2005.
Scarcella, Mike. "Disney Must Face Consumer Antitrust Claims in TV Streaming Lawsuits." Reuters, October 2, 2023.
Schmitt, Carl. *Political Theology: Four Chapters on the Concept of Sovereignty.* Translated by George Schwab. University of Chicago Press, 2005.
Schreckinger, Ben. "The Alt-Right Manifesto That Has Trumpworld Talking." *Politico,* August 23, 2019.
Schüll, Natasha Dow. *Addiction by Design: Machine Gambling in Las Vegas.* Princeton University Press, 2014.
Sedgwick, Eve Kosofsky. *Epistemology of the Closet.* University of California Press, 1990.
———. "Paranoid Reading and Reparative Reading, or, You're So Paranoid, You Probably Think This Essay Is About You." In *Touching Feeling: Affect, Pedagogy, Performativity.* Duke University Press, 2003.
Sedgwick, Eve Kosofsky, Stephen M. Barber, and David L. Clark. "This Piercing Bouquet: An Interview with Eve Kosofsky Sedgwick." In *Regarding Sedgwick: Essays on Queer Culture and Critical Theory,* edited by Stephen M. Barber and David L. Clark. Routledge, 2002.
Sen, Ari, and Ben Zadrozny. "QAnon Groups Have Millions of Members on Facebook, Documents Show." *NBC News,* August 10, 2020.
Serazio, Michael, and Emily Thorson. "Weaponized Patriotism and Racial Subtext in Kaepernick's Aftermath: The Anti-politics of American Sports Fandom." In Stanfill, "Reactionary Fandom."
SerialBrain2. "Decoding and Deciphering Q." In WWG1WGA, QAnon.
Shannon, Claude Elwood, and Warren Weaver. *The Mathematical Theory of Communication,* University of Illinois Press, 1949.
Shapiro, Ben. "**Spoiler Alert**: TDKR Magnificent . . . and Most Conservative Film Ever." *Breitbart,* July 20, 2012.
Sharratt, Bernard. "The Politics of the Popular?—From Melodrama to Television." In

Performance and Politics in Popular Drama: Aspects of Popular Entertainment in Theatre, Film and Television 1800–1976, edited by David Bradby, Louis James, and Bernard Sharratt. Cambridge University Press, 1980.

Shaw, Brent. "The Myth of the Neronian Persecution." *Journal of Roman Studies* 105 (2015): 73–100.

Shen, Dianna. "Taylor Swift's Biggest Music Easter Eggs Over the Years." *L'Officiel* [online], October 21, 2022.

Shone, Tom. "The Dark Knight Trilogy as Our Generation's Godfather." *Guardian*, July 20, 2012.

Slack, Kevin. *War on the American Republic: How Liberalism Became Despotism*. Encounter Books, 2023.

Smith, Amy. "Taylor Swift Signs a Huge New Record Deal that Also Secures Money for Other Musicians." *NME* [online], November 19, 2018.

Smith, Blake. "Bronze Age Pervert's Dissertation on Leo Strauss. *Tablet*, February 14, 2023.

Smith, David. "Belief in QAnon Has Strengthened in U.S. since Trump Was Voted Out, Study Finds. *Guardian* [online], February 24, 2022.

Smith, Matthew. "World's Most Admired 2021." *YouGov*, December 13, 2022.

Smith, Naomi, and Clare Southerton. "FreeBritney and Pleasures of Conspiracy." *M/C Journal* 25, no. 1 (2022).

Smith, Stephen W., and Travis Curtright, eds. *Shakespeare's Last Plays: Essays in Literature and Politics*. Lexington Books, 2002.

Snyder, Jeffrey Aaron. "America Will Never Move Beyond the Culture Wars." *New Republic* [online], April 23, 2015.

Southern Poverty Law Center. "Greg Johnson." n.d. https://www.splcenter.org/resources/extremist-files/greg-johnson.

SpaceShot76 and RedPill78. "When Will it Become Mathematically Impossible?" In WWG1WGA, *QAnon*.

Spark, Alasdair. "New World Order." In *Conspiracy Theories in American History: An Encyclopedia*, edited by Peter Knight. Vol. 2. ABC-CLIO, 2003.

"Speech: Donald Trump Holds a Political Rally in Tampa, Florida—July 31, 2018." *Roll Call*, https://rollcall.com/factbase/transcript/donald-trump-speech-maga-tampa-july-31-2018.

Spelling, Ian. "Why Are There No More G-Rated Films?" *AV Club*, August 22, 2023.

Spencer, Leland G. "Performing Transgender Identity in the Little Mermaid: From Andersen to Disney." *Communication Studies* 65, no. 1 (2014): 112–27.

Spencer, Richard, Andy Nowicki, and Colin Lidell. "Batman—Anarcho-Fascist?" *Vanguard*, July 23, 2012. Podcast.

Spiekerman, Tim. *Shakespeare's Political Realism: The English History Plays*. State University of New York Press, 2001.

St. James, Emily. "Why Elsa from *Frozen* Is a Queer Icon—and Why Disney Won't Embrace That Idea." *Vox,* November 22, 2019.

Stanfill, Mel. *Fandom Is Ugly: Networked Harassment in Participatory Culture.* New York University Press, 2024.

———, ed. "Introduction: The Reactionary in the Fan and the Fan in the Reactionary." In "Reactionary Fandom."

———, ed. "Reactionary Fandom." Special issue, *Television & New Media* 21, no. 2 (2020).

Stano, Simona. "The Internet and the Spread of Conspiracy Content." In Butter and Knight, *Routledge Handbook of Conspiracy Theories.*

Stempel, Carl, Thomas Hargrove, and Guido H. Stempel III. "Media Use, Social Structure, and Belief in 9/11 Conspiracy Theories." *Journalism and Mass Communication Quarterly* 84, no. 3 (2007): 357–72.

Stewart, Kathleen. "Conspiracy Theory's Worlds." In George Marcus, *Paranoia Within Reason: A Casebook on Conspiracy as Explanation.* University of Chicago Press, 1999.

Strauss, Leo. *The City and Man.* University of Chicago Press, 1964.

———. "Exoteric Teaching." In *Reorientation: Leo Strauss in the 1930s,* edited by Martin D. Yaffe and Richard S. Ruderman. Palgrave Macmillan, 2014.

———. "On a Forgotten Kind of Writing." *Chicago Review* 8, no. 1 (1954): 64–75.

———. *Persecution and the Art of Writing.* University of Chicago Press, 1988.

———. "Plato's *Gorgias.*" Transcript. Department of Political Science, University of Chicago (Winter 1957).

———. *Thoughts on Machiavelli.* University of Chicago Press, 1958.

Strauss, Leo, and Joseph Cropsey, eds. *History of Political Philosophy.* 3rd ed. University of Chicago Press, 1987.

Stroude, Will. "Disney's Gaston Was Based on Gay 'Trade,' Beauty and the Beast Director Reveals." *Attitude,* March 2, 2017.

———. "How One Gay Man's Battle with Aids Shaped Disney's 'Beauty and the Beast.'" *Attitude,* March 1, 2017.

Sunderland, Mitchell. "Beauty and the Plague." *Vice,* December 25, 2013.

Suskind, Alex. "New Reputation: Taylor Swift Shares Intel on TS7, Fan Theories, and Her Next Era." *Entertainment Weekly* [online], May 9, 2019.

Swan, Jonathan. "Why Trump's White House Never Says Sorry." *Axios,* May 14, 2018.

Tabatabai, Ariane. "QAnon Goes to Iran." *Foreign Policy,* July 15, 2020.

Taibbi, Matt. "Batman Shrugged." *Rolling Stone,* no. 1163 (August 16, 2012).

Tan, Rebecca. "A Timeline of Trump's Clearly Made-Up 'Secret Plan' to Fight Isis." *Vox,* July 3, 2017.

Tanner, Tony. *City of Words: American Fiction 1950–1970.* Jonathan Cape, 1971.

"Taylor Swift Inspires Teen to Come Out as Straight Woman Needing to Be at Center of Gay Rights Narrative." *The Onion,* June 17, 2019.

Teiry, Eliose C. *Your Thoughts Alone.* Parapet Press, 1999.

Terrill, Robert E. "Put on a Happy Face: *Batman* As Schizophrenic Savior." *Quarterly Journal of Speech* 79, no. 3 (1993): 319–35.

———. "Spectacular Repression: Sanitizing the Batman." *Critical Studies in Media Communication* 17, no. 4 (2000): 493–509.

Thalmann, Katharina. *The Stigmatizing of Conspiracy Theory Since the 1950s: "A Plot to Make Us Look Foolish."* Routledge, 2019.

Thrash, Steven. "15 Shocking Things You Didn't Know About The Dark Knight Trilogy." *Screen Rant,* July 28, 2017.

"Top 100 Most Popular Superheroes and Villains in Comic Books." *Ranker,* March 19, 2022.

Tovey, Barbara. "The Golden Casket: An Interpretation of *The Merchant of Venice.*" In Alvis and West, *Shakespeare as Political Thinker.*

Trafton, Dain A. "Shakespeare's *Henry IV:* A New Prince in a New Principality." In Alvis and West, *Shakespeare as Political Thinker.*

Tsjeng, Zing. "'Mulan' Was the Most Bisexual Cartoon Ever." *Vice,* January 19, 2018.

Turner, Patricia A. *I Heard It Through the Grapevine: Rumor in African-American Experience.* University of California Press, 1993.

U.S. Department of Energy. "Departmental Vetting Policy and Outreach FAQs." https://www.energy.gov/ehss/security-policy-guidance-reports/departmental-personnel-security-faqs.

U.S. Federal Bureau of Investigation. "Anti-Government, Identity Based, and Fringe Political Conspiracy Theories Very Likely Motivate Some Domestic Extremists to Commit Criminal, Sometimes Violent Activity." Intelligence bulletin, FBI Phoenix Field Office, May 30, 2019, https://www.justsecurity.org/wp-content/uploads/2019/08/420379775-fbi-conspiracy-theories-domestic-extremism.pdf.

van Prooijen, Jan-Willem, and Mark van Vugt. "Conspiracy Theories: Evolved Functions and Psychological Mechanisms." *Perspectives on Psychological Science* 13, no. 6 (2018): 770–88.

van Prooijen, Jan-Willem, Iris Wahring, Laura Mausolf, Nicole Mula, and Shayda Shwan. "Just Dead, Not Alive: Reconsidering Belief in Contradictory Conspiracy Theories." *Psychological Science* 34, no. 6 (2023): 670–82.

Victor, Jeffrey S. *Satanic Panic: The Creation of a Contemporary Legend.* Open Court, 1993.

Voght, Kara, and Ashley Parker. "A Taylor Swift Endorsement? It's Delicate." *Washington Post* [online], February 4, 2024.

von Delden, Jayn. "Sex, Gender, Sexuality, and Victimology." In *Sex, Sexuality, Law, and (In)Justice,* edited by Henry F. Fradella and Jennifer M. Sumner. Routledge, 2016.

Walker, Jess. "This Just In: Conspiracy Theorists Not Quite as Kooky as Previously Reported." *Reason,* March 22, 2023.

Walt Disney Company. *Annual Report, 1999*. https://thewaltdisneycompany.com/app/uploads/2015/10/1999-Annual-Report.pdf.

Warren, Spencer. "A Conservative Generation Gap: How Younger Conservative Critics Gave In to Aesthetic Relativism." *Precepts*, January 10, 2003, https://www.claremont.org/writings/030110warren.html. Archived June 18, 2003, at the WayBack Machine.

Washington, Harriet A. *Medical Apartheid: The Dark History of Medical Experimentation on Black Americans from Colonial Times to the Present*. Doubleday, 2006.

Watkins, Ali. "A Conspiracy Theorist, Anthony Comello, and a Mystery Motive in Gambino Murder." *New York Times* [online], March 22, 2019.

Way, Katie. "Taylor Swift's Very First Cheating Ex Bragged About Screwing Her Over on Twitter, and Her Fans Ate Him Aliiive." *babe*, February 26, 2018.

Weaver, Richard M. "Language Is Sermonic." In *Richard M. Weaver on the Nature of Rhetoric*, edited by Richard L. Johannesen, Rennard Strickland, and Ralph T. Eubanks. Louisiana State University Press, 1970.

Weldon, Glen. *The Caped Crusade: Batman and the Rise of Nerd Culture*. Simon and Schuster, 2016.

Welsh, Daniel. "How the Little Mermaid Found a Place in the Hearts of LGBTQ Fans." *HuffPost*, November 16, 2019.

Whitbrook, James. "As the Punisher Skull Re-Emerges on Cops in U.S. Protests, Marvel Comics Reckons with Its Imagery." *Gizmodo*, June 5, 2020.

White, Howard B. *Copp'd Hills Towards Heaven: Shakespeare and the Classical Polity*. Martinus Nijhoff, 1970.

Whitten, Sarah. "Disney Accounted for Nearly 40% of the 2019 U.S. Box Office." CNBC [online], December 29, 2019.

Wilson, Edmund. *Axel's Castle: A Study of the Imaginative Literature of 1870–1930*. Farrar, Straus and Giroux, 2004.

Wilson, Jonathan. "Reddit Crackdown on 7,000 Hate Pages, as Facebook Boots Out QAnon 'Extremists.'" *Engineering and Technology*, August 21, 2020.

Windsor, Will. "A Dark Knight Without a King." In Johnson and Hood, *Dark Right*.

Winterhalter, Benjamin. "The Politics of the Inner: Why *The Dark Knight Rises* Is Not a Conservative Allegory." *Journal of Popular Culture* 48, no. 5 (2015): 1030–47.

Winters, Michael, and Tasia Jensen. "Egg Prices Increased 70% Over the Last Year—Here's Why." CNBC [online], March 3, 2023.

Winthrop-Young, Geoffrey. "Cultural Techniques: Preliminary Remarks." *Theory, Culture & Society* 30, no. 6 (2013): 3–19.

Wiseman, Andreas. "Disney/Pixar's 'Onward' Banned in Multiple Middle East Countries Due to Lesbian Reference." *Deadline*, March 6, 2020.

Wolf, Z. Byron. "Donald Trump Is Not Sorry. Ever." CNN, May 15, 2018.

WWG1WGA [pseud.]. *QAnon: An Invitation to the Great Awakening.* Relentlessly Creative Books, 2019.

Yack, Bernard. "*Philosophy Between the Lines: The Lost History of Esoteric Writing.*" Review. *Notre Dame Philosophical Reviews,* October 27, 2014.

Yahr, Emily. "How the Search for Clues in Taylor Swift's Music Became All-Consuming." *Washington Post,* October 20, 2022.

Yodovich, Neta. "'A Little Costumed Girl at a Sci-Fi Convention': Boundary Work as a Main Destigmatization Strategy Among Women Fans." *Women's Studies in Communication* 39, no. 3 (2016): 289–307.

Zadrozny, Brandy, and Ben Collins. "How Three Conspiracy Theorists Took 'Q' and Sparked Qanon." *NBC News* [online], August 14, 2018.

Zerofsky, Elisabeth. "How the Claremont Institute Became a Nerve Center of the American Right." *New York Times Magazine* [online], updated June 15, 2023.

Zuckerman, Esther. "Watching 'The Dark Knight Rises' and Seeing Politics." *Atlantic* [online], July 17, 2012.

Zuckert, Catherine H., and Michael P. Zuckert. *The Truth About Leo Strauss: Political Philosophy and American Democracy.* University of Chicago Press, 2006.

INDEX